**FREE DVD**  **FREE DVD**

Essential Test Tips DVD from Trivium Test Prep

Dear Customer,

Thank you for purchasing from Cirrus Test Prep! Whether you're looking to join the military, get into college, or advance your career, we're honored to be a part of your journey.

To show our appreciation (and to help you relieve a little of that test-prep stress), we're offering a **FREE *FTCE Essential Test Tips DVD*** by Cirrus Test Prep. Our DVD includes 35 test preparation strategies that will help keep you calm and collected before and during your big exam. All we ask is that you email us your feedback and describe your experience with our product. Amazing, awful, or just so-so: we want to hear what you have to say!

To receive your **FREE *FTCE Essential Test Tips DVD***, please email us at 5star@ cirrustestprep.com. Include "Free 5 Star" in the subject line and the following information in your email:

1. The title of the product you purchased.

2. Your rating from 1 – 5 (with 5 being the best).

3. Your feedback about the product, including how our materials helped you meet your goals and ways in which we can improve our products.

4. Your full name and shipping address so we can send your **FREE *FTCE Essential Test Tips DVD***.

If you have any questions or concerns please feel free to contact us directly at 5star@cirrustestprep.com.

Thank you, and good luck with your studies!

* Please note that the free DVD is <u>not included</u> with this book. To receive the free DVD, please follow the instructions above.

FTCE Professional Education Test Prep 2018 – 2019

FTCE Professional Education Test Study Guide and Practice Test Questions

Table of Contents

Ethics

Practice Test

Online Resources

To help you fully prepare for your FTCE Professional Education exam, Cirrus includes online resources with the purchase of this study guide.

PRACTICE TEST

In addition to the practice test included in this book, we also offer an online exam. Since many exams today are computer based, getting to practice your test-taking skills on the computer is a great way to prepare.

FLASH CARDS

A convenient supplement to this study guide, Cirrus's flash cards enable you to review important terms easily on your computer or smartphone.

CHEAT SHEETS

Review the core skills you need to master the exam with easy-to-read Cheat Sheets.

FROM STRESS TO SUCCESS

Watch From Stress to Success, a brief but insightful YouTube video that offers the tips, tricks, and secrets experts use to score higher on the exam.

REVIEWS

Leave a review, send us helpful feedback, or sign up for Cirrus promotions—including free books!

Access these resources at:

www.cirrustestprep.com/ftce-professional-education-online-resources

Introduction

Congratulations on choosing to take the Florida Teacher Certification Examinations: Professional Education Test (PEd) (083)! By purchasing this book, you've taken the first step toward becoming a teacher.

This guide will provide you with a detailed overview of the FTCE PEd, so you know exactly what to expect on test day. We'll take you through all the concepts covered on the test and give you the opportunity to test your knowledge with practice questions. Even if it's been a while since you last took a major test, don't worry; we'll make sure you're more than ready!

WHAT IS THE FTCE?

The FTCE is a requirement of teaching licensure in Florida. In conjunction with completion of the General Knowledge Test and a subject matter examination, FTCE (PEd) (083) scores are used to complete a state application for teacher certification. The FTCE exams ensure that the examinee has the skills and knowledge necessary to become an educator in Florida public schools.

WHAT'S ON THE FTCE?

The content in this guide will prepare you for the FTCE PEd (083) exam. This multiple-choice test assesses whether you possess the knowledge and skills necessary to become a teacher. You have a maximum of two hours and thirty minutes to complete the entire test, which consists of approximately 120 questions.

FTCE PEd (083) Content		
Skill	**Approximate Number of Questions**	**Percentage**
Instructional design and planning	22	18%
Appropriate student-centered learning environments	18	15%
Instructional delivery and facilitation through a comprehensive understanding of subject matter	22	18%
Various types of assessment strategies for determining impact on student learning	17	14%
Relevant continuous professional improvement	14	12%
The Code of Ethics and Principles of Professional Conduct of the Education Profession in Florida	11	9%
Research-based practices appropriate for teaching English Language Learners (ELLs)	8	7%
Effective literacy strategies that can be applied across the curriculum to impact student learning	8	7%
Total (2 hours and 30 minutes)	**120 multiple-choice questions**	

You will answer approximately twenty-two questions (18 percent of the test) on instructional design and planning. You should have a solid understanding of educational theories, student diversity, and learning goals and objectives; instructional plans and assessment should apply all of this knowledge. These aspects will affect student learning, so you should know how to plan instruction and assessment that is engaging, effective, and appropriate.

You will answer approximately eighteen questions (15 percent of the test) on appropriate student-centered learning environments. This section will assess your aptitude for managing the behavior of students and creating a productive and organized learning atmosphere. As a teacher, your classroom should feel safe for your students and be conducive to excellence, equity, and learning.

You will answer approximately twenty-two questions (18 percent of the test) on instructional delivery and facilitation through a comprehensive understanding of subject matter. You should be able to engage and motivate students in order to build student knowledge. This section will also assess your ability to analyze gaps in knowledge and apply instructional techniques based on student assessment.

You will answer approximately seventeen questions (14 percent of the test) on various types of assessment strategies for determining impact on student learning. Your teaching should incorporate assessment that monitors student achievement, understanding, and performance as well as feedback that is helpful, flexible, and timely. You should be able to use communication methods and technology to help deliver instruction in different contexts.

You will answer approximately fourteen questions (12 percent of the test) on relevant continuous professional improvement. Your role as a teacher will include reflection on your own effectiveness through the review of relevant data and thorough collaboration with colleagues and parents. You will need to be able to identify professional growth opportunities that will enhance your teaching skills throughout your career.

You will answer approximately eleven questions (9 percent of the test) on the Code of Ethics and Principles of Professional Conduct of the Education Profession in Florida. As a teacher, you will be expected to apply these codes and principles in real-life personal and professional situations. This section will assess your knowledge of an educator's ethical and legal requirements that ensure students' safety.

You will answer approximately eight questions (7 percent of the test) on research-based practices appropriate for teaching ELLs. As a Florida teacher, you will be expected to create a learning environment that is effective for a multicultural and multilingual student population. You should understand the nature of culture and be familiar with the major theories and research related to it. This section will test your knowledge of diverse learners and your ability to apply pedagogy in order to reach learners of different backgrounds and needs.

You will answer approximately eight questions (7 percent of the test) on effective literacy strategies that can be applied across the curriculum to impact student learning. You will be expected to select and apply instructional practices and content to promote literacy development as appropriate for learners with differing needs.

How is the FTCE Scored?

On the FTCE, the number of correctly answered questions is used to create a scaled score. The minimum passing score is 200, which is equivalent to answering approximately 71 percent of the questions correctly. There is no penalty for guessing on FTCE tests, so be sure to eliminate incorrect answer choices and answer every question. If you still do not know the answer, guess; you may get it right! Keep in mind that a small number of multiple-choice questions are experimental for the purpose of the FTCE test-makers and will not count toward your overall score. However, as those questions are not indicated on the test, you must respond to every question.

Scores are released on Tuesdays within four weeks of the testing date. Your score report will be available to you on your FTCE/FELE account for sixty days. Although scaled, your score will be reported simply as "Pass" (200 or above) or "No Pass" (below 200). Passing scores are automatically submitted to the Department of Education's Bureau of Educator Certification.

How is the FTCE Administered?

The FTCE is administered year round at testing centers located throughout Florida and across the nation. To register for a test and find a testing site near you, go to http://www.fl.nesinc.com/FL_Register.asp. At this site, you can create an FTCE/FELE account, check testing appointment times, and take a tutorial about computerized testing.

On the day of your test, arrive thirty minutes before your appointment time, and be sure to bring your admission ticket (which is emailed to you after you register) along with proper identification. The testing facility will provide any necessary paper and pencils and an area outside of the testing room to store your personal belongings. You are allowed no personal effects in the testing area. Cell phones and other electronic, photographic, recording, or listening devices are not permitted in the testing center at all, and bringing those items may be cause for dismissal, forfeiture of your testing fees, and cancellation of your scores. For details on what to expect on testing day, refer to http://www.fl.nesinc.com/FL_DayOfTest.asp.

About Cirrus Test Prep

Cirrus Test Prep study guides are designed by current and former educators and are tailored to meet your needs as an incoming educator. Our guides offer all of the resources necessary to help you pass teacher certification tests across the nation.

Cirrus clouds are graceful, wispy clouds characterized by their high altitude. Just like cirrus clouds, Cirrus Test Prep's goal is to help educators "aim high" when it comes to obtaining their teacher certification and entering the classroom.

About This Guide

This guide will help you master the most important test topics and also develop critical test-taking skills. We have built features into our books to prepare you for your tests and increase your score. Along with a detailed summary of the test's format, content, and scoring, we offer an in-depth overview of the content knowledge required to pass the test. Our sidebars provide interesting information, highlight key concepts, and review content so that you can solidify your understanding of the exam's concepts. Test your knowledge with sample questions and detailed answer explanations in the text that help you think through the problems on the exam and two full-length practice tests that reflect the content and format of the FTCE. We're pleased you've chosen Cirrus to be a part of your professional journey.

Students as Learners

If every student was the same, the teaching and learning process would be simple. Students come to school with a wide variety of cultural experiences, background knowledge, intellectual abilities, developmental levels, and learning styles, and this requires professionals with an arsenal of tools to meet each learner's needs. Fortunately, there is a large body of research about the learning process. This chapter discusses how students learn, what motivates them to succeed, and how to set up the learning environment to maximize student success.

STUDENT DEVELOPMENT AND THE LEARNING PROCESS

How does human development affect the learning process? Each child develops at a different rate, but there are consistencies in the way children move through developmental stages as they grow. Students' developmental stages should be considered when planning lessons because students who are not ready to learn a new skill will likely become resistant. Researchers have discovered instructional strategies that enable teachers to implement learning activities that match each child's cognitive needs. This section will review the learning process and human development, and how these affect instructional decisions in the classroom.

THEORETICAL FOUNDATIONS OF STUDENT LEARNING

What happens when learning takes place? Research by some top educational theorists points to constructivism as the key to cognition. Constructivism theorizes that **knowledge** (acquired information) constructed by the learner through collaboration and real-world experiences is better understood. Under this premise, teachers are facilitators of learning, rather than lecturers. **Cognitive processes** are more than just acquisition of knowledge and **skills** (abilities); cognition includes the ability to apply new information to other settings and to draw conclusions.

Cognitive processes include perception, attention, language, memory, and thinking. Perception describes the way students use their senses to deliver signals to the brain to form insights and opinions about the world around them. Attention refers to which stimuli students focus on. Language is the way in which students both receive and articulate learning concepts. Memory refers to the way the brain categorizes new information and makes connections so that it can be retrieved at a later time. Thinking includes all aspects of reasoning and problem-solving.

When a student is able to draw on the knowledge that he or she learned in school, such as adding and subtracting, and use those cognitive processes to create a budget and make purchases in the grocery store, it is called transfer. This also works in reverse. Students may be able to use what they learn at home about baking a cake to help solve measurement problems at school. By making connections between contexts, learning is transferred and expanded.

In addition to being able to transfer knowledge to new contexts, students need to be able to make reasonable assumptions from the connections they form. For example, students may recite a mnemonic device that reminds them that Earth is closer to the sun than Jupiter. They also know that Earth's seasons are determined by its proximity to the sun. Are they able to draw the conclusion that the temperature of Jupiter's atmosphere is colder than the temperature of Earth's atmosphere? If they are given the average temperatures of Earth and Jupiter, are they able to form a reasonable conclusion about the temperature of Mars? Students who have learned to think, or activate cognition, will form these types of connections, rather than passively receive a list of facts.

> **QUICK REVIEW**
>
> What types of activities would be found in a constructivist classroom?

Teachers who understand constructivism encourage instructional conversations among peers, the use of manipulatives to solve problems, student choice, reflection, and self-regulated progress monitoring that focuses on learning. The days of teacher-centered classrooms with one-size-fits-all learning and assessment for the sole purpose of assigning grades are gone for good.

SAMPLE QUESTIONS

1) **Which of the following activities is most appropriate for the constructivist classroom?**

   A. The teacher lectures while the class takes notes about historical documents that were written by America's forefathers.

   B. Students recite the Preamble to the Constitution.

   C. Students work in groups of four to research, write, and act out a play about the First Constitutional Convention.

   D. Students memorize and recite the names of all of the US Presidents and their years of service.

Answers:

A.   Incorrect. Lectures, even with note-taking, are teacher-centered approaches to teaching.

B.   Incorrect. Cognitive processes are not at play during rote memorization of facts.

C.   **Correct.** This activity inspires students to construct their own learning through cooperation and application.

D.   Incorrect. Once again, this is rote memorization that does not require active thinking.

2)   **After learning about renewable and nonrenewable energy sources, which of the following students is demonstrating a deep cognitive understanding of this unit?**

A.   Matilda designs and presents an experiment in which she compares the heat of burning vegetable oil to that of motor oil to determine whether both renewable and nonrenewable sources give off the same amount of energy.

B.   Devin creates a power-point presentation that lists all of the nonrenewable energy sources and provides the advantages and disadvantages of using those sources, including economic and ecological factors.

C.   Celeste creates a video that outlines the timeline of research and development of biomass fuels, including some promising new theories from current sources.

D.   Austin writes a report about the impact that hybrids have had on the environment within the last five years.

Answers:

A.   **Correct.** Matilda is using a hands-on, real-world approach to demonstrate her understanding of the difference between renewable and nonrenewable resources, as well as potential challenges that will need to be considered. She has demonstrated application as well as understanding.

B.   Incorrect. Devin did a great job of creating his presentation and backing it up with research from secondary resources. This is not a bad assignment, but it pales in comparison to creating a primary source through experimentation.

C.   Incorrect. Celeste, just like Devin, applied her research to a new format, which makes this assignment acceptable, but it still deals primarily with facts instead of thoughts and application.

D.   Incorrect. Austin also used secondary resources to create a report of facts.

FOUNDATIONAL THEORISTS

Foundational theorists provide the framework by which all current knowledge of cognitive processes is based. This chapter provides an overview of some of the psychologists and philosophers who contributed to the understanding of teaching and learning through research.

The psychologist **Jerome Bruner** contributed the three modes of representation to the field of cognitive development. According to Bruner, children integrate learning experiences in the following semisequential order. The enactive stage (up to one year) is characterized by learning through action. In this stage, acquisition of knowledge can be attributed to muscle memory. During the iconic stage (one to six years), cognition comes through mental pictures. Children approximately seven years and older enter the symbolic stage, where abstractions such as language, symbols, and classifications play a bigger role in learning. In contrast to Piaget, Bruner believed that education is not about developmental readiness, but instead it is about providing active and engaging experiences for students to construct their own knowledge through discovery learning and spiraling the curriculum. Children learn so that they can understand and communicate the patterns of events in their environment. Children comprehend the world around them by classifying, sorting, and organizing their thinking patterns. Beyond understanding facts and solving problems, the cognitive process involves applying what they have learned to new situations in order to make predictions. In a constructivist classroom that followed the advice of Jerome Bruner, the teacher is a facilitator who promotes symbolic thinking and problem-solving skills that can be applied to a variety of situations. For example, a teacher might show children a picture of a ladybug and ask them to think of what else it is: ladybug is a beetle; it is an insect; it is an organism because it has life; it is a predator because it hunts for food …

.

Albert Bandura is a Canadian psychologist who developed the social learning theory. Bandura believes that learning is a combination of cognition, behavior, and environment. Children learn through the combination of conditioned response and by imitating those models around them with whom they most identify. According to Bandura, behavioral changes occur when the following four processes are present:

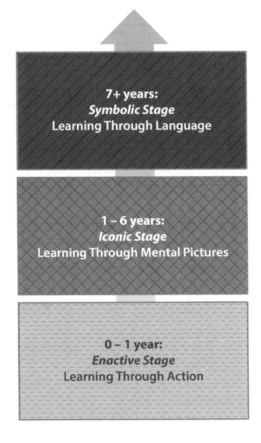

Figure 1.1. The Three Modes of Representation

attention, retention, reproduction, and motivation. Attention must be given to a behavior to entice someone to copy it. Retention means that it must have enough meaning to be memorable beyond immediate mimicry. Reproduction requires the learner to have the skill and ability to be able to recreate the behavior. Motivation relates to positive and negative reinforcement related to the behavior. Behavior has an effect on the environment, and vice versa. Aspects of social learning theory in the classroom would include using an attention-getting hook, explaining the learning goals, recalling background knowledge, modeling, guided practice, feedback, more guided practice, assessment, and then spiraling the objective back into the curriculum, but at a deeper level, after a period of time.

John Dewey was a pragmatic philosopher who viewed learning as a series of scientific inquiry and experimentation. Dewey's approach to education balances the teacher's role of understanding content knowledge and modeling a passion for learning with the child's necessity to construct knowledge using hands-on and relevant learning activities. Real-world challenges that provide students the opportunity to impact society should be the goal. Dewey believed that truth is a tool for problem-solving. However, as problems change, truth also changes. Teachers using the John Dewey philosophies in their classrooms will help students understand how the learning objectives relate to the world outside the classroom. The teacher includes social responsibility, such as tolerance, active listening, and volunteerism through curriculum standards.

Jean Piaget was a Swiss psychologist who was the first to study cognition in children. Piaget's identified stages of development are sensorimotor, preoperational, concrete operational, and formal operational. The sensorimotor stage, from birth to two years of age, is when children develop the concept of object permanence. The preoperational stage, from two to seven years of age, is when children engage in symbolic play, but they do not have the ability to think abstractly or to see another person's perspective. From approximately the ages of seven to eleven years, children are in the concrete operational stage of learning. Children in this stage are more capable of thinking logically, making inferences, and viewing things from more than one perspective. Having acquired the ability to identify several attributes in a single object, students are able to make classifications. In the formal operational stage from age eleven into adulthood, people are able to think abstractly, transfer knowledge, and mentally process information. Piaget also introduced the concepts of assimilation and accommodation. Refer to the next section on learning theories to find out more about assimilation and accommodation in Piaget's schema theory. Teachers can apply Piaget's theories by providing a variety of hands-on experiences for students to explore and by focusing on the process of learning rather than the end result. Understanding that students develop at different

QUICK REVIEW

In a sixth-grade classroom, some students may be in the concrete operational stage while others have moved to the formal operational stage. How can instruction be differentiated to meet the needs of all students?

rates, the teacher does not push students toward knowledge or skills for which the student has not yet demonstrated readiness.

Lev Vygotsky was a Russian psychologist who researched what has become social development theory; however, because of his death at a young age, his work was not completed. Some of Vygotsky's notable points that differ from those of his contemporaries involve the degree to which culture and social influences determine learning. The two main tenets of his philosophy include more knowledgeable other (MKO) and the **zone of proximal development (ZPD)**. The MKO who models a new activity may be a teacher, peer, or even technology program. Refer to the next section on learning theories for more information about scaffolding instruction within the student's ZPD. In the classroom, lots of fun and cooperative learning activities that emphasize language at each student's instructional level are recommended.

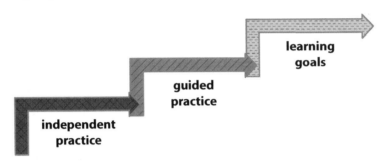

learning
goals

guided
practice

independent
practice

Figure 1.2. Scaffolding Learning Goals

Lawrence Kohlberg worked to further develop Piaget's ideas on moral development. Kohlberg identified the following stages of moral development.

- ▶ Level 1: Preconventional morality
    - ▷ Stage 1: Obedience and Punishment Orientation: The child behaves to keep from getting in trouble.
    - ▷ Stage 2: Individualism and Exchange: There is more than one point of view and the authority is not always right.
- ▶ Level 2: Conventional morality
    - ▷ Stage 3: Good Interpersonal Relationships: The child behaves to gain social acceptance.
    - ▷ Stage 4: Maintaining the Social Order: The child behaves to feel good about doing his or her part to keep society running smoothly.
- ▶ Level 3: Postconventional morality
    - ▷ Stage 5: Social Contract and Individual Rights: The individual understands that laws are usually in the best interest of society, but that there are times when individual circumstances create a gray area in determining what is right and what is wrong.

▷ Stage 6: Universal Principles: While not everyone reaches this stage, in this stage, people determine what is right and wrong based on their own moral principles. People in this stage are not concerned about fitting in or about consequences to doing the right thing.

Moral development in the classroom would include student participation in creating a social contract that all students are expected to adhere to for the good of the classroom society as a whole. Cooperative learning, role-playing, and self-assessment help move students toward Stage 5.

Benjamin Bloom was an American psychologist who contributed to the taxonomy of educational objectives and the theory of mastery learning. Within the theory of mastery learning, Bloom proposed increasing cooperation over competition and using assessments as learning tools. Mastery learning gives credit for success to hard work over innate talent. Bloom's contributions to early childhood education research led to the development of Head Start programs. He recognized the crucial role of child development in the first four years of life and presented his findings before the US Congress. Bloom's taxonomy is a more holistic approach to education, providing for affective, psychomotor, and cognitive domains of learning. The affective domain deals with emotions and attitudes, the psychomotor domain deals with motor skill development, and the cognitive domain deals with acquiring intellect. Teachers apply Bloom's research in the classroom by asking questions and assigning tasks that promote higher-level thinking. Although obtaining some prerequisite knowledge may necessitate some recall, teachers should be digging deeper with application and synthesis of new information.

SAMPLE QUESTIONS

3) **According to Piaget, at approximately what age are children in the preoperational stage, in which they engage in symbolic play but do not have the ability to think abstractly or to see another person's perspective?**

   A. birth to two years

   B. two to seven years

   C. seven to eleven years

   D. eleven years and older

Answers:

A. Incorrect. Birth to two years of age is the sensorimotor stage.

B. Correct. Two to seven years of age is the preoperational stage.

C. Incorrect. Seven to eleven years of age is the concrete operational stage.

D. Incorrect. Eleven years of age into adulthood is the formal operational stage.

4)   **Which educational theorist identified the zone of proximal development?**

A.   Bandura

B.   Dewey

C.   Piaget

D.   Vygotsky

Answers:

A.   Incorrect. Bandura developed social learning theory.

B.   Incorrect. Dewey was a proponent of hands-on learning.

C.   Incorrect. Piaget was the first psychologist to study cognition in children.

D.   Correct. Vygotsky identified the zone of proximal development.

LEARNING THEORIES

Learning theories have applied research to describe how genetics, development, environment, motivation, and emotions affect a student's ability to acquire and apply knowledge. One of the first learning theories to emerge was **classical conditioning**. Ivan Pavlov documented that a neutral stimulus becomes associated with a reflex response through conditioning. For example, when a teacher rings a bell, students stop what they are doing and pay attention to the teacher. **Operant conditioning** provides rewards or punishment as a motivation for desired performance. Rewards and consequences can be intrinsic or extrinsic. Using hands-on, inquiry-based, and relevant learning activities provides intrinsic motivation to learn. Extrinsic rewards, such as stickers, praise, and certificates of achievement, also have a place in motivating behavior but can actually reduce engagement over time. If a student receives an unpleasant consequence for failure, it is negatively extrinsic. If a student prefers not to comply with the teacher's expectations, it is negatively intrinsic.

Metacognition is simply teaching students to think about their learning. For example, when students come to a word they are unfamiliar with, they are reminded of ways to figure out meaning. They can look at the words around it to see whether context clues help. They can use reference materials or technology. They can ask a friend. They can look for the word in other places. Some strategies for metacognition that are frequently used in the classroom include think-pair-share and metacognitive journaling. There are several ways to structure a think-pair-share, but it is important to try to be consistent so that once students have learned the procedure, their attention can be turned to the learning rather than the process. The first step is to give students think time to formulate their

QUICK REVIEW

One example of metacognition is understanding that good readers ask themselves comprehension questions while they are reading. How could a teacher model this process for students?

own response to either a thought-provoking question or a reflection on something they have read. The next step is to have the students share their thoughts with an identified partner. Finally, partners share their discussion with the group. Metacognitive questions may lead students to identify learning goals or stimulate background knowledge before a lesson. They may also be used to guide comprehension or offer opportunities for reflection during and after a lesson. Metacognition brings focus and clarity to a new learning experience.

Table 1.1. Motivators

Extrinsic Motivators	Intrinsic Motivators
praise	relevant learning activities
awards	choice
preferred activity	competence
positive phone calls home	progress

Assimilation and accomodation are methods by which people resolve cognitive dissonance when presented with new information. Most new information meshes with existing **schema**, or frameworks for understanding. Schema are like file folders in the brain that learners naturally sort information into. However, there are times when the learner's schema does not reconcile with a new piece of information. In this instance, the learner must make accommodations to his or her schema in order to process new learning. As people progress through the stages of cognitive development, they can more effectively **transfer**, or apply, knowledge to make inferences about new thoughts and ideas.

The social learning model identifies how emotions related to learning impact the retention of information. Teachers promote self-efficacy by helping students write learning goals, providing opportunities for choice, and providing focused feedback. **Self-efficacy** is when a person believes that he or she is capable of achieving a learning goal. Keeping students within their zone of proximal development (ZPD) prevents students from feeling discouraged and giving up. The ZPD is the space between what a child can do independently and the learning goal. By scaffolding instruction, the student is able to independently work on material that once required guidance and support. Scaffolding is breaking the curriculum up into smaller pieces and then providing support so that students can acquire mastery. Once students have a firmer understanding of the materials, the scaffold may be removed.

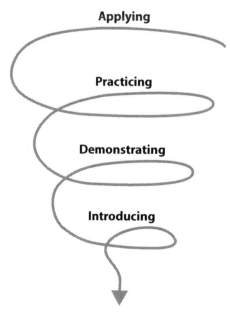

Applying

Practicing

Demonstrating

Introducing

Figure 1.3. Spiraling Curriculum

Another way to promote self-efficacy in students is through spiraling the curriculum. Spiraling the curriculum involves reteaching a concept multiple times throughout the year with steadily increasing levels of rigor and depth.

When a teacher attempts to engage students in learning, emotional responses that determine the students' motivation level fall into three categories: approach, avoid, or attack. Ideally, students will be willing to approach a new challenge. There are many ways that students avoid learning, including sleeping, drawing, and socializing. If students attack the work, the teacher, or other students, the disruption to the learning environment will be felt by all. Teachers can help students understand their emotional response so that they are better able to **self-regulate**. It is not just students who need to maintain control of their emotional responses, but teachers also need to be aware and in control of their emotional responses to stressors. Teachers who are unable to self-regulate have a negative impact on student learning.

SAMPLE QUESTIONS

5) **Which of the following is an example of an extrinsic reward?**

   A. lunch with the teacher

   B. hands-on learning activities

   C. relating knowledge to students' interest

   D. a student's pride in his or her own project

Answers:

   A. **Correct.** Lunch with the teacher is an extrinsic reward because it motivates students with something outside of the learning experience.

   B. Incorrect. Hands-on learning activities are intrinsically motivating because students enjoy activities in which they are able to physically manipulate materials to solve a problem.

   C. Incorrect. Relating curriculum to students' interest is intrinsically motivating.

   D. Incorrect. A student's pride in his or her own learning is intrinsically motivating.

6) **Using the zone of proximal development, most of a student's instruction will take place at which of the following levels?**

   A. below the student's independent level

   B. at the student's independent level

   C. above the student's instructional level

   D. at the student's instructional level

Answers:

A.   Incorrect. This student is past this level. It's time to increase the depth and rigor of instruction.

B.   Incorrect. Independent practice will take place at the student's independent level, but most instruction will be at the student's instructional level.

C.   Incorrect. A student may be exposed to instruction that is above his or her instructional level, but most instruction will take place within the instructional level.

D.   Correct. Most work will be within the student's guided instructional level.

HUMAN DEVELOPMENT

What do children need in order to grow? In the 1950s, Dr. Benjamin Bloom led a group of researchers who studied learning processes. His team identified three domains, or categories, of learning: cognitive (knowledge), social (attitude), and psychomotor (skills). Each domain has its own hierarchy, which means that it is divided into categories, or degrees of complexity, that must be mastered before moving to the next level.

The **cognitive domain** deals with intellectual development. Some of Dr. Bloom's students revised the categories of the cognitive domain in the 1990s. The new categories of the cognitive domain, in order from simplest to most challenging, are as follows: remembering, understanding, applying, analyzing, evaluating, and creating.

Verbs for each category in the cognitive domain of Bloom's taxonomy are as follows:

▶ Level 1, Remembering: define, describe, identify, know, label, list, match, name, outline, quote, recall, recognize, recite, reproduce, retrieve, select, state

▶ Level 2, Understanding: comprehend, convert, defend, distinguish, estimate, explain, extend, generalize, infer, interpret, paraphrase, predict, provide examples, rewrite, summarize, translate

▶ Level 3, Applying: apply, change, compute, construct, demonstrate, discover, manipulate, modify, operate, predict, prepare, produce, relate, show, solve, use

▶ Level 4, Analyzing: analyze, compare, contrast, deconstruct, differentiate, discriminate, distinguish, identify, illustrate, infer, outline, relate, select, separate

▶ Level 5, Evaluating: appraise, compare, conclude, contrast, criticize, critique, defend, describe, discriminate, evaluate, explain, interpret, justify, relate, summarize, support

▶ Level 6, Creating: build, categorize, combine, compile, composes, creates, design, devise, explain, generate, modify, organize, plan, rearrange, reconstruct, relate, reorganize, revise, rewrite, summarize, support

Dr. Bloom's committee elected not to further explore the psychomotor domain since the committee was composed of people who worked at the college level who did not have direct experience in this domain, but E. Simpson expounded on the physical domain in 1972. The **physical domain**, also called the psychomotor domain, deals with all aspects of motor skill development. Simpson's categories of the physical domain in order of complexity are as follows: perception (awareness), set (readiness), guided response (imitation), mechanism (proficiency), complex or overt response (skilled), and adaptation and origination (modification and construction). For example, in the perception domain, a child may sense that squiggles on a page form letters and make words. At the set stage, students are interested in learning to write the letters for themselves. During the guided response stage, the student is able to copy or trace letters with teacher support. During the mechanism phase, the student is proficient in writing letters and no longer needs support. During the complex or overt response stage, the student begins to show some talent in fine motor skills. During the adaptation and origination stage, the student can create impressive designs that most others could not.

The **social domain** is referred to as the affective or social-emotional domain. The affective domain includes emotions, motivation, and attitudes. The categories of the social domain are receiving phenomena (attentive/aware), responding to phenomena (participation), valuing (respect), organizing (balance/prioritization), and internalizing values (discriminating). For example, a student in the receiving stage might learn about a local animal shelter. In the responds to phenomena stage, the child may tell his or her parents that he or she would like to adopt a shelter pet. In the valuing stage, the student may volunteer at the shelter. In the organization stage, the student will teach others to spay and neuter their animals and to adopt shelter pets. In the internalizes values stage, the student will participate in establishing a no-kill shelter.

The **moral domain** theory is not part of Bloom's domains of learning but was developed by Lawrence Kohlberg based in theories by Jean Piaget. The moral domain deals with the acquisition of morals and values. The categories of the moral domain are preconventional morality, conventional morality, and postconventional morality (refer to Kohlberg in the section Foundational Theorists for more information). During preconventional stages, the child behaves because it is in his or her own best interest. During the conventional stage, the child conforms to societal expectations. During the postconventional stage, the person is driven by his or her ethics and morals, even when it is not popular.

As children grow, researchers have identified what is considered typical behavior for each age range. The following developmental milestones are generally accomplished by the time a child reaches the end of the phase. However, there is a great deal of variance among students at each grade level. If a student consistently fails to meet milestones, the teacher will need to provide further assistance to the student, which may come in the form of small group or individual intervention within the classroom setting, or may require support from special services.

0 – 2 years old: Children in the sensorimotor stage are beginning to understand object permanence. They begin to learn through imitation and through action. By the end of the second year, they should be able to use two-word phrases and identify some pictures, which is the beginning of symbolic thought. By the end of this stage, they will know a few people by name and be able to follow simple directions. The typical attention span is three minutes or less. Most will learn to walk by the end of the first year and may be able to climb stairs by the end of the second year. The child will be able to build simple towers and identify some body parts. The child can throw or kick a ball and run by age two. He or she can draw lines and circles. The child is attached to the parent and may suffer from separation anxiety. The child engages in parallel play and imitation. The child may begin to become willful or throw tantrums. The child judges right from wrong based on how he or she feels.

2 – 3 years old: Children at this age are egocentric and illogical. They have a difficult time differentiating reality from fantasy. Vocabulary improves drastically, but receptive language is much better than expressive language. They are unaware that others may have a different perspective. Children learn through mental pictures. Toddlers can follow two- to three- step instructions. They know their own name and age and can communicate using two to three sentences. The typical attention span ranges from two to eight minutes. Toddlers have a hard time sitting still. They hop, jump, climb, and ride tricycles. The child can cut with scissors and draw basic shapes. Most are toilet trained by three and a half years of age. Children this age can do simple puzzles and turn book pages. They are capable of alternating feet when walking up and down stairs. The child begins to have empathy for others and will independently show affection. The child may have a security object, such as a toy or blanket, but by the end of this stage, should be able to separate from parents. The child begins to cooperate, share, and take turns with peers and begins to understand and use possessive pronouns. The child feels badly if he or she disappoints his or her parents. Children during this stage begin to get better at controlling their emotions, but they prefer routine and may act out emotionally if it is changed. The child learns right from wrong based on what other people tell him or her.

4 – 7 years old: The child is able to communicate using language. The child begins to understand other perspectives but is unable to be empathetic. The child is beginning to think rationally and remember past events. For most of this stage, the child continues to think through mental pictures. Children in this stage want to make more of their own decisions. The typical attention span ranges from four to fifteen minutes. Motor skills are improving. Children are developing more controlled movements and demonstrate better coordination and balance. The child changes friends frequently. Structured play and rules provide a sense of security, although rules sometimes change. They still need a structured routine but are better able than toddlers to be flexible if there are occasional changes to the routine. The child has a strong sense of justice and begins to understand expectations and consequences.

8 – 11 years old: The child is beginning to understand other perspectives and understands the difference between "on purpose" and "by accident." Children are able to learn through abstractions, such as language and symbols. The child can sort, organize, and make deductions based on similarities. Reciprocal relationships make sense. Writing should be several paragraphs and may be edited by the child for grammatical and spelling errors. The typical attention span ranges from fifteen to twenty minutes. Some children begin to enter puberty. Depth perception and the ability to predict movement improve. At the beginning of this stage, the child strictly follows rules but begins to see them as negotiable toward the end of this stage. The child takes on more responsibilities at home. Structured activities, such as sports and games, are preferred to fantasy play. Children begin to question authority and have a strong sense of justice. Identifying with their social groups becomes important for the first time. They begin to be able to delay gratification. Children may have questions about pregnancy and sex.

12 – 18 years old: The child is able to think logically and draw conclusions. Abstract thinking and metacognition begins. The child understands and considers the perspectives of others. Emotions influence cognition. The typical attention span is about twenty minutes. This stage is marked by hormonal changes. Children begin to distance themselves psychologically from their parents. They conform to peers. They choose friends and adults based on loyalty, respect, and honesty. In the beginning of this stage, adolescents tend to be self-conscious about their appearance. They enjoy dramatic, intense experiences. Frequently, they overreact to questions or criticisms from parents. By the end of this stage, adolescents begin to form a positive self-image. Children place more importance on peer over adult opinions and begin to develop their own value system. They may experiment in an effort to find the best fit. Young teens (twelve to fifteen years old) may be moody and argumentative with adults. Older teens (fifteen to eighteen years old) are more concerned about their future, are more independent, and have fewer conflicts with their parents.

SAMPLE QUESTIONS

7) **Which of the learning domains deals with the intellectual acquisition?**

   A.   cognitive domain

   B.   physical domain

   C.   social domain

   D.   moral domain

   Answers:

   A.   **Correct.** The cognitive domain is related to intellectual development.

   B.   Incorrect. The physical domain relates to motor skill development.

   C.   Incorrect. The social domain relates to emotions and attitudes.

   D.   Incorrect. The moral domain relates to the development of values.

8) **Which of the following behaviors is atypical for a fourteen-year-old girl?**

   A.   enjoys creating drama among her peer group

   B.   separation anxiety when away from her parents

   C.   overreacts to questions from her mother

   D.   complains about her appearance

   Answers:

   A.   Incorrect. Adolescents enjoy intense experiences and often create them.

   B.   **Correct.** Separation anxiety is typical for a toddler, but by adolescence, the child should prefer peers.

   C.   Incorrect. Children at this stage are beginning to distance themselves from their parents and may overreact to parenting.

   D.   Incorrect. Early adolescents are still trying to get used to the body changes that occur during puberty. Body image issues are normal.

IMPLICATIONS FOR INSTRUCTION

How does the research done by the foundational theorists help teachers in the classroom? The information that theorists have provided about how students learn is only useful if classroom teachers understand how to put it into practice. Inquiry-based learning is based on constructivism. It involves asking a thought-provoking question followed by providing opportunities for students to research and discover answers for themselves. Inquiry-based learning gives students the opportunity to actively participate in their learning in lieu of simply learning facts, as is common with direct teach. For example, the teacher might ask what would be different if we used a base-5 instead of a base-10 number system. Students may explore aspects of numeracy, operations, and algebraic reasoning as they work through the differences in money, time, and measurement.

Direct teach is a teacher-centered approach to instruction that often involves lectures. Direct instruction is the oldest and most frequently used type of instruction, although its long-term value is questionable. Direct teach conflicts with the constructivist approach of allowing students to form their own conclusions through discovery because direct instructions are teacher guided. For example, a teacher teaches from a power-point presentation that includes vocabulary, lecture points, and an embedded video. Even though there are several elements to this presentation, the students are passively taking in information.

Another method of instruction that is inspired by research is project-based learning. Project-based learning is rooted in pragmatism and involves increasing the depth of understanding by developing real-world solutions to problems. For example, the teacher might present a newspaper article about a cat falling twelve stories from a building and surviving. Students may research why the cat survived and whether there is anything that a human being in a similar circumstance could do to survive. In the process, students are learning about a variety of concepts, including momentum, friction, surface area, acceleration, and natural selection.

Jean Piaget's work about assimilation and accommodation resulted in schema theory. By using advanced organizers, stimulating background knowledge, and categorizing information, students are able to resolve conflicts within their schema. One way to build schema is through interdisciplinary learning, or cross-curricular instruction. Interdisciplinary learning is teaching across content areas in order to build schema and enable students to transfer knowledge to different types of situations. For example, the art teacher, history teacher, and English teacher work together to teach students about propaganda. The art teacher may have students develop advertisements. The history teacher may review propaganda used by political parties during World War II. The English teacher might read a dystopian novel in which the government uses propaganda to control its citizens.

How can teachers ensure that students are moving in the right direction? Vgotsky's social learning theory leads to scaffolding. It involves breaking apart the curriculum so that an MKO (more knowledgeable other) can provide a variety of experiences within the student's ZPD (zone of proximal development) to lead the learner to mastery. For example, response to intervention (RTI) provides a framework for a tiered approach to student support in which all students are given universal supports, but students who do not respond to the regular curriculum are given additional support, with small-group instruction, or individualized instruction if needed.

Social learning theorists promote teaching students the learning objectives and activating prior knowledge before modeling and practicing with students. KWL charts activate prior knowledge and guide students through learning goals. The *K* stands for *What do I know about this subject?* The *W* stands for *What do I want to learn about this subject?* The *L* stands for *What did I learn?* Using a KWL chart establishes prior knowledge, sets learning goals, and summarizes learning.

Students arrive at school at varying developmental stages, cognitive abilities, and learning styles. Differentiation, or providing different types of instruction and learning environments, is necessary to meet the needs of all students.

SAMPLE QUESTIONS

9) **Why would a teacher use a KWL chart?**

A.   to focus learning goals

B.   to differentiate instruction

C.   to help students construct knowledge

D.   to provide prerequisite knowledge

Answers:

A.   **Correct.** KWL charts outline background information and learning goals, and provide a summative of learning.

B.   Incorrect. KWL charts document what happens before, during, and after instruction.

C.   Incorrect. KWL supplements social learning theory rather than constructivism.

D.   Incorrect. KWL documents and retrieves prior knowledge. It does not provide new knowledge.

10) **A teacher reads a book about rain and then asks students to work in small groups to brainstorm other types of precipitation and draw conclusions about how snow, hail, sleet, and fog are formed. Which strategy is the teacher using?**

A.   project-based learning

B.   schema theory

C.   direct teach

D.   zone of proximal development

Answers:

A.   Incorrect. Project-based learning involves using real-world scenarios to solve problems.

B.   **Correct.** Schema learning puts new information into an existing framework by categorizing things. In this scenario, students are assimilating new knowledge about snow, hail, sleet, and fog into what they already know about rain.

C.   Incorrect. Direct teach is teacher centered.

D.   Incorrect. The zone of proximal development is the individual child's instructional level.

Students as Diverse Learners

Factors Affecting Student Learning

Learning styles research indicates that children learn in different ways. Rather than trying to adapt children to fit into a traditional classroom, students gain and retain intellect by teachers adapting the curriculum to fit their needs. The general categories of learning styles are visual, auditory, and kinesthetic. Visual learners use graphic organizers, word maps, and images to understand information. Auditory learners benefit from discussions and lectures. Kinesthetic learners use action and manipulation of objects to solve problems. Matching learning activities to each student's preferred mode of comprehension will yield the best results.

Howard Gardner, a professor of education at Harvard University, expanded learning styles research into nine separate categories called Gardner's Theory of Multiple Intelligences. According to Gardner's research, using a person's area of gift-edness to demonstrate intellect will help learners achieve their potential. Gardner's intelligences are verbal-linguistic (language), logical-mathematical (abstractions and patterns), spatial-visual (thinks in pictures), bodily-kinesthetic (movement), musical (rhythm, pitch, and timber), interpersonal (empathy), intrapersonal (self-aware), naturalist (plants, animals), and existential (deep thinker). For example, if James has a verbal-linguistic learning style and Stephanie has a spatial-visual learning style, James may learn the vocabulary words for a new unit by role-playing their meaning or brainstorming words with similar meanings, whereas Stephanie will learn the words better using graphic organizers or word maps.

Although there is no difference in cognitive abilities between male and female learners, there are big differences in the way they learn. Research indicates that girls tend to rely heavily on one learning style, whereas boys tend to prefer more variety. Another difference between the sexes is attention span. The younger the child, the greater the difference, but boys need to change activity much more frequently than girls do. The desire to please adults is much more pronounced in girls, as are their expectations of themselves. In addition, boys tend to inflate their academic successes, whereas girls are overly critical of their own performance.

Researchers have concluded through both observational and data-based research that gender and cultural differences in learning styles exist but advise caution when applying to generalities to individual students within the group. Each student is unique and deserves to be taught in the way that best serves him or her as an individual. Nature and nurture have an effect on learning styles, so the best way to determine the needs of individual students is to administer a learning-style inventory and offer a variety of learning modalities.

Children from families with a low socioeconomic status have more problems in school not only because of a lack of early childhood experiences but also because less language is used in homes marked by poverty and prolonged stress. Families in poverty are unable to afford tutoring or preschool programs, and the teacher turnover rate is abnormally high at schools in poverty-stricken areas, which further contribute to differences in achievement. Many students of poverty begin to feel as if they do not belong and drop out of school, thus perpetuating the cycle of poverty for another generation. Early intervention through public preschool programs and access to learning materials and books help students build prior knowledge that reduces the achievement gap upon entering school.

Emotional factors, such as motivation and confidence, affect learning. Motivation is what stimulates a person to want to do something. All students are motivated by something. The trick is to find the motivator and channel it in a positive direction. Motivation affects the attention, effort, and energy that the students put into learning. Ideally, the work itself will be stimulating and motivating, but extrinsic rewards may also be effective. Student confidence in achievement of learning goals has been proven to make a big difference in success; however, the same results have not been found when comparing self-esteem to intellectual success. Self-esteem refers to the way students feel about themselves, whereas confidence is related to the child's ability to perform. Boosters to self-esteem have been shown to produce children with an exaggerated sense of self, whereas confidence boosters result in academic gains.

Factors such as cognitive development, maturity, and language development must be considered. Children grow, learn, and develop at different rates, but as long as they are progressing at a steady rate, there is no cause for concern. If a child is not making progress, more research should be done to find out if the issue is chronic or temporary. Teachers need to be aware of health issues, such as ear infections, that have the potential to create delays in language development so that accommodations may be made.

SAMPLE QUESTIONS

11) **Which of the following learning activities would be most appropriate for a visual learner?**

   A. cooperative learning

   B. constructing a model

   C. creating a graphic organizer

   D. lectures

Answers:

   A. Incorrect. Cooperative learning groups are most beneficial to auditory learners.

   B. Incorrect. Constructing a model would benefit a kinesthetic learner.

C. **Correct.** Graphic organizers provide visual representations of the material.

D. Incorrect. Lectures benefit auditory learners.

12) **Which of the following is true of gender differences between learners?**

A. Boys tend to have lower attention spans.

B. Boys and girls equally want to please their teachers.

C. Boys typically prefer one learning style.

D. There is a gap in cognitive ability between girls and boys.

Answers:

A. **Correct.** Younger children tend to have wider gaps, but boys typically need to change activities more frequently than girls.

B. Incorrect. Girls generally want to please their teachers. Boys tend to be more concerned with mastery.

C. Incorrect. Boys often prefer multiple learning styles. Girls often seem to prefer one style.

D. Incorrect. There is no difference in cognitive ability between the sexes.

STUDENTS WITH EXCEPTIONALITIES

Exceptionality is strength or weakness in academic functioning that requires extra attention to meet the needs of the student. Exceptionalities include giftedness, mental illness, speech disorders, physical disabilities, intellectual disabilities, and medical issues that interfere with school performance.

Gifted and talented students are also considered intellectually exceptional because adaptation must be made to the regular curriculum to meet their needs. Typically, these students are identified as having IQs over 130.

Cognitive disabilities are impairments in intellectual functioning and adaptive behavior. A cognitive disability may be mild, moderate, or severe. Most students with cognitive disabilities are mildly impaired with IQ scores between 55 and 70. Students with moderate cognitive disabilities typically have IQ scores between 30 and 55. Students with severe cognitive disabilities have IQ scores below 30. Cognitive disabilities may be caused by genetic disorders, such as Down syndrome, or can be caused by injuries to the brain, such as fetal alcohol syndrome.

Physical disabilities are impairments that require assistance during the school day. Students with chronic health conditions may need physical therapy, repositioning, or changing. Students with **visual** impairments, such as blindness, may need access to materials in Braille. **Motor skill** impairments, which are characterized by loss of movement, may be caused by injury or disease. Students with motor skill impairments may need access to assistive technology, such as wheelchairs, walkers, prosthesis, and communication technology.

Communication disorders include all deficits in **speech** and **language**, including autism and hearing impairments. Students with speech disorders have difficulty forming words. Students with language impairments have difficulty with comprehension. Whereas speech disorders may stifle expressive language, language disorders negatively affect both expressive and receptive language.

Behavioral exceptionalities interfere with educational performance of the student or other students. Students with behavioral disorders may find it difficult to form relationships with other people. They could have difficulty recognizing social cues and conforming to expectations. Behavior issues include attention-deficit/hyperactivity disorder, emotional disorders, or conduct disorders.

SAMPLE QUESTIONS

13) **Which of the following is an example of a child with an exceptionality?**

   A.   Hannah has an IQ of 85.

   B.   Brynn has pneumonia.

   C.   Jaimie has an IQ of 145.

   D.   Hallie has been acting out since the death of her father two weeks ago.

Answers:

   A.   Incorrect. IQ scores between 70 and 130 are considered normal.

   B.   Incorrect. Brynn's illness is not chronic.

   C.   **Correct.** Students with IQs over 130 are considered gifted and talented.

   D.   Incorrect. Hallie's behavior is a reaction based on circumstances rather than a chronic disorder.

14) **Damien has exceptional comprehension but struggles with forming words to express himself. Which possible exceptionality should be explored?**

   A.   cognitive disorder

   B.   language disorder

   C.   speech disorder

   D.   behavioral disorder

Answers:

   A.   Incorrect. Cognitive disorders are intellectual disabilities that are reflected in IQ scores.

   B.   Incorrect. Since Damien has good receptive language skills, as demonstrated through comprehension, it is unlikely a language disorder.

   C.   **Correct.** Problems with expressive language may indicate a speech disorder.

   D.   Incorrect. There is no indication of a behavioral disorder.

Legislation and Students with Exceptionalities

To ensure that students with exceptionalities are guaranteed their right to a free and appropriate public education, the following legislation has been passed.

The **Americans with Disabilities Act** prohibits discrimination based on disabilities. In schools, this includes activities that take place both on and off campus, including athletics and extracurricular activities. Typically, building modifications must be made to make facilities wheelchair accessible, but if that is cost prohibitive, other accommodations must be made to give disabled students equal access to services.

The **Individuals with Disabilities Education Act (IDEA)** Part B serves students aged three to twenty-two. IDEA provides guidelines to schools to help address the individual needs of special education students. IDEA establishes the framework for identification, parental rights, placement decisions, modifications and accommodations, behavior supports, transitioning to adulthood, and handling disputes between parents and schools. Part C provides state-run early intervention services for children from birth to three years of age. Each child who is identified as eligible for special services must have an **Individualized Education Plan (IEP)** developed each year. The IEP outlines the student's learning goals and identifies the supports and services that the school will provide for the child. The IEP is a legal document that must be followed by all school personnel.

Section 504 of the Rehabilitation Act provides services to all students in federally assisted programs who have physical or mental impairments that substantially limit one or more life activities. Identification does not come from a single source but from a combination of assessments, teacher recommendations, and doctor's statements. Once a 504 plan is in place, the regular classroom is legally responsible to provide all outlined modifications and accommodations for the child.

There are additional pieces of legislation that affect all students, including those with exceptionalities. Teachers should be familiar with The Family Educational Rights and Privacy Act of 1974 (FERPA), The Every Student Succeeds Act (which replaced No Child Left Behind [NCLB]), the McKinney-Vento Homeless Assistance Act, and Title IX of the Education Amendments of 1972.

The Family Educational Rights and Privacy Act of 1974 prohibits schools from sharing identifiable information about students. Further, it gives parents and students, once they reach the age of eighteen years, the right to review their records and request that amendments to those records be made.

NCLB was federal legislation passed in 2002 that held schools to high standards using high-stakes testing to determine federal funding. NCLB was replaced in December 2015 with the Every Student Succeeds Act (ESSA). ESSA continues to require annual testing, but states, rather than the federal government, have the authority to determine performance standards.

Title IX of the Education Amendments of 1972 protects students against gender discrimination in all federally funded education programs, including colleges that receive federal funding.

The McKinney-Vento Homeless Assistance Act provides services, such as transportation to a child's home school or enrollment without appropriate documentation, for students who do not have a consistent home. This includes children who are living with family/friends; students who live in temporary housing, such as motels and campgrounds; children living in shelters; and children who live in cars, parks, or public spaces. Each school must have a homeless liaison to provide support for families of homeless children.

SAMPLE QUESTIONS

15) **Which of the following is a violation of legislation that has been designed to protect children with disabilities?**

   A. Dalton has a doctor's statement that he has attention-deficit/ hyperactivity disorder, but he was not placed on a 504 plan because his teachers have demonstrated that it is not affecting his classroom performance.

   B. The aisles of the school library are too narrow to accommodate a wheelchair, so the media specialist brings books to Sabrina.

   C. Rhonda's parents have been denied their teacher of choice for science in a regular classroom setting.

   D. Tyler has been denied enrollment in football during the regular, open-enrollment period because he is autistic.

   Answers:

   A. Incorrect. A doctor's statement alone is not the determining factor when deciding to have a child placed on a 504 plan.

   B. Incorrect. Ideally, the building will be accessible to all learners, but if that is cost prohibitive, other accommodations may be made.

   C. Incorrect. Teacher selection is not within parents' rights.

   D. Correct. Students may not be discriminated against in athletics based on disability.

16) **Which piece of federal legislation provides state intervention services to disabled students from birth to three years of age?**

   A. Americans with Disabilities Act

   B. Individuals with Disabilities Education Act

   C. Section 504 of the Rehabilitation Act

   D. Title IX

Answers:

A.   Incorrect. Americans with Disabilities Act provides antidiscrimination legislation.

B.   **Correct.** IDEA, Part C, provides state services to disabled children from birth to three years.

C.   Incorrect. Section 504 provides services to physically or mentally impaired students who may not qualify under IDEA.

D.   Incorrect. Title IX prohibits discrimination based on gender.

GIFTED STUDENTS

Intellectually gifted students typically have an IQ greater than 130, but it is recommended that in addition to aptitude tests, multiple measures (portfolio assessments, anecdotal records, and student achievement) should be considered when placing students. Gifted children are typically alert, curious, and imaginative. At a young age, they have comparatively advanced vocabulary, memory, and sense of humor. However, gifted children also have a tendency toward radicalism, impulsivity, and emotionality.

Gifted students are typically **divergent thinkers**, meaning that they think more deeply and differently from other people. While some openly display eccentricities, others may hide their opinions. What may seem like common sense to others may not make sense to a divergent thinker. The differences in thought processes may irritate peers and teachers. Frequently, gifted students prefer to immerse themselves in one thing at a time, finding it difficult to multitask. They are seen as irresponsible because they view homework as a waste of time. Understanding what the teacher wants from them is often elusive. Gifted students need support building relationships and understanding which parts of the assignment require the use of a format and which parts of the assignment are more flexible so that they know where their creativity can shine through.

> **QUICK REVIEW**
>
> How might a reward system for a class of gifted students differ from one used with on-level students?

Successful **differentiation** supports the use of advanced curricula that favor inquiry-based learning activities. The use of independent study is not supported by research. Challenges to educators of gifted students include staying ahead of the children on content knowledge, being organized enough to have multiple activities happening simultaneously, and competently modifying curricula to meet the needs of advanced learners.

SAMPLE QUESTIONS

17) Which of the following is a typical behavior of a gifted student?

    A.   Howell makes great grades and always completes his homework on time.

    B.   Lynn is a popular student who tries to please her parents and teachers.

    C.   Grayson is the class president, quarterback on the football team, and at the top of his class.

    D.   Delaney is funny, has a high vocabulary, and excels in AP Calculus, but she rarely turns in her homework.

Answers:

    A.   Incorrect. Howell is an ideal student but does not display the characteristics of giftedness.

    B.   Incorrect. Lynn has excellent social skills but does not display the characteristics of giftedness.

    C.   Incorrect. Grayson is a hard worker who is capable of multitasking and excelling in multiple areas, but he does not display the characteristics of giftedness.

    D.   **Correct.** Delaney's advanced humor, vocabulary, and high level of interest in an advanced subject paired with her lack of organization and interest in mundane tasks like homework may indicate giftedness.

18) Which of the following traits might indicate that a four-year-old is gifted?

    A.   sorts objects by shape and color

    B.   speaks in five to six word sentences

    C.   dresses and undresses self

    D.   becomes obsessed with spiders

Answers:

    A.   Incorrect. This is an example of typical development.

    B.   Incorrect. This is an example of typical development.

    C.   Incorrect. This is an example of typical development.

    D.   **Correct.** A gifted child may become obsessed with one thing and want to learn everything there is to know about that subject before moving on to something else.

ENGLISH–LANGUAGE LEARNERS

English-language learners (ELL) face a unique set of challenges. Learning a new language at the same time as learning content objectives is different from acquisition of the native language through the preschool years. Many of the rules about how language works differ from one language to the next, which requires relearning language patterns. Five stages of **second-language acquisition** have been identified.

Stage one is when the student is just beginning to learn receptive language. Students learn through pictures, diagrams, and body language. In this stage, students listen more than they speak and will become fatigued from being immersed in a new language. Teaching strategies that work at this stage include choral reading, peer tutoring, and total physical response (TPR). TPR involves role-playing phrases in English. It should be noted that textbook language is much different from the language English speakers use in conversation. Whenever possible, **authentic language** from storybooks, newspapers, the Internet and from other sources should be used.

Stage two is the emerging stage that occurs approximately six months after students begin to learn receptive language. Students will begin using short phrases. Teaching strategies include the use of graphic organizers, charts, graphs, and labeling. For the next several years, students may fall into **code-switching**, or slipping into their second language while speaking their native language. As the new language becomes dominant, they will reverse code-switching.

Stage three is developing. The student may initiate conversations with peers and can understand modified curriculum. At this point, the child has developed **basic interpersonal communication skills (BICS)**, which is basically conversational English. Professionals may be confused into thinking the student is more ready for academic independence than they are. Teaching strategies for stage three include flashcards and choral reading.

Stage four is expanding. Students are becoming fluent speakers but continue to struggle with writing and sentence structure. Learning activities should focus on writing and comprehension.

Stage five is bridging. Students will be exited from ELL programs but may continue to need teacher support for several years. **Cognitive academic language proficiency (CALP)** refers to a student's ability to comprehend academic vocabulary in English. Typically, it takes five to seven years for students to reach this level.

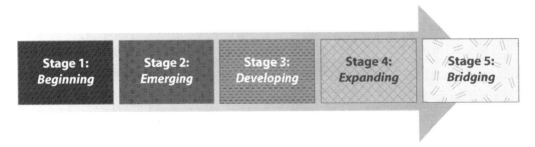

Figure 1.4. The Five Stages of Second-Language Acquisition

English-Language Proficiency Standards (ELPS) are designed not only to support ESL instruction but also to be used in the content areas to increase students' academic readiness. There are ten identified ELPS.

1. Students will be able to construct meaning from literary and informational text or presentations.

2. Students will be able to exchange information orally and in writing.

3. Students will be able to speak and write about literary and informational text.

4. Students will be able to construct and defend oral and written statements.

5. Students will be able to solve problems using research.

6. Students will be able to critique the claims of others both orally and in writing.

7. Students will be able to make appropriate word choices orally and in writing in relationship to the audience and purpose.

8. Students will be able to comprehend the meaning of words in literary and informational text.

9. Students will be able to speak and write clearly and coherently.

10. Students will be able to accurately use English when speaking and writing.

SAMPLE QUESTIONS

19) **Which of the following is NOT a source of authentic language?**

    A.   textbooks

    B.   newspapers

    C.   storybooks

    D.   Internet

Answers:

    A.   **Correct.** The academic language that is used in textbooks is different from conversational language and may confuse beginners.

    B.   Incorrect. Newspapers have a conversational tone and structure.

    C.   Incorrect. Storybooks have a conversational tone and structure.

    D.   Incorrect. Internet has a conversational tone and structure.

20) **Approximately how long does it take students to acquire cognitive academic language proficiency (CALP)?**

    A.   six months to a year

    B.   one to two years

    C.   three to five years

    D.   five to seven years

Answers:

A.   Incorrect. Students will likely be emerging with short phrases during this time.

B.   Incorrect. During this time period, the student may be able to participate in social language but will not understand academic language.

C.   Incorrect. At this point, students will communicate proficiently but may need continued support with writing and academic comprehension.

D.   Correct. For a student to become academically proficient in a new language takes five to seven years.

ACCOMMODATING STUDENTS WITH EXCEPTIONALITIES

Students with exceptionalities may need accommodations and modifications to the curriculum and learning environment to meet their learning goals. **Accommodations** in the classroom give a student access to the same curriculum as their grade-level peers, but information is presented in a different way. Accommodations may be instructional or environmental. Some examples of accommodations include the following:

▶   audiobooks and other media in lieu of text
▶   item presented in a larger print with fewer words per page
▶   oral instructions presented
▶   notes provided
▶   visual organizers
▶   written instructions
▶   calculator or word processor use
▶   setting isolated
▶   extra time
▶   frequent breaks
▶   supplementary materials
▶   a behavior contract
▶   check-in/check-out sheet

Modifications are changes made to the curriculum or environment because students are so far behind that they are unable to progress using the same curriculum or settings as their peers. Modifications include the following:

▶   shortened assignments
▶   modified grading
▶   modified assignments
▶   alternate assignments

Annually, teachers, parents, administrators, and support personnel have a meeting for each special education student where the IEP is developed. The IEP outlines the student's learning goals and identifies the accommodations and modifications that the school must legally provide for the child. Modifications may be made to the IEP at any time by having an IEP meeting.

SAMPLE QUESTIONS

21) **Which of the following is considered a modification?**

   A.   audio recordings of text

   B.   calculator use

   C.   alternate assignments

   D.   large print

Answers:

   A.   Incorrect. This is an example of an accommodation. Accommodations present the same information in a different way.

   B.   Incorrect. This is an example of an accommodation. Accommodations present the same information in a different way.

   C.   Correct. This is an example of a modification. Modifications are changes in the curriculum that are necessary because the student is so far below grade level.

   D.   Incorrect. This is an example of an accommodation. Accommodations present the same information in a different way.

22) **Elijah's IEP says that he may use calculators on tests as a modification. Mrs. Jones does not think that he needs one for the algebra test. What are her options?**

   A.   Mrs. Jones has the option of denying Elijah a calculator based on her professional opinion.

   B.   Mrs. Jones could talk to Elijah to see if she can convince him not to use the calculator.

   C.   Mrs. Jones can call Elijah's parents to see if they agree with her.

   D.   Mrs. Jones can request an IEP meeting to see if the team agrees to have the calculator modification removed.

Answers:

   A.   Incorrect. The teacher does not have the flexibility to make changes to the IEP independent of the IEP team.

   B.   Incorrect. The student must be provided modifications and accommodations as they are written in the IEP.

   C.   Incorrect. The student's parents may not make changes to the IEP independent of the IEP team.

>   **D.**   **Correct.** Accommodations and modifications that are written into the IEP must be followed until another IEP meeting is held to discuss changes.

STUDENT MOTIVATION AND LEARNING ENVIRONMENT

What part does motivation play in cognition? No matter how great the lesson is, students will not learn if they are not engaged. Foundational behaviorists have researched methods of motivating students to behave and attend to learning tasks. This section will review classroom management and student motivation.

FOUNDATIONAL BEHAVIORISTS

Foundational behaviorists created the basis for what we now know about behaviorism. **Edward Thorndike** was a psychologist whose research initially led to operant conditioning. Operant conditioning is learning how to behave because of rewards or punishments that are given in response to conduct. Thorndike's three laws of learning are the law of effect, the law of readiness, and the law of exercise. The law of effect states that pleasant consequences lead to repetitive behavior, whereas unpleasant consequences extinguish behavior. The law of readiness explains that learners will be resistant to learning before they are ready. The law of exercise states that what is practiced gets stronger, whereas what is not practiced becomes weaker.

John Watson coined the term *behaviorism*. He was the first psychologist who believed that subjectivity needed to be removed from psychology. **Behaviorism** objectively measures and controls behavior in response to stimuli. Believing that the three emotions of children (fear, rage, and love) could be conditioned, Watson performed what would now be considered unethical experiments to create phobias in an orphaned infant using negative stimuli for operant conditioning. Behaviorism in the early 1920s was for data and observation only, rather than for improving life, until about thirty years later. One example in the classroom might be test anxiety. Many children have been conditioned to feel fear during high-stakes testing.

Abraham Maslow developed Maslow's Hierarchy of Needs, which he theorized to be the unconscious desires that motivate people. According to Maslow, as each stage is achieved, a person may turn his or her attention to the next stage. In stage one, physical needs of air, food, water, shelter, comfort, sex, and sleep are the primary sources of motivation. If all of stage one needs are met, the person will progress to stage two, which consists of the safety needs, which include security, stability, and freedom from fear. The third stage includes needs of love and belonging from coworkers, family, friends, and romantic partners. The fourth stage involves self-esteem, which includes success, independence, status, and respect. The fifth state is self-actualization; although not everyone makes it to this level, those who self-actualize have realized their potential and seek fulfillment and growth. Classroom application of Maslow's theory means that a student's physical and emotional needs must be met before that child can feel successful.

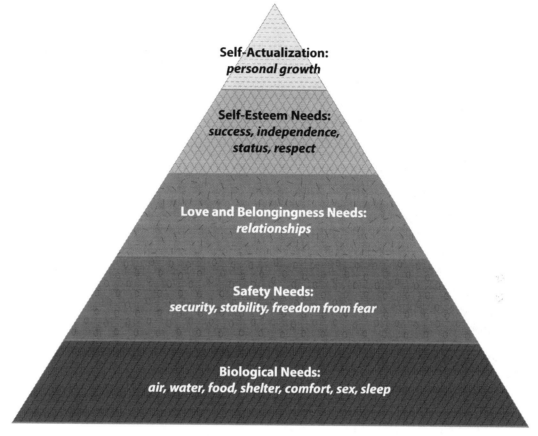

Figure 1.5. Maslow's Hierarchy of Needs

B.F. Skinner was a psychologist who expanded on Thorndike and Watson's work on operant conditioning. Skinner's work involved learning by responding to the environment rather than in response to stimuli. Successfully training several animals to do some extraordinary things, including teaching pigeons to play ping-pong, he was able to prove that learning happens when the teacher facilitates self-paced learning activities and provides rewards for success. He concluded that reinforcement must be part of learning behavior. In the classroom, this means allowing the learner time to meet learning goals and offering lots of praise and positive reinforcement along the way.

Erik Erikson is a psychologist who expanded on Sigmund Freud's ideas with his own theory of psychosocial development. For each stage, the individual must reconcile his or her own personal needs with the needs of society. Failure at any stage can result in personality disorders and stunt future stages, but all is not lost, as the individual may resolve any issues that develop later. During the first stage, trust versus mistrust, infants learn how to trust themselves and others based on the response of caregivers to their cries. In the second stage, autonomy versus shame and doubt, toddlers become willful as rules are introduced. Self-control and independence come from the ability to be independent within a structured environment. The third stage, initiative versus guilt, children are exposed to peer relationships and begin to develop personality traits, such as independence and leadership. In the fourth stage, industry versus inferiority, chilren are in school and are exposed to new materials, new people, and new experiences. For the first time, they are compared to a standard and assessed by others. By the end, they will feel successful or like failures. In the fifth stage, teenagers resolve identity versus role confusion. They may try out different friends, styles, and belief systems on their way to figuring out who they are. Erikson's sixth stage is intimacy versus isolation. In early adulthood, individuals learn to love other people. The last two stages, generativity versus stagnation and integrity versus despair, occur in middle and

Trust vs. Mistrust (birth – 18 months)

If the primary caregivers are nurturing, children will be hopeful. If they are unpredictable, children will become anxious. Children need caregivers to answer their cries, or they will not feel safe or trust other people.

Autonomy vs. Shame (18 – 36 months)

If caregivers are supportive and patient while children try new things, they will become independent, but if the caregivers are critical, children become overly dependent. As children are toilet training, they are beginning to exercise more control over their lives and their bodies. Children will want to do things for themselves, such as making choices and getting themselves dressed.

Initiative vs. Guilt (3 – 5 years)

If children are allowed to explore, they will learn to become leaders and decision makers. If parents are overly controlling, children will feel like a nuisance and lack initiative.

Industry vs. Inferiority (5 – 12 years)

Peer groups and teachers, in addition to parents, begin to play a role in children's social development. If initiative is reinforced and children are able to achieve goals valued by society, they will feel confident in their abilities. Otherwise, children may feel inferior. This is the first stage where performance, rather than participation, is judged by others as students enter school.

Identity vs. Role Confusion (12 – 18 years)

During this stage, adolescents are trying to find their sexual and occupational identity. Success will result in acceptance of others. Failure to establish an identity or being forced into an identity may result in rebellion or an identity crisis. Children during this stage make frequent identity changes as they attempt to "find themselves." Some rebellion against adults is normal at this age, as peer groups become more important, but should be resolved by the end of this stage.

Intimacy vs. Isolation (18 – 40 years)

Successful completion results in love. Failure to commit can result in depression.

Generativity vs. Stagnation (40 – 65 years)

Successful careers, family, and community involvement results in care. Failure results in stagnation.

Ego Integrity vs. Despair (65 + years)

When reflecting on life, if proud of their accomplishments, individuals will feel wise and face death without fear. If dissatisfied, individuals will become depressed.

Figure 1.6. Erikson's Theory of Psychosocial Development

late adulthood. Teachers at each grade level can contribute to the psychosocial development of their students in a variety of ways. Preschool students need to feel safe to try new things, make choices, and make mistakes. Elementary students also build confidence by taking responsibility, making decisions, and realizing that it is okay to mess up sometimes. Middle and high school students need teachers who model respect, expose them to career choices, and help them build confidence in their abilities.

SAMPLE QUESTIONS

23) According to Maslow's Hierarchy of Needs, children will not be able to form healthy relationships if which of the following needs has not been met?

   A.   success

   B.   freedom from fear

   C.   independence

   D.   personal growth

Answers:

   A.   Incorrect. Success is a stage four need that comes after relationships.

   B.   Correct. Freedom of fear is a stage two need that must be realized before students can develop healthy relationships in stage three.

   C.   Incorrect. Independence is a stage four need that comes after relationships.

   D.   Incorrect. Personal growth is a stage five need that comes after relationships.

24) Which of the following researchers did NOT research operant conditioning?

   A.   Edward Thorndike

   B.   John Watson

   C.   Abraham Maslow

   D.   B. F. Skinner

Answers:

   A.   Incorrect. Edward Thorndike was the first psychologist to study operant conditioning.

   B.   Incorrect. John Watson expanded Edward Thorndike's studies with operant conditioning experiments using an orphaned child exposed to negative stimuli to create phobias.

   C.   Correct. Abraham Maslow developed a hierarchy of unconscious motivators.

D.   Incorrect. B. F. Skinner expanded on Thorndike's and Watson's work but added the element of using operant conditioning to help people.

MOTIVATION THEORIES

Motivation theory explains the driving forces behind conduct. There are several motivation theories. According to **self-determination theory**, everyone has a perceived locus of causality (PLOC). People with a higher internal PLOC are more likely to feel in control of their circumstances and are motivated by internal rewards, or **intrinsic motivation**. People with an external PLOC feel that outside forces are controlling their behavior and are motivated by external rewards, or **extrinsic motivation**. Helping students understand their PLOC will move them toward feeling more in control of their own behavior.

Attribution theory suggests that internal attribution, or personality flaws, are assumed when other people make mistakes. Victim-blaming occurs because people tend to view the victim as a predictable stereotype. When an individual makes a mistake, he or she tends to view the cause as external. People tend to think of themselves as more complex than they give others credit for being. Blaming others and making excuses destroy relationships. Teachers should be careful about applying internal attributions to students and should help students understand that others are as multifaceted as they are. Care should be taken to recognize when limited internal attributions are made by students, parents, and coworkers about other students, parents, and coworkers.

Cognitive dissonance theory refers to the uneasiness that is felt when an individual has conflicting thoughts. To resolve cognitive dissonance, individuals will change their behavior, change their thoughts about the behavior, or justify the behavior. Creating cognitive dissonance carries with it the power of persuasion. Recognizing and helping students recognize where the internal conflict is coming from will help resolve it. For example, Tammy and Tiffany are good friends who have a lot in common. They agree on everything. Tammy loves art and is excited that Tiffany is in her class. After the first week, Tiffany begins complaining that art is dumb and boring. Tammy is confused because either her feeling about art is wrong or her feeling about agreeing with Tiffany about everything is wrong. Tammy will feel uncomfortable until she is able to resolve that inner conflict.

Classic conditioning involves learning a response to stimuli or the environment. If students view a classroom as safe, inviting, and interesting, they are less likely to miss class and more likely to pay attention. **Operant conditioning** involves eliciting a response through rewards or punishment. Intermittent rewards, such as preferred activities, praise, and tangible rewards, are powerful tools for modifying classroom behavior.

SAMPLE QUESTIONS

25) Jaylen is an eighth-grade student who has always followed the rules and had good relationships with peers and adults. Recently, she has been accepted into a social group that talks about smoking cigarettes, doing drugs, and writing graffiti. Jaylen is torn between knowing what is right and wanting to be accepted. What is she experiencing?

 A.   extrinsic motivation

 B.   external attribution

 C.   cognitive dissonance

 D.   response to stimuli

Answers:

 A.   Incorrect. Extrinsic motivation describes an external reward. While Jaylen may be extrinsically motivated by peer acceptance, the torn feeling describes cognitive dissonance.

 B.   Incorrect. External attribution involves blaming outside circumstances for mistakes and judging others more harshly than an individual judges himself or herself.

 C.   Correct. Cognitive dissonance describes Jaylen's two conflicting thoughts.

 D.   Incorrect. Jaylen could potentially make bad choices in response to the stimulating effect of peer acceptance, but the feeling of having difficulty resolving conflicting thoughts describes cognitive dissonance.

26) Abraham is a second-grade student who completes very little work because he prefers play. Concerned about his disruption to the learning environment and lack of progress because of his behavior, Mr. Sissons places him on a behavior plan. Every fifteen minutes, Mr. Sissons places a stamp on Abraham's card if Abraham is attentive. Which motivation theory is Mr. Sissons putting into action?

 A.   classic conditioning

 B.   attribution

 C.   cognitive dissonance

 D.   operant conditioning

Answers:

 A.   Incorrect. Classic conditioning uses neutral or environmental stimuli to evoke a response.

 B.   Incorrect. Attribution blames other people for their mistakes and misfortunes but excuses oneself.

 C.   Incorrect. Cognitive dissonance involves reconciling two conflicting thoughts.

D.   **Correct.** Operant conditioning uses rewards and consequences to modify behavior.

CLASSROOM MANAGEMENT

Classroom management involves the strategies and procedures that are used to engage (inspire interest) and produce positive behavior outcomes for most students. Good classroom management provides a safe, orderly learning environment where time and attention is paid to academic pursuits in lieu of correcting student behavior. In contrast, poor classroom management contributes to teacher stress and reduced time on task. Good classroom management includes proactively teaching student expectations, providing engaging instruction, arranging the environment to reduce behavior issues, developing consistent classroom routines and procedures, and determining consequences for discipline problems. Consequences may include the following:

- ▶ private verbal warning
- ▶ nonverbal warning
- ▶ parent phone call
- ▶ loss of minutes from preferred activity
- ▶ seat reassignment
- ▶ private student–teacher conference
- ▶ loss of privileges
- ▶ alternate assignment

When students are intrigued by a learning experience that is well-planned, structured, and challenging, discipline issues diminish. Learning experiences such as these do not come by accident or even teacher experience. It takes time and thought to put together lessons that inspire students to learn.

Although there are occasional interruptions to the regular classroom schedule, students perform better when they are able to predict what will happen next. A class schedule should be posted and adhered to as much as possible. Consistency and structure make a classroom environment feel safe for all students.

Discussions about learning improve the retention and quality of the educational experience. Therefore, it is recommended that students have the opportunity to work with cooperative groups or pairs; however, students must be explicitly taught inclusivity. Proactively creating a culture in which every student feels welcome will reduce conflict. In addition to rules, procedures, and routines, adequate consideration should be given to developing plans for making every student feel wanted and capable.

Fear, embarrassment, frustration, and boredom can all lead to the fight-or-flight syndrome. The fight-or-flight syndrome means that when an individual feels stress, he or she will either fight back or run away. The teacher's awareness of the emotional state of students and the reasons behind strong emotions can de-escalate a situation that could lead to a disruption of learning.

Attention-getters, such as hand signals and sounds, can be taught to help students refocus. When teaching the attention-getter, the teacher needs to ensure that students understand and follow expectations. For example, the teacher may count down from three with the expectation that by the time he or she gets to zero, all eyes will be on the teacher, movement will stop, and there will be no talking. If the attention-getter is overused or underenforced, it will become ineffective.

When arranging a classroom, teachers should consider whether it is a teacher-centered classroom with all students facing the direction of the teacher, or a student-centered classroom, where students are arranged in groups or pairs and collaboration is encouraged. Researchers recommend a student-centered classroom. Some things to keep in mind are ensuring that every student has access to the learning materials, including the whiteboard, smart board, or projector screen, and that the teacher can easily circulate the room to monitor the progress of students and offer additional assistance when necessary. Students should have assigned seats, but those seats should be changed regularly so that students have an opportunity to work with many other students. The teacher must keep in mind individual student needs, such as hearing, vision, or attention issues, when selecting seat assignments. Members of the class need some personal space to put their things, as well as space to move around in the event that they need to change position. Regardless of age, students are proud to see their work on display. There should be a location for student work.

Positive behavior support is an example of a tiered behavior management system. Eighty percent or more of students fall into tier one in a tiered model of support. By establishing clear and consistent expectations, modeling expected behavior, and tracking data for the purpose of decision making, most students will comply with rules. Teachers at all grade levels should be careful about making assumptions that students will walk in the door understanding classroom expectations. Rules and procedures should not just be taught at the beginning of the year, but throughout the year, and as part of each transition of activity. For example, when teaching a full-group assignment, it might be reasonable to expect students to raise their hand to speak, but when students move into a cooperative learning group, expectations change. Students need to be explicitly taught the expectations each and every time the expectations change. It is important that rules are clear, nonnegotiable, and enforced. Student dignity should be maintained as consequences are applied. **Positive reinforcement**, such as praise and other rewards, should be tailored to the needs of the student. All high school students are not motivated by grades and may need other rewards. Fewer problems exist when students are intrinsically motivated by a curriculum that is relevant, interesting, at the appropriate level, and involves some degree of choice. It is much easier to **redirect**, or distract students from negative behavior, by channeling it into something positive if students are enjoying the learning experience. Inappropriate behavior occurs when students are attempting to escape boredom. Some methods for redirecting students without interrupting the flow of the lesson include proximity and nonverbal communication. Proximity is simply moving closer to the student or students who are having trouble staying focused. Many times, being near a potential problem averts it. Nonverbal communication includes eye contact, body language, hand signals, pointing to the assignment, and other ways of silently letting students know the expectations.

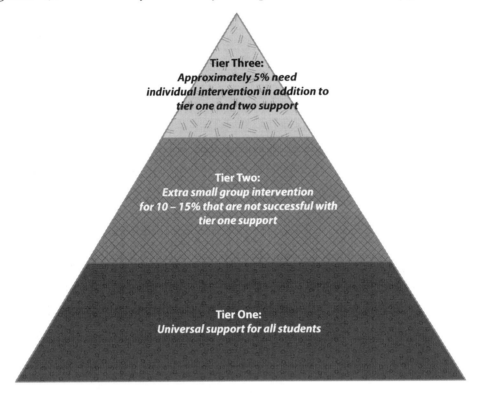

Figure 1.7. Tiered Behavior Management System

Between 10 and 15 percent of students fall into tier two and may need some additional support. Students who are not responding to the universal interventions in tier one may need small-group social skill training or mentoring to monitor and improve behavior.

Approximately 5 percent of students fall into tier three, which requires individualized intervention. A committee of school personnel should arrange for a functional behavior assessment and meet to create an individualized behavior plan, which may include a behavior contract.

There is a certain degree of record-keeping that teachers need to maintain as part of their professional responsibilities. Accurate attendance records are tied to school funding. While it is easy to become distracted by all of the other things teachers are thinking about during the school day, this is not something to let slip. However, it is also not recommended to let teachers' paperwork interfere with student learning. Seating assignments allow teachers to quickly make note of who is missing without taking time from instruction for roll call.

Grading and records of grades should be maintained throughout the year. Although some assignments may be quickly checked as a participation grade, each student should have at least two grades per week that assess skill mastery so that teachers, parents, and students will be aware of student achievement levels. (The exact number of assessment required will vary by school and district.) Parent contact and discipline reports offer crucial information that can be used in parent conferences, IEP meetings, and meetings with administrators. It is always advisable to make positive parent contact before it is necessary to report a problem.

Quality lesson plans are a necessary professional responsibility. Even experienced teachers who may be able to pull off an adequate lesson without lesson plans will deliver a better lesson if it has been thought out and committed to paper. Lesson plans should include thoughts about engagement, necessary materials, timing, and metacognition. Preparedness and timing go a long way toward improving classroom management.

SAMPLE QUESTIONS

27) **When should high school students be taught classroom expectations?**

   A. Rules and procedures should be mastered at a whole school assembly at the beginning of the year.

   B. High school students have been in school long enough to know the rules.

   C. Rules and procedures should be reviewed in the classroom on the first day of every month.

   D. Rules and procedures should be reviewed at every transition in activity.

Answers:

   A. Incorrect. If classroom rules are consistent throughout the school, this might be beneficial but not sufficient.

   B. Incorrect. Rules are different in different places and under different circumstances. Students of all ages need to be educated about expectations frequently.

   C. Incorrect. An introduction of classroom rules, perhaps with students help in their formation, is beneficial but not sufficient.

   D. Correct. Rules need to be clearly taught regularly throughout the year. Each time expectations change, they need to be reviewed.

28) Toby is a kindergarten student who acts out aggressively toward other boys in his class. The classroom management system that the teacher has in place is sufficient for almost all of the students, but he does not seem to be responding to it. What is his teacher's next step?

    A.   send the student to the principal's office and request suspension

    B.   refer the student to the school counselor for individual counseling

    C.   change the classroom management system

    D.   provide small-group social skills instruction

Answers:

    A.   Incorrect. Removing a child from class should be avoided.

    B.   Incorrect. Individual counseling may be necessary if other interventions do not work, but this teacher has not yet tried other interventions.

    C.   Incorrect. If the classroom management system is working for at least 80 percent of the students, it likely does not need to be changed.

    D.   **Correct.** Small-group social skills instruction or mentoring would be an appropriate intervention for a student who is not responding to universal interventions.

STUDENT SELF-MOTIVATION

Self-motivation is acquired as an individual makes movement toward a goal. Goals must reflect something that the child views as a need; therefore, the student must be involved in goal selection and other instructional decisions. Frequently, long-term goals may seem overwhelming for students, but broken into smaller parts, they begin to feel achievable, which is motivating. Subgoals are not intended to be easy but involve manageable movement in the right direction. The SMART goal format ensures that goals are specific, measurable, attainable, relevant, and time-bound.

Building and maintaining self-efficacy through positive reinforcement and frequent **feedback** is a necessary part of motivation. Self-efficacy is the belief that one is capable of accomplishing his or her goals. Student feedback may come in the form of positive reinforcement, such as praise, recognition, or rewards. Positive reinforcement is encouraging a behavior to continue or improve by providing the student with something he or she values. Although positive reinforcement from teachers is effective, it is more effective if the student feels the reward intrinsically. Feedback may also come in the form of negative reinforcement, which includes negative feedback and punishment. Negative feedback is intended to extinguish a behavior. More damage is done to self-efficacy by negative messages than positive messages do to increase it.

> **QUICK REVIEW**
>
> If more than 20 percent of the students are underperforming and seem unmotivated to learn, what steps should a teacher take?

Research has shown that when students are asked to self-monitor, they are more likely to keep their focus on learning than if grades are emphasized. De-emphasizing grades and allowing students to track their own progress, filling out self-assessments, and then meeting with teachers about their results are suggestions for self-monitoring.

SAMPLE QUESTIONS

29) **Which of the following is a key ingredient to self-motivation?**

  A.   consequences for failure

  B.   goal-setting

  C.   emphasis on grades

  D.   parent involvement

Answers:

  A.   Incorrect. Negative reinforcements damage self-efficacy that is necessary to stay self-motivated.

  B.   Correct. Goal-setting and achievement of subgoals is related to self-motivation.

  C.   Incorrect. De-emphasizing grades through self-regulation improves learner outcomes.

  D.   Incorrect. Parent involvement is extremely important through the education process, but self-motivation comes from within the student.

30) **Which of the following grading practices is most ineffective?**

  A.   formal self-assessments

  B.   students tracking their own progress

  C.   basing 30 percent of a student's grade on a semester final

  D.   student–teacher conferences

Answers:

  A.   Incorrect. Self-assessments are a way to keep students focused on learning as they see themselves moving closer to their learning goals.

  B.   Incorrect. Progress monitoring is a type of self-assessment that keeps students focused on learning.

  C.   Correct. Emphasizing grades as a measure of achievement toward learning goals deflects the focus away from learning.

  D.   Incorrect. Conferences between students and teachers are a way for students to monitor their own progress and keep focused on learning.

TERMS

Abraham Maslow: Maslow developed the Hierarchy of Needs, which he theorized to be the unconscious desires that motivate people.

accommodations: Accommodations provide students access to the same curriculum as their grade-level peers, but information is presented in a different way.

Albert Bandura: Bandura is a Canadian psychologist who developed the social learning theory.

Americans with Disabilities Act: This act prohibits discrimination based on disabilities. In schools, this includes activities that take place both on and off campus, including athletics and extracurricular activities.

attribution theory: Internal attribution is assumed when other people make mistakes or are victims, since individuals tend to see others as a predictable stereotype. When an individual makes a mistake, he or she tends to view the cause as external.

B.F. Skinner: Skinner expanded on operant conditioning but focused on responding to environment in lieu of responding to stimuli.

Basic interpersonal communication skills (BICS): BICS is conversational English.

Benjamin Bloom: Bloom contributed to the taxonomy of educational objectives and the theory of mastery learning.

classic conditioning: This practice involves learning a response to stimuli or the environment.

classical conditioning: A neutral stimulus becomes associated with a reflex response through conditioning.

code-switching: Code-switching happens when students slip into native language while speaking their second-language, or vice versa.

cognitive academic language proficiency (CALP): CALP is a student's ability to comprehend academic vocabulary in English.

cognitive disabilities: Cognitive disabilities are impairments in intellectual functioning and adaptive behavior.

cognitive dissonance theory: Uneasiness is felt when an individual has conflicting thoughts.

cognitive domain: Cognitive domain deals with acquiring intellect.

cognitive processes: Cognitive processes involve acquiring new knowledge and skills and being able to apply new learning to new situations and draw conclusions from it.

differentiation: Differentiation means providing curricula for students based on their individual needs, including learning styles and level.

divergent thinkers: Divergent thinkers are people who think more deeply and differently from other people.

Edward Thorndike: Thorndike's research initially led to operant conditioning; Thorndike's learning laws include the law of effect, the law of readiness, and the law of exercise.

engage: Engage means inspiring interest or motivation.

English-language learner (ELL): ELLs are students whose native language is not English.

English Language Proficiency Standards (ELPS): ELPS are objectives that not only support ESL instruction but also increase students' academic readiness in the content areas.

Erik Erikson: Erikson's theory of psychosocial development focuses on reconciling individual needs with the needs of society through stages.

exceptionality: Exceptionality is strength or weakness in academic functioning that requires extra attention to meet the needs of the student.

extrinsic motivation: Extrinsic motivation describes an external reward.

feedback: Feedback is information about performance.

foundational theorists: Foundational theorists are the people who provided the framework by which all current knowledge of cognitive processes is based.

individualized education plan (IEP): IEP is an annual meeting for each special education student that outlines the student's learning goals and identifies the accommodations and modifications that will be offered to the student.

Individuals with Disabilities Education Act (IDEA): This act provides guidelines to schools to help address the individual needs of special education students.

intellectually gifted: Students with an IQ greater than 130 are considered intellectually gifted.

intrinsic motivation: Intrinsic motivation describes an internal reward.

Jean Piaget: Piaget was a Swiss psychologist who was the first to study cognition in children. He identified stages of development and contributed to schema learning.

Jerome Bruner: Bruner was a constructivist theorist who contributed the three modes of representation to the field of cognitive development.

John Dewey: Dewey was a pragmatic philosopher who viewed learning as a series of scientific inquiry and experimentation; he advocated real-world experiences and volunteerism.

John Watson: Watson coined the term *behaviorism*, which objectively measures behavior in response to stimuli.

knowledge: Knowledge is acquired intellectual information.

language acquisition: Language acquisition is the process by which a new language is learned.

language impairments: Students with language impairments have difficulty with comprehension.

Lawrence Kohlberg: Kohlberg identified the stages of moral development.

learning styles: Learning styles research indicates that children learn in different ways.

learning theories: Learning theories describe how genetics, development, environment, motivation, and emotions affect a student's ability to acquire and apply knowledge.

Lev Vygotsky: Lev Vygotsky was a Russian psychologist who researched what has become the social development theory; more knowledgeable other (MKO) and zone of proximal development (ZPD) are the two main tenets of his philosophy.

metacognition: Metacognition means thinking about the learning process.

modifications: Modifications are changes made to the curriculum because students are so far behind that they are unable to use the same curriculum as their peers.

moral domain: Moral domain deals with the acquisition of morals and values.

motivation theory: Motivation theory explains the driving forces behind conduct.

motor disabilities: Motor disabilities, which are characterized by loss of movement, may be caused by injury or disease.

operant conditioning: Operant conditioning provides rewards or punishment as a motivation for desired performance.

physical disabilities: Physical disabilities are impairments that require assistance during the school day.

physical domain: Physical domain, also called the psychomotor domain, deals with all aspects of motor skill development.

positive reinforcement: Positive reinforcement, such as praise, recognition, or rewards, is encouraging a behavior to continue or improve by providing the student with something he or she values.

redirect: To redirect means to distract students from negative behavior by channeling their attention into something positive.

schema: Schema are frameworks for understanding.

Section 504 of the Rehabilitation Act: This section provides services to all students in federally assisted programs who have physical or mental impairments that substantially limit one or more life activities.

self-determination theory: According to self-determination theory, everyone has a perceived locus of causality.

self-efficacy: Self-efficacy is when a person believes that he or she is capable of achieving a learning goal.

self-motivation: Self-motivation is the drive from within that inspires a person to work toward something.

self-regulate: Self-regulate means to maintain control of one's own emotional responses.

skills: Skills are abilities to apply what has been learned.

social domain: Social domain is referred to as the affective or social-emotional domain and includes emotions, motivation, and attitudes.

speech disorders: Students with speech disorders have difficulty forming words.

transfer: To transfer means to apply knowledge to make inferences about new thoughts and ideas.

visual impairments: These impairments are problems with eyesight, such as blindness.

zone of proximal development (ZPD): ZPD is the space between what a child can do independently and the learning goal.

2

The Instructional Process

Chapter Two will focus on planning instruction, instructional strategies, questioning techniques, and communication techniques. When writing lesson plans, teachers must align the instructional objectives with learning activities and assessments while working within the framework of district planning tools. Research-based educational theories are married with available curriculum and the needs of individual students to develop plans that best serve the diverse classroom population. Teachers consider the way students think and adopt learning experiences that help students build schema and move information from short-term to long-term memory. There are a variety of questioning techniques and discussion strategies that help students and teachers effectively communicate with one another in a way that helps students reach their full potential.

PLANNING INSTRUCTION

This section discusses how to effectively plan a lesson by using backward design to implement a given learning objective determined by state and district frameworks. Lesson planning involves the alignment of standards, assessments, and learning materials. Frequently, the district will supply a scope and sequence that helps teachers determine the timeline, pacing, and depth of instruction for each learning objective. Beyond this, there are several considerations that help a teacher plan effectively. Educational theories such as cognitivism, social learning theory, behaviorism, and constructivism contribute to the planning process as teachers consider strategies to meet the needs of all learners.

Dr. Benjamin Bloom identified three domains of learning for the educational community. Each domain breaks down further into categories. Within the cognitive domain, there are question stems that may be used to assess standards within the cognitive, affective, and psychomotor domains using a hierarchy of depth and rigor. A classroom generally displays a large range of background knowledge and individual abilities that will call for differentiation of instruction. Enrichment provides more challenging experiences to broaden the learning of students who have mastered the standards. Enrichment does not mean more work; it means more meaningful work that often takes place in a higher level of Bloom's taxonomy. On the other hand, remediation strategies assess the learning needs of each student and provide targeted instruction when there are gaps in a student's background knowledge that prohibit him or her from moving forward at the expected rate. Resources and personnel with whom a teacher may collaborate to enhance the learning experiences of students will be explored.

THE ROLE OF STANDARDS AND FRAMEWORKS

Since the early 1990s, educational researchers and practitioners have been endorsing **standards-based education** in an effort to improve learner outcomes. Standards-based education involves clearly set goals that all students are expected to achieve.

The US Department of Education's role is to encourage high standards and a system of accountability for schools. However, each state is ultimately responsible for adopting its own curriculum standards and developing a system for accountability. When federal funds (such as Title I funds) are used to supplement curricula, the state still maintains responsibility, but there are increased expectations for the quality of programs and materials selected.

All schools in the state are required to use the state-adopted curriculum. Generally, the state will contract with a standardized testing company to develop and score testing materials based on the state's curriculum standards. Individual districts will frequently break down the state standards into a framework that includes the scope and sequence. District standards support state standards but sometimes provide more detail by identifying the emphasis that should be placed on each standard, as well as providing suggestions from available curriculum materials to cover each standard to the suggested depth.

Teachers should plan for their classroom using the concept of backward design. In other words, the teacher should begin by identifying the **lesson objective**, or student learning goals for a lesson, and the timeline for achieving the goals and subgoals as identified through state standards. The next step is to determine the **assessment**, or process of gathering data to determine the extent to which learning goals have been met. The third step is to determine the learning experiences that will provide students with the skills they need to move toward mastery. Materials and resources are selected based on their alignment with learning goals.

> **QUICK REVIEW**
>
> Why is alignment such an important part of the planning process?

SAMPLE QUESTIONS

1) **Which of the following entities bears the greatest responsibility in determining what second-grade students should be taught in science?**

    A.   the US Department of Education

    B.   the state department of education

    C.   the district board of education

    D.   the classroom teacher

Answers:

    A.   Incorrect. The US Department of Education urges states to adopt high standards but leaves it up to the state to make the decision.

    B.   Correct. Each state reviews and adopts curricular standards and accountability protocols.

    C.   Incorrect. Districts frequently clarify state-adopted standards, provide timelines, and recommend curricula, but the districts are required to implement state standards.

    D.   Incorrect. The classroom teacher designs instruction by planning for delivery of instruction of the objectives determined by the state and district.

2) **Which of the following is the first step in using backward design to plan a lesson?**

    A.   Identify the lesson objective.

    B.   Identify materials to be used.

    C.   Find engaging activities.

    D.   Assess mastery.

Answers:

    A.   Correct. Objectives are determined by the state, but before planning, the teacher needs to identify which objectives will be taught in this lesson.

    B.   Incorrect. Identifying materials to be used is the last step in planning a lesson.

    C.   Incorrect. Activities do need to be engaging, but they must be aligned to the learning objective; therefore, the objective must be identified first.

    D.   Incorrect. How to assess mastery of the objectives is the second step after determining what the objectives are.

THE ROLE OF EDUCATIONAL THEORIES

When developing lesson plans, the teacher should be mindful of educational theories that can contribute to the effectiveness of instruction. Cognitivism is the process by which a learner receives new information and processes it within his or her existing **schema**, or framework of understanding. The development of schema for information processing is encouraged using **mapping**. Mind maps graphically organize thoughts by starting with a main idea. Particularly when working with visual learners, the use of graphic organizers helps students connect new learning to prior knowledge.

Albert Bandura's social learning theory describes learning as occurring when another, more knowledgeable person engages in **modeling**, or demonstrations, that students are able to duplicate. **Reciprocal determinism** theorizes that a combination of cognitive factors, the environment, and stimuli determines behavior. Among the stimuli is **vicarious learning**, which means that when learners observe the consequences and emotions of others, they learn. In classroom terms, when a teacher models a skill or behavior, including appropriate reactions and consequences, students can determine which skills and behaviors are desirable and then replicate them. A teacher may guide students through a skill and then allow students to practice or watch other students practice that skill before attempting it themselves. Although this is a bit more teacher-centered than some other theories, the element of guided practice is essential when using social learning in lesson plans.

Constructivism is the theory that students construct their own knowledge through learning experiences. Advocates of constructivism support **problem-based learning**, in which the teacher facilitates activities that present open-ended questions—**inquiries**—for students to solve, and **discovery learning**, in which students perform experiments or research information as a means for comprehending new concepts. Teachers use **scaffolds**, or supports, within the zone of proximal development to gradually move students to higher levels of mastery. Although constructivism is not always easy to plan, the use of student-led constructivist techniques motivates students to stay on task, while scaffolding keeps students moving forward at their instructional level.

Behaviorism describes how the use of rewards and punishments conditions students to behave and learn. Teachers use **reinforcements** to strengthen behavior based on behavior goals. **Intrinsic rewards** mean that learners are internally satisfied by doing work because it is interesting, challenging, or relevant, or makes them feel successful; intrinsic rewards are more beneficial than extrinsic rewards. However, **extrinsic rewards**, or external rewards such as trinkets, praise, or recognition bestowed upon someone for doing a good job, may also be used to motivate students. **Punishment** is penalizing a student for the purpose of extinguishing behavior. Although punishments can be effective, they may also interfere with student motivation by diminishing a student's self-efficacy. Typically, behaviorism is used during lesson planning as the teacher considers aspects of instruction, such as engagement, motivation, transitions, and classroom management.

The following are positive reinforcements for students of all ages:

- time to listen to music
- homework passes
- a free pass to a school activity
- extra computer time
- positive phone call to parents
- preferred activity time
- praise
- permission to work with a peer
- stickers

SAMPLE QUESTIONS

3) Mrs. Paget is a fifth-grade teacher who is planning a lesson and needs to connect what the students already know about prehistoric plants and animals to new information about energy sources. Which strategy best connects new information to existing schema?

   A.   scaffolding
   B.   modeling
   C.   reinforcement
   D.   mapping

Answers:

   A.   Incorrect. Scaffolding provides support for students at their instructional level and is gradually removed so that students can work more independently. It is part of constructivism.

   B.   Incorrect. Modeling is when a more knowledgeable person, like the teacher, shows students how to do something. It is part of social learning theory.

   C.   Incorrect. Reinforcement is part of behaviorism and is used to condition students to learn or behave using a system of rewards.

   D.   Correct. Schema learning is part of cognitivism in which sorting new information within the existing frameworks of the mind can be accomplished through the use of mapping and other graphic organizers.

4) Mrs. Whitlock is a biology teacher who provides students with a question and then supports them as they design a lab and research project to determine a solution. Which theory is Mrs. Whitlock using?

   A.   cognitivism
   B.   behaviorism
   C.   constructivism
   D.   social learning

Answers:

A.   Incorrect. Cognitivism would support the use of advanced organizers to help students categorize elements of learning.

B.   Incorrect. Behaviorism is conditioning to support classroom management and engagement.

C.   **Correct.** The inquiry-based approach to learning is an example of constructivism.

D.   Incorrect. Social learning relies on modeling and mimicry while the teacher provides support.

The Role of Scope and Sequence

Typically, districts will develop a scope and sequence for planning that further explains how state standards will be taught in the district; in some cases, however, grade-level teams or individual teachers may be tasked with this duty as part of planning for the academic year. The **scope** outlines which learning objectives will be taught to students, which supporting standards need to be mastered for students to fully understand the objective, and the level of complexity that students need to attain. For example, if a state standard reads that students should be able to compose and decompose numbers to 1000, the scope may add some important details, such as using pictorial models or using standardized notation.

The **sequence** is the order in which learning objectives are taught to maximize student success. The sequence might include a suggested window of instruction and a pacing guide, as well as embedded opportunities to reteach related material.

SAMPLE QUESTIONS

5)   **Mr. Donaldson wants to know how much time he should devote to teaching his students about force and motion. Which document should he consult?**

A.   state standards

B.   the scope

C.   the sequence

D.   the textbook

Answers:

A.   Incorrect. State standards will tell Mr. Donaldson what needs to be mastered but will not provide him with a timeline.

B.   Incorrect. The scope will help Mr. Donaldson determine the level of complexity with which students need to understand the objective.

C.   **Correct.** The sequence provides a suggested timeline and pacing for a lesson.

D.   Incorrect. Textbooks are limited in their ability to provide this type of information for individual districts and classrooms.

6)   **Ms. Adams is teaching a lesson on the impact of plate tectonics on geological events. To find out which geological events students need to understand, which document would she consult?**

A.   state standards

B.   the scope

C.   the sequence

D.   the textbook

Answers:

A.   Incorrect. The state standards give Ms. Adams the objective, but she may need additional details.

B.   **Correct.** The scope provides the details that will help Ms. Adams understand how deeply students need to understand this concept.

C.   Incorrect. The sequence explains the order and pacing in which material is taught.

D.   Incorrect. The textbook may provide some examples but may not be aligned with the scope and sequence.

CONTENT SELECTION

A teacher should consider several things when selecting the appropriate materials for a lesson. First, the learning activities need to be aligned with the standards and assessments. It does not help students to participate in a fun, engaging learning experience that is only vaguely aligned to their learning goals.

An understanding of the students' developmental levels, cultural contexts, and background knowledge will help a teacher select materials that are engaging rather than distracting. Students are put off by books at reading levels that are too low for them, just as they are overwhelmed by hard-to-understand tasks that are beyond their level of understanding. Additionally, teaching about biomass fuels to students who think corn comes from a can in the grocery store will be frustrating unless some of those gaps are acknowledged and filled.

Materials should be checked for validity based on current research. For example, a book written about the planets in 1984 will have some incorrect information about Pluto because scientific discoveries about the dwarf planet have been made since that time.

Availability also plays a role in which materials work best to teach a lesson. There are some amazing Web-based programs available for students, but if the school's Internet capabilities are limited, students will be constantly frustrated. The best advice for material selection is to know the standards, the students, and the content, and to understand any constraints that may exist.

The following are quick-check questions for sources:

- ▶ What bias does the source show and does that interfere with the learning goal?
- ▶ How does the material help advance the learning goal?
- ▶ What student bias or prejudice might interfere with their reading/understanding of the source?
- ▶ What other sources might accomplish the same goal?
- ▶ Is this the best source for the lesson?
- ▶ What will students do with the material?
- ▶ How is the concept being delivered?

SAMPLE QUESTIONS

7) **Mr. Cavitt is teaching a unit about how to vote in an election. Which of the following materials would be most appropriate?**

A. a book published in 1985

B. the Democratic National Committee website

C. the state election board's publications

D. the Republican National Committee website

Answers:

A. Incorrect. Electronic voting was not part of the election process until 2004. This book is out of date.

B. Incorrect. The Democratic National Committee is biased toward candidates from the Democratic Party.

C. Correct. Each state's election board has up-to-date information about the voting process.

D. Incorrect. The Republican National Committee is biased toward Republican candidates.

8) **Ms. Gorman found a free website that contains self-correcting math games. She should consider all the factors EXCEPT which of the following?**

A. What technology is available at the school?

B. How closely do the lessons align with the standards?

C. Are the graphics and text developmentally appropriate?

D. Have the students mastered all the concepts introduced in this game?

Answers:

A. Incorrect. She does need to consider the availability of technology, including Internet capabilities of the school, but that is not the only factor.

B.   Incorrect. The lessons must align with standards to be an appropriate use of instructional time, but there are other factors as well.

C.   Incorrect. Developmental stages of the students should be considered to keep them engaged and at their instructional level, as well as other factors.

D.   Correct. A self-correcting game may introduce some challenging new concepts to students.

INSTRUCTIONAL OBJECTIVES

Dr. Benjamin Bloom outlined three domains of learning. The **learning domains** are cognitive, affective, and psychomotor. The **cognitive domain** controls the development of intellect. The ways students process new information, store knowledge, and retrieve it to apply to new circumstances fall within the cognitive domain. Most of the academic knowledge that students learn in school takes place within the cognitive domain. The **affective domain** controls the development of emotions, values, and attitudes. For example, students may have strong feelings about work ethic, human rights advocacy, or environmental protection. The ways students align their priorities and form opinions about things that matter most to them are part of the affective domain. Student motivation and engagement are tied to the affective domain. The **psychomotor domain** controls motor skill development. Separate from simply being kinesthetic, activities within the psychomotor domain are designed to specifically improve motor or perceptual skills. For example, playing soccer, writing the letters of the alphabet, and creating art take place within the psychomotor domain.

When developing instructional objectives within the cognitive domain, teachers can use Bloom's hierarchy of cognitive skills designed to move students to more rigorous thought processes. **Bloom's taxonomy** classifies cognitive processes from simple to abstract.

The basic level is remembering facts. Although there is a certain amount of recall that students must develop in order to have enough background information to move forward, teachers should be cautious of spending too much time developing this low-level skill. Ideally, a big majority of instructional time should be spent in the higher levels of thought. The second level is applying the information students have learned. Next is analysis, which involves making inferences and drawing conclusions. The fourth level is evaluating, which includes developing and defending a position. Finally, creating gives students the opportunity to pull the information together to develop a unique solution.

The levels of Bloom's taxonomy:

- Level one: remembering facts
- Level two: applying information
- Level three: making inferences and drawing conclusions
- Level four: evaluating and defending opinions
- Level five: creating unique solutions

Within the affective domain, there are also five levels. The receiving level is awareness of something. For example, a student might read a book about bullying. The next level is responding. A child might share information about the book with someone or be able to identify when bullying behaviors are happening. The third level is valuing. At this level, the student has integrated the beliefs within his or her character. Next, at the organization level, the individual has prioritized a new belief system and may begin leading others in the same direction. The final level is characterization, in which the belief has become a defining part of the person.

The levels of the affective domain:

- Level one: awareness
- Level two: responding
- Level three: valuing
- Level four: organization
- Level five: characterization

The levels of the psychomotor domain were not developed by Dr. Bloom, but they have been studied and outlined by three other researchers. Basically, the levels of motor skill development are observing, imitating, practicing, and adapting.

The levels of the psychomotor domain:

- Level one: observing
- Level two: imitating
- Level three: practicing
- Level four: adapting

When creating instructional objectives for each domain, the teacher should determine at which level the students are performing and which level will be considered mastery according to the standards that have been set by the state and district. Differentiation and enrichment exist within a learning goal through making adjustments to the level of questioning according to Bloom's taxonomy.

QUICK REVIEW

Why would a teacher need to understand the levels of the affective domain?

SAMPLE QUESTIONS

9) **In which of the learning domains would fall an activity designed to help a student form letters with a pencil?**

  A. affective domain

  B. psychomotor domain

  C. cognitive domain

  D. psychological domain

Answers:

  A. Incorrect. The affective domain focuses on behavior, values, and motivation.

B. **Correct.** The psychomotor domain, which is the development of motor skills, would include fine motor skills necessary for writing.

C. Incorrect. The cognitive domain includes the development of intellect.

D. Incorrect. The psychological domain is not part of the learning domains identified by Dr. Bloom.

10) **In which of the learning domains would an antiracism rally fall?**

A. affective domain

B. psychomotor domain

C. cognitive domain

D. psychological domain

Answers:

A. **Correct.** The affective domain includes the development of the student's values.

B. Incorrect. The psychomotor domain focuses on physical movement.

C. Incorrect. Within the cognitive domain, the development of knowledge takes place.

D. Incorrect. The psychological domain is not part of the learning domains.

ENRICHMENT AND REMEDIATION RESOURCES

Students come to school with various experiences and background knowledge and require differentiation in instruction in order to meet their needs. One way to meet the needs of students is by providing remediation. **Remediation** is additional support provided to regular education students to bridge gaps in learning specific objectives. More than just reteaching, remediation is targeted instruction based on the needs of the individual student. It may involve small-group instruction, one-on-one teaching, peer tutoring, computer-based intervention, or a combination of settings. To determine which areas need to be targeted for remediation, a teacher may use error analysis or formal or informal assessments. Grouping should be flexible and based on the learning needs of the students.

Enrichment is the opportunity to learn objectives at a deeper level than outlined in the curriculum standards and will frequently be used when a student masters the required curriculum more quickly than others in the class. Enrichment does not mean more work or independent study. Each student, even those who are ahead, deserves to have challenging and engaging learning experiences. As mentioned in the previous section, questioning students at a higher level of Bloom's taxonomy than is required by the standards provides enrichment without changing the structure of the learning experience.

> **QUICK REVIEW**
>
> What is the difference between enrichment and remediation?

SAMPLE QUESTIONS

11) **When would remediation be an appropriate intervention for a student?**

A.   The child has been found to have a learning disability.

B.   The child is working ahead of his or her classmates.

C.   Each child should receive remediation regardless of achievement levels.

D.   The child has a gap in learning that is preventing him or her from moving forward.

Answers:

A.   Incorrect. While a student with a disability may receive remediation, it is not an automatic indicator, nor is it the only indicator.

B.   Incorrect. Generally, a child who is mastering skills more quickly than his or her classmates will receive enrichment rather than remediation.

C.   Incorrect. Not every child needs remediation, and not every child who needs remediation needs it with every learning experience.

D.   Correct. Remediation is intended to find where students are making mistakes and correct those errors so that learning can move forward.

12) **Which of the following is most appropriate for providing enrichment to a student?**

A.   asking higher-order questions

B.   giving extra homework

C.   asking the student to tutor others

D.   implementing independent practice

Answers:

A.   Correct. Higher-order thinking questions give students enrichment without altering the structure of the assignment.

B.   Incorrect. Students will not be motivated to work to their ability if they are punished with extra work.

C.   Incorrect. Tutoring others may help the other students and it may help the teacher, but it does not provide the higher-level students with the learning challenges they need to continue growing.

D.   Incorrect. Independent practice has not been shown to help students grow academically.

The Role of Materials, Resources, and Support Personnel

Some districts have more available resources than others. This section discusses in detail the different types of resources that may be available to support student learning. Many school districts have technology resources for students. Technology may be in the form of computers, tablets, or other resources that are connected to the Internet. The Internet is a valuable tool for educators, since there is a wealth of information available as well as engaging interactive activities for nearly every imaginable objective. However, there are also dangers that should not be minimized when using online resources. Most districts have filtering software that prevents students from engaging with strangers or accessing inappropriate sites, but these are not foolproof. Teachers should explore in advance any site that students will be using and should closely monitor students to make sure that they limit their explorations to acceptable sites. Another area of caution when using the Internet is using legitimate sites as sources. Nearly anyone can publish a website, so care needs to be taken when finding information that is relevant and valid. Museums, educational institutes, libraries, online encyclopedias, and some news sources provide useable information. Tabloids, social media, and community boards are much less reliable. Students need to learn to be critical consumers of available media.

Most schools have a school library that contains a wealth of books, videos, and audiovisual equipment in nearly every content area. Students need access to materials at their instructional level to challenge them to grow. Community members and guest speakers can provide enrichment for students in their areas of expertise from a real-world vantage point. Some districts have the ability for students to go on field trips where students can view artifacts and models. **Artifacts** are created by a person and tell the story of a past event. This might refer to objects from history, such as historical documents from Early America or clay pots from ancient tribes, but students can also create their own artifacts to document a learning experience. **Models**, on the other hand, are representations of something. For example, a natural history museum may have an exhibit where models of pre-historic animals are displayed. An artifact is a genuine object or document, whereas a model is a created example. **Manipulatives**, which are items that students are able to move or change during hands-on instruction, may be purchased or created by students. Manipulatives are especially helpful when teaching students a conceptual understanding of mathematics concepts.

Students of all grade levels absorb information more readily when it is presented using an integrative framework. An **integrative framework** is a plan for achieving goals in all subject areas by combining content across disciplines. Using **interdisciplinary units**, which are units of study in which content from all subject areas is integrated, helps students understand that the perimeter of their art project is related to the perimeter of a geometric shape, which may then be transferred to finding the perimeter of their yard when purchasing fencing material. Teachers of multiple disciplines can collaborate to find ways to teach the learning standards from each content area using similar language.

Thematic units, which integrate curricula across content areas under a general theme, help students make connections between different content areas. To build a thematic unit, the teacher first selects a theme and then designs assessments and integrated learning activities related to the theme and aligned with standards, and also selects resources.

Likely, teachers have instructional partners with whom they will collaborate while planning for instruction. Special education teachers are an invaluable resource for regular classroom teachers since they must make modifications and/or accommodations to meet the individual needs of identified students. The special education teacher is just one member of the Individualized Education Plan team, which will meet at least once yearly to determine what is in the best interest of a child with exceptionalities.

Depending on which exceptionalities are exhibited, the Individualized Education Plan team may include a **speech therapist**, a certified professional who diagnoses and treats communication disorders; a **physical therapist**, a certified professional who evaluates and treats mobility issues; and/or an **occupational therapist**, a certified professional who assesses and provides treatment for the development of life skills among disabled individuals.

Sometimes special education students work with **paraprofessionals**, who are trained teacher assistants. Paraprofessionals receive some training and are often very familiar with the children with whom they work, but it is important to note that the teacher is ultimately responsible for developing the curriculum and making sure that it is delivered to students in an effective way.

Teachers of gifted and talented students can be helpful when determining enrichment activities that will challenge the students who have demonstrated giftedness. Guidance counselors are available to provide support for emotional and social skill development. Library media specialists may help identify resources and coordinate interdisciplinary planning. Teachers may also share a course with a colleague or have a subject or grade-level department that determines the local content scope and sequence for the required state and district curriculum.

SAMPLE QUESTIONS

13) **Which of the following types of websites will most likely contain relevant, valid, and reliable information for students researching historical content?**

   A. social media

   B. museum

   C. community board

   D. tabloid news

Answers:

   A. Incorrect. Anyone can post anything on social media whether it is true or not. Social media is not a reliable source.

   B. **Correct.** Museums typically have reliable information for students.

C.   Incorrect. Community boards have few restrictions and do not always contain valid information.

D.   Incorrect. Tabloid news sources are inconsistently reliable.

14)   **Which of the following professionals assess and coordinate life skill development for disabled students?**

A.   a paraprofessional

B.   a speech therapist

C.   a physical therapist

D.   an occupational therapist

Answers:

A.   Incorrect. Paraprofessionals are trained, but not certified, teacher assistants.

B.   Incorrect. Speech therapists are certified professionals who work with students who have been found to have a language or speech deficit.

C.   Incorrect. Physical therapists assist with motor skill development of disabled students.

D.   **Correct.** Occupational therapists help disabled students develop life skills.

INSTRUCTIONAL STRATEGIES

In this section, the reader will learn more about the cognitive processes and identify instructional models. For each of the instructional models, the reader will learn instructional strategies that support both cognition and motivation. This section describes various configurations of students and discusses how to select the best configuration and strategy to meet the instructional objectives. Finally, this section will teach how to best monitor learning and adjust instruction so that students will master standards.

COGNITIVE PROCESSES

The goal of education is not just to impart knowledge but also to produce critical and creative thinkers who can participate and contribute to a changing, global economy. **Critical thinking** is looking at evidence with deliberate and analytical thought to make inferences or draw conclusions. One aspect of critical thinking is to be able to view the flood of information that is available on the Internet and social media and to critique its validity. **Creative thinking** is a cognitive process, such as brainstorming, that is designed to generate new thoughts, ideas, and solutions to existing problems. Students who have only been taught to **recall**, or retrieve, facts and information have a difficult time with critical and creative thinking.

When lesson **planning**, professional educators are putting forethought into the implementation and design of instructional activities in order to achieve the desired outcome. To develop students into critical and creative thinkers, specific consideration should be paid to **questions**, or inquiries that are used to help focus instruction and assess understanding. Students should be actively engaged in **problem-solving** using both inductive and deductive reasoning.

Inductive reasoning is when students draw likely conclusions by putting together specific circumstances and applying their conclusions to general circumstances. For example, Emily is a Lhasa apso. Emily is smoky gray. Therefore, all Lhasa apsos are smoky gray. Inductive reasoning does not always produce an accurate result, since Lhasa apsos can actually range in color from cream to black, but inductive reasoning can bring the student close to an accurate conclusion: Some Lhasa apsos are smoky gray. When students draw conclusions using inductive reasoning, it is important for them to understand that their conclusions are an approximation rather than an absolute.

Students are better able to draw absolute conclusions when using deductive reasoning. **Deductive reasoning** occurs when conclusions are drawn by using known information and narrowing it to a specific circumstance. For example, if all Lhasa apsos are dogs, and my pet Emily is a Lhasa apso, then deductive reasoning tells me that Emily is a dog.

There will be times when the facts are important to commit to **memory**, or stored to be retrieved at a later time, but more often students will need to remember the thinking process and procedures instead. The teacher should consider student goals for the end of the unit when planning activities.

Table 2.1. Inductive Versus Deductive Reasoning

Inductive Reasoning	Deductive Reasoning
The results from a small sample are applied generally (not always accurate).	General information is narrowly applied to a specific situation (usually accurate).

SAMPLE QUESTIONS

15) **Which of the following is an example of inductive reasoning?**

   A. Fish have gills. Salmon are fish. Therefore, salmon have gills.

   B. All fish are animals. Salmon are fish. Therefore, salmon are animals.

   C. All dinosaurs are extinct. Stegosaurus is a dinosaur. Therefore, stegosaurus are extinct.

   D. Salmon are fish. Salmon are pink. Therefore, fish are pink.

Answers:

A. Incorrect. This is an example of deductive reasoning because the reasoning begins with the general category, fish, and then applies what is true of all fish to a certain type of fish, salmon.

B. Incorrect. This is an example of deductive reasoning because it is a true conclusion based on the broader evidence. What is true about the broad category of fish is also true about all types of fish, including salmon.

C. Incorrect. The conclusion is absolutely correct because it draws from true generalities, which makes it an example of deductive reasoning. If dinosaurs are extinct, then every type of dinosaur is also extinct.

D. Correct. Inductive reasoning develops a somewhat reasonable yet not always correct conclusion by applying information about a small or specific sample and turning it into a generality. Just because a type of fish is pink, it does not mean that all fish are pink.

16) **Which of the following is an example of deductive reasoning?**

A. Rational numbers are numbers that can be written as a ratio. The number one can be written as a ratio (1:1). Therefore, one is a rational number.

B. One is a prime number. One is a rational number. Therefore, all rational numbers are prime numbers.

C. One is a prime number. One is a rational number. Therefore, all prime numbers are rational.

D. One is a prime number. One is an odd number. Therefore, all odd numbers are prime.

Answers:

A. Correct. Moving from general to specific allows the learner to draw an accurate conclusion in this example of deductive reasoning. The general category is *numbers that can be written as ratios*. The sample from that group is the number one.

B. Incorrect. Moving from specific to general often results in an example of inductive reasoning. Just because one example, the number one, is both a rational number and a prime number, it does not mean that all rational numbers will also be prime.

C. Incorrect. Sometimes using inductive reasoning will lead the learner to a correct answer, but oftentimes it does not. In this case, the number one is a specific example of a prime number that is also rational. In reality, all prime numbers are rational, but be wary of drawing that conclusion based on just one sample.

D. Incorrect. Inductive reasoning is an effort to draw a conclusion from a small sample, but it sometimes produces an inaccurate result. One is a sample odd number that happens to also be prime, but fifteen, for example, is an odd number that is not prime.

INSTRUCTIONAL MODELS

Some instructional models are more effective and engaging than others. All instructional models have their place in an effective unit; however, because most teachers move among different types of instruction in order to keep students interested, students attend best when their activities change every ten to twenty minutes, depending on their developmental level.

Direct teaching is a form of teacher-centered instruction in which the teacher focuses on disseminating facts to students. Although this may be the form of instruction most people think of when picturing American schools, it is viewed by most as being the least effective because the students are passively receiving information rather than constructing their own knowledge. A more effective teaching model is **indirect teaching**. Indirect teaching is student-centered instruction in which the teacher facilitates opportunities for students to construct their own learning. Indirect teaching can be independent, experiential, or interactive.

Independent learning is student-centered instruction that focuses on developing autonomy with minimal teacher support. When using independent instruction, some guided practice usually precedes autonomous learning. Many make the mistake of giving advanced and gifted learners independent projects in lieu of other types of instruction. Independent learning is an accessory, not a replacement for other types of instruction.

Experiential learning is acquiring knowledge through experiences, including hands-on learning. Experiential learning is highly engaging and gives students opportunities to categorize their learning according to their schema. Students tend to remember experiences and be able to apply them better than with other types of instruction.

Interactive learning is an approach that relies heavily on social interaction and cooperative grouping. The social experience and ability to formulate learning into words while working within a group are highly engaging for some students and tend to develop schema and commit information into long-term memory. When determining which types of instructional models to include in lesson plans, teachers should consider the depth of the standard, the background knowledge and experiences of the students, and the time and materials that are available.

SAMPLE QUESTIONS

17)   **Which model of instruction represents a traditional, teacher-centered approach?**

    A.   direct teaching

    B.   independent learning

    C.   experiential learning

    D.   interactive learning

Answers:

    A.   **Correct.** In traditional classrooms, direct teaching is the most common form of instruction. Direct teaching places students in a passive learning role.

    B.   Incorrect. Independent learning is not commonly used, except in working with gifted students. Independent study has its place but should not be relied upon heavily as an instructional model.

    C.   Incorrect. Experiential learning is very effective because students are actively creating their knowledge.

    D.   Incorrect. Interactive learning is effective as the social aspect provides for the development of schema and long-term retention.

18)   **Which of the following is an example of interactive learning?**

    A.   The teacher lectures for half an hour followed by students independently answering questions from the book.

    B.   The students break into cooperative groups to jigsaw the text and present their findings.

    C.   Each student researches, creates a PowerPoint presentation, and presents on an element of the unit.

    D.   The class goes on a field trip to a local pond and runs tests on water samples.

Answers:

    A.   Incorrect. This is an example of direct teaching followed by independent practice.

    B.   **Correct.** Cooperative learning groups define interactive learning.

    C.   Incorrect. This is an example of independent learning.

    D.   Incorrect. This is an example of experiential learning.

STRATEGIES ASSOCIATED WITH INSTRUCTIONAL MODELS

Under each model there are several instructional strategies from which a teacher may choose for planning purposes. Instructional strategies for direct instruction include **explicit teaching**, which is focused and unambiguous teaching of a specific skill or standard; **drill and practice**, which is repetitive practicing of skills to promote memorization of facts; **lecture**, which is when the teacher talks while students listen and possibly take notes; **demonstration**, in which the teacher shows the students evidence to an observable conclusion; and **reading**, **listening**, and **viewing guides**. Guides contain statements or questions that provide instructional focus while reading text, listening to a lecture, or viewing media.

Strategies for indirect instruction include **problem-solving**; **inquiry**; **case studies**; **concept mapping**, which is using graphic organizers to present thoughts or information; **reading for meaning**; and **cloze procedures**, which is omitting words from the text as a reading comprehension activity. Each of these types of activities provides opportunities for students to construct meaning for themselves.

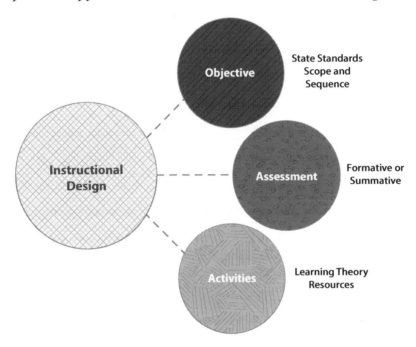

Figure 2.1. Concept Map

Independent instruction can take many different forms. Some teachers develop a **learning contract** with students as an agreement that defines expectations when working independently. Learning contracts typically provide some degree of creativity on the part of the student but also keep focus on the mastery of learning objectives. **Research projects** give students the opportunity to study specific concepts in depth using scientific principles for gathering information. The use of learning centers is a form of independent instruction as well. In **learning centers**, segments of the classroom are set aside for independent learning activities.

Technology increasingly plays a role in how students are taught. Within the classroom, **computer-mediated instruction**, or learning activities facilitated through computer technology, may be used to target student learning needs and move students forward using highly engaging instruction. Outside the classroom,

distance learning is becoming a popular option for students who are not able to attend school during the school day for various reasons.

Experiential and virtual instruction may include **field trips**, **experiments**, **games**, or **observations**. **Simulations** model a real-world process, while **role-playing**, or playacting, may also be used to demonstrate concepts in ways that make learning more memorable for students.

Interactive instruction takes advantage of social interactions with students to improve learning. Some modes of interactive instruction include **brainstorming**, **cooperative learning groups**, **interviews**, **discussions**, **peer practice**, and **debates**.

Brainstorming involves generating ideas related to a specific problem or concept. When brainstorming, students feed off of each other's ideas and make connections to learning. Peer practice is a popular form of interactive instruction that uses social interaction among students to promote learning goals. Structured debates are formal discussions about opposing arguments that give students insight into a subject from multiple viewpoints.

SAMPLE QUESTIONS

19) Which of the following learning activities is a form of direct teaching?

    A.   demonstration

    B.   concept mapping

    C.   computer-mediated instruction

    D.   role-playing

Answers:

    A.   **Correct.** A demonstration in which the teacher shows students an example that leads to a logical conclusion is a form of direct instruction.

    B.   Incorrect. Concept mapping is a form of indirect instruction.

    C.   Incorrect. Computer-mediated instruction is independent.

    D.   Incorrect. Role-playing is a method of experiential learning.

20) Which of the following interactive learning experiences provides students with the opportunity to formally discuss a subject from multiple perspectives?

    A.   peer practice

    B.   debate

    C.   cooperative learning groups

    D.   brainstorming

Go on ⟶

Answers:

A.   Incorrect. Peer practice is guided practice with the assistance of one's peers.

B.   **Correct.** Debate is a formal discussion in which students must be able to view a subject from multiple perspectives in order to defend their point of view.

C.   Incorrect. Cooperative learning groups socially interact in the learning process but do not actively work from opposing viewpoints.

D.   Incorrect. Brainstorming is openly generating ideas.

COGNITIVE STRATEGIES

Cognition is a complicated process that involves many steps. One of the first steps in cognition is learning to classify information by topic, or **concept learning**. Consider a small child who is learning to identify colors: first, he or she must be able to sort them by blocks to indicate understanding of the difference in attributes. The same process takes place at higher grade levels. For example, when a child is learning about the geography of Europe, he or she will classify cities, countries, and continents, as well as sort countries in Europe from countries in other continents, such as Asia. **Categorizing**, or putting things into groups by characteristic, helps the learner organize new information within his or her schema. **Comparing**, or noting the similarities between things, and **contrasting**, which is noting the differences between things, are appropriate learning activities for helping students learn by concept.

Problem-solving requires the ability to **infer** using critical thinking or reasoning skills. When a child approaches a problem, he or she will need to be able to **synthesize**, or bring together knowledge from various learning experiences, to apply to a new challenge. Using transfer of background knowledge and reasoning skills, students may **predict** what will happen if a specific solution is applied. As students **analyze** the outcome, they will need to **evaluate** the process. By doing this, they draw conclusions to determine whether there is any **bias** that might invalidate the objectivity of the experience before **generalizing** that their conclusions would apply in broader terms.

Metacognition refers to the student's ability to consider the way he or she thinks or learns as part of the learning process. For example, one metacognitive strategy would be to have students explain which strategy they used to solve a problem and why that strategy works best for them. At the end of an experience, students should be able to **summarize**, or explain the process and the outcome of their experience in a condensed form.

Some additional specific activities that assist students in developing their cognitive skills, thereby improving their abilities to solve problems and accurately assess outcomes, include differentiating between fact and opinion, and decision making. Improving their abilities to be able to consider appropriate sources of information and the precision by which processes are implemented are skills that may be applied to all areas of learning and life beyond school.

SAMPLE QUESTIONS

21) **Which of the following is an example of concept learning?**

A. The student considers the way he or she best learns.

B. The student sorts pictures based on the phoneme with which the name of each begins.

C. The student anticipates what will happen next.

D. The student explains the learning process and outcomes using condensed language.

Answers:

A. Incorrect. This is an example of metacognition.

B. Correct. Sorting things into categories is an example of concept learning.

C. Incorrect. This student is using prediction.

D. Incorrect. Summarizing skills are used when students are able to explain what they have learned.

22) **Which of the following is an example of detecting bias?**

A. James categorizes numbers as rational or irrational.

B. Zoe realizes that she is a visual learner; therefore, she creates a graphic organizer from her notes.

C. Abraham is disqualified as a judge in the art contest because his sister is a contestant.

D. Ysenia uses what she learned in history class to understand the literature about the Holocaust in English.

Answers:

A. Incorrect. This is an example of concept learning using categorization.

B. Incorrect. This is an example of metacognition because Zoe is thinking about the way she thinks.

C. Correct. Abraham may be a biased judge with leanings toward or against his sister.

D. Incorrect. Ysenia is transferring knowledge from one subject to another.

STRATEGIES THAT SUPPORT STUDENT LEARNING

Teachers provide support for student learning experiences both directly and indirectly. Teachers provide direct support through **modeling**, **scaffolding**, and **guided practice**. Through modeling, teachers show students how to solve problems. Then, gradually, the teacher releases the scaffolded support as students engage in guided practice.

Teachers provide indirect support by helping students develop self-regulation skills to monitor their progress and to take an active role in developing and assessing their learning goals. Differentiating instruction provides learning experiences that meet the learning needs of each student and may address learning styles, achievement levels, and/or student preferences. Differentiation promotes student engagement, which helps motivate students to self-regulate. **Coaching** provides training toward the achievement of a goal while maintaining the learner as the lead participant in the learning process.

SAMPLE QUESTIONS

23) **Which of the following is an example of scaffolding through multiple opportunities to address the content?**

   A.   After learning new vocabulary, students turn and talk to a peer about the new words before completing a graphic organizer with their cooperative groups.

   B.   The student looks up definitions of words in the dictionary before independently reading the text.

   C.   The teacher tells students the definitions of new words and then reminds them of the meaning each time the words come up in the text.

   D.   The student engages in learning activities according to his or her learning style.

   Answers:

   A.   **Correct.** This teacher is providing multiple opportunities for the students to practice skills with various levels of support.

   B.   Incorrect. The teacher is not providing support to the students in this scenario. The student is participating in an independent learning experience.

   C.   Incorrect. The teacher is providing direct, explicit instruction, but he or she is not gradually releasing the student to work independently.

   D.   Incorrect. This is an example of differentiated instruction.

24) **Which of the following is an example of self-regulation?**

   A.   Brianna is an auditory learner; therefore, audiobooks are used to support her.

   B.   Xavier has demonstrated behavior issues since moving to a new school. His teacher has set up a reward system for work completion.

   C.   Carolyn consistently scores the highest in the class on reading assessments; therefore, she is allowed to choose independent reading to complete and report on to the class.

D.   Warren has a goal to increase his fluency to 170 words per minute. Each week, he tracks his progress using fluency passages and graphs it on a chart.

Answers:

A.   Incorrect. This is an example of differentiation based on learning styles.

B.   Incorrect. This is an example of behavioral conditioning.

C.   Incorrect. In this case, the teacher is providing the student an opportunity for enrichment, not an opportunity to monitor her own progress.

D.   **Correct.** Warren is self-regulating because he has set a learning goal and is tracking his progress toward that goal.

PROMOTING SELF-REGULATION

Self-regulation helps motivate students, keeps them engaged, and builds self-efficacy. The first step in self-regulation is for the teacher and student to work together to set learning goals. Once the student understands what is expected of him or her and what it will take to show mastery, he or she sets subgoals that may be celebrated along the way. When the student begins to reach the subgoals, it helps him or her to feel accomplished and capable. Along with goal setting, students should be coached on how to manage their time efficiently and stay organized. As the student monitors his or her progress, opportunities should be set aside at regular intervals to reflect on outcomes and determine whether or not learning is moving in the right direction.

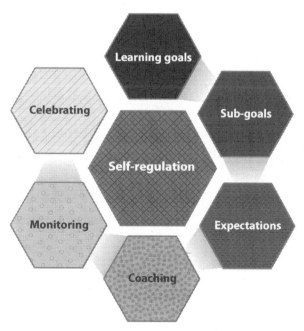

Figure 2.2. Steps of Self-Regulation

Establishing a productive work environment for students includes making sure that every student feels included and safe both physically and emotionally. Routines, schedules, and behavioral expectations all contribute to making the classroom feel safe for all students. In addition to setting rules, explicit instruction that fosters mutual respect among students, staff, and guests is appropriate at all grade levels. Responsibility is another key component of a productive learning space. Students must learn to be responsible for themselves, their learning, and the classroom. Materials need to be cared for and the space needs to be kept tidy. The classroom should contribute to a student's desire to come to school and learn rather than serve as a distraction.

SAMPLE QUESTIONS

25) **What is the first step in self-regulation?**

    A.   setting learning goals

    B.   developing assessments

    C.   monitoring progress

    D.   reflecting on outcomes

Answers:

    A.   **Correct.** Students must set learning goals and subgoals to self-regulate.

    B.   Incorrect. Developing assessments, timelines, and organizing materials occurs after the learning goals have been set.

    C.   Incorrect. Students should regularly monitor progress toward the goals they have set.

    D.   Incorrect. Reflecting on outcomes should take place at regular intervals to determine if the learning activities are effectively moving students toward the goals they have set.

26) **Which of the following contributes to a productive learning environment for students of all ages?**

    A.   mandatory curriculum

    B.   technology

    C.   independence

    D.   routine

Answers:

    A.   Incorrect. Curriculum that is required by the district may assist with learning goals but not necessarily with developing a productive learning environment.

    B.   Incorrect. Technology is a wonderful resource but not necessary to make the environment productive.

C.   Incorrect. A great curriculum may allow students some room for independence within the framework of a learning contract but is not part of the work environment.

D.   **Correct.** Routine, structure, and high expectations play a role in keeping the learning environment safe and productive for all students.

STUDENT GROUPING

There are multiple ways that students can be configured, all of which are used by teachers regularly depending on the instructional goal. **Whole-class** instruction is delivered to all of the students in the class at the same time in the same way. Although whole-class instruction is typically the most efficient way for a teacher to impart knowledge, it is not the most effective way for students to internalize it. **Small-group** instruction is provided to a group composed of learners with similar instructional needs. For example, after teaching a mini-lesson about order of operations, there may be some students who struggle with exponents and others who struggle with the overall concept. The teacher may pull each of those sets of students into a small-group setting for additional instruction.

Independent-learning experiences are activities that are completed autonomously by the student. When making independent learning assignments, the student will still need significant monitoring and coaching to stay on target. **One-on-one** instruction is when a teacher works with one individual student on a concept. Generally, this is used as an additional intervention when a small group is not successful or when a student's abilities stand apart from those of other students. Pair-share is a remarkable way to be able to get all students involved in the learning process during whole-group instruction. The teacher pauses instruction to give students the opportunity to work with a partner to discuss learning that has just taken place.

> **QUICK REVIEW**
>
> Why would a teacher divide students up into different configurations throughout the school day?

Table 2.2. Student Grouping Configurations

Configuration	Goal	Example
whole class	impart knowledge to the entire class in the same way at the same time	The teacher teaches a fifteen-minute mini-lesson to the entire class on author's voice before students begin a writing assignment.
small group	serve the collective learning needs of a small group of students based on results of monitoring	The teacher pulls together a group of five students who are struggling with transition words to do a small-group lesson.

Table 2.2. Student Grouping Configurations (continued)

Configuration	Goal	Example
independent learning	teach students to be autonomous; provide students the opportunity to work more deeply within their areas of interest	The student uses a self-editing checklist to try to correct his or her own work.
one-on-one	provide intense remediation or feedback to an individual student	The teacher has a writing conference with an individual student to help him or her edit a writing assignment.

SAMPLE QUESTIONS

27) **Which of the following configurations would be used to provide support for some students with similar instructional needs?**

 A. whole class

 B. small group

 C. one-on-one

 D. independent learning

Answers:

 A. Incorrect. Whole-class instruction is delivered to all students in the same way; therefore, it has limited capacity to provide support for students with needs.

 B. **Correct.** Students with similar learning needs are configured in small, flexible groups to which the teachers can provide instruction within the students' instructional level.

 C. Incorrect. One-on-one instruction is effective but not practical in all situations. If students have similar learning needs that can be addressed within a small group, that is more efficient.

 D. Incorrect. Independent learning allows the student to be autonomous but may be limited in its ability to meet the needs of students.

28) **When is the most appropriate time to use the pair-share configuration?**

 A. to provide remediation for students who are very far behind

 B. to provide enrichment for students who are ahead of the class

 C. with students who have similar learning needs

 D. throughout instruction with all students regardless of ability

Answers:

A.   Incorrect. Students who are very far behind will need small-group and one-on-one instruction that targets learning needs.

B.   Incorrect. Students who are ahead need enrichment through higher-order questioning.

C.   Incorrect. Students with similar learning needs benefit from small-group instruction.

D.   **Correct.** Pair-share is beneficial to all students throughout instruction.

STRATEGY SELECTION

Each of the research-based instructional strategies has a place in the classroom depending upon the learning goals. When selecting a strategy, the first steps are to identify the objective and how that objective will be assessed to determine mastery. Next, the teacher will determine which strategies will net the desired results.

In the event that the goal is to transmit facts or clear up misunderstandings, direct teaching strategies, such as lectures, demonstrations, and explicit instruction, are the most effective. On the other hand, if the intention is to support students in becoming independent and to give them the opportunity to more deeply study a facet of interest within a unit of study, independent study, such as research projects, will help students reach their goals.

Group discussions, cooperative learning groups, and pair-share are options that help students benefit from each other's background knowledge. By working cooperatively, students learn to view things from other perspectives, defend their positions, and critically evaluate the things they learn. Experiential learning opportunities, such as field trips, labs, and learning centers, help students think critically and respond to the learning environment in a real-world setting.

SAMPLE QUESTIONS

29)   **Which of the following strategies would be used to clear up student misunderstandings?**

A.   cooperative learning groups

B.   labs

C.   independent study

D.   lectures

Answers:

A.   Incorrect. Cooperative learning groups help students benefit from each other's background knowledge.

B.   Incorrect. Labs are used to help students respond metacognitively to learning.

C.   Incorrect. Independent study teaches students to work autonomously.

D.   Correct. Lectures and other methods of direct instruction help clear up misunderstandings.

30) **Which of the following learning strategies helps students think critically in real-world settings?**

A.   research projects

B.   explicit instruction

C.   pair-share

D.   field trips

Answers:

A.   Incorrect. Research projects help students learn more about facets of interest within a unit.

B.   Incorrect. Explicit instruction transmits facts and information directly to students.

C.   Incorrect. Pair-share helps students learn from each other and evaluate their opinions.

D.   Correct. Field trips provide experiential learning in a real-world setting.

Monitoring and Adjusting Instruction

Research has consistently shown that learning improves when teachers continuously monitor student learning, provide relevant feedback to students, and adjust learning strategies based on students' needs. There are a variety of ways that teachers can monitor student learning. Questioning techniques may be used to assess student understanding in a whole-group, small-group, or individual configuration. Monitoring seatwork and homework, while providing extra help to those who need it, will help teachers track how individual students are performing. Informal assessments, such as checklists, pop quizzes, periodic learning probes, and exit tickets, which are short statements about learning that students complete at the end of a lesson, are effective ways of monitoring learning during the learning experience. Summative assessments, such as weekly tests, end-of-unit tests, benchmarks, and standardized tests, provide information for remediation after learning has taken place but have a limited ability to guide instruction while learning is taking place.

Monitoring is effective only if teachers review the assessments and use the information to meet the learning needs of their students. If 75 to 80 percent of students understand the concept, intervention for the others may take place through small-group, individual, or computer-based instruction, but if more than 75 percent of students are struggling, it is an indication that either concepts need to be retaught using a different strategy or students lack the background knowledge to absorb the information.

SAMPLE QUESTIONS

31) Which of the following assessments is most effective for guiding instruction?

    A.   standardized tests

    B.   benchmarks

    C.   unit tests

    D.   periodic quizzes

Answers:

    A.   Incorrect. Summative assessments, such as standardized tests, are better for testing knowledge after learning has taken place than they are for guiding instruction.

    B.   Incorrect. Benchmarks, like standardized tests, are an example of a summative assessment. Formative assessments are better for guiding instruction.

    C.   Incorrect. Unit tests are intended to be summative reviews of an entire unit once it is complete.

    D.   **Correct.** Periodic quizzes are short tests that are given to students in the middle of instruction to help guide the teacher toward the next steps.

32) Which of the following strategies is most effective if 75 percent of students have not mastered the objective?

    A.   one-on-one instruction

    B.   whole-class reteaching

    C.   small-group instruction

    D.   independent study

Answers:

    A.   Incorrect. One-on-one instruction would be for an individual who is very far behind.

    B.   **Correct.** If more than 75 percent of students have not mastered the objective, it needs to be retaught using a different instructional technique.

    C.   Incorrect. Small-group instruction is for small groups of students with similar learning needs. In this scenario, large groups of students have similar learning needs.

    D.   Incorrect. Independent study is for students who have mastered learning goals and need enrichment to explore concepts at a deeper level.

Evaluating Instructional Effectiveness

Just as students continue to grow and learn, teachers also should take every opportunity to improve their practice. This section discusses some reflective teaching practices that are designed to improve the instructional effectiveness of classroom teachers.

Viewing instruction from an objective vantage point is a powerful tool. Many teachers will create video recordings of their instruction that they critique, or they ask peers to watch them teach to provide feedback. This type of feedback is most effective if the teacher focuses on just a few elements of instruction that they want to improve. For example, a teacher may want to improve the questioning techniques and active student engagement. A critique of a short lesson will provide sample data to help the teacher identify areas of need and growth targets.

Survey data from students, parents, and colleagues can provide valuable insight regarding how others view the teacher's use of instructional time, relationships with students, and content knowledge. Student achievement data that focus on growth may be used to determine the relationship between student learning and teacher effectiveness. If students are not making progress, the teacher needs to find out why.

Insight about how to put instructional strategies into practice can be garnered from watching other teachers. Peer observation is one of the most potent ways to develop teachers. It is well worth a teacher's time, regardless of experience level, to spend some time watching colleagues in action.

SAMPLE QUESTIONS

33) **How should a teacher, when viewing a video of his or her own instruction, reflect on the lesson?**

   A. holistically

   B. by targeting a few areas for growth

   C. by justifying teaching practices

   D. by identifying student conduct issues

Answers:

   A. Incorrect. It can be overwhelming to look at all teaching practices at once.

   B. Correct. Identifying a few areas for growth is most beneficial for teacher improvement.

   C. Incorrect. Justifications interfere with continuous growth.

   D. Incorrect. The purpose of reflecting is to improve the teacher's instruction, which will likely impact student behavior. However, the purpose is not to "catch" misbehavior.

34) **Which of the following is the biggest advantage of peer observation as a professional practice?**

  A. Teachers can make sure that class sizes are consistent across the grade level.

  B. Peer observation allows teachers to determine which instructional supplies are available in the building.

  C. It provides ideas about how to implement new instructional strategies.

  D. Viewing shared struggles improves self-esteem.

Answers:

  A. Incorrect. The purpose of peer observation is as a reflective practice to improve the teacher's own performance.

  B. Incorrect. Taking inventory of supplies during a peer observation is a wasted opportunity to learn from a colleague.

  C. **Correct.** Observation has the advantage of practical application of new practices.

  D. Incorrect. The purpose of peer observation is for teachers to learn from one another.

THE ROLE OF MEMORY

Learning and memory are closely related because learning changes thoughts and behavior but depends on memory to retrieve the information that has been learned, in order to apply it to future circumstances. Memory provides the schema, or framework, necessary to make connections between prior knowledge and new learning.

Short-term memory includes information that enters the conscious memory but is not stored for recall at a later time. Short-term memory typically lasts less than a minute unless a learner consciously attempts to store the information into the long-term memory. During planning, teachers consciously choose activities that will provide opportunities for students to assimilate new information with existing schema by activating prior knowledge. Information that is appropriately encoded may be stored in long-term memory and retrieved for use at another time. **Long-term memory** is information that is stored for a long period and may be recalled. Although long-term memory appears to have infinite capacity, memories may become distorted over time.

Another method for transitioning short-term memory into long-term memory is repetition. Simply repeating the information sometimes works, but an even more successful strategy is to repeatedly teach the information using multiple modalities. The key to maximizing student learning through memory is to help the student form a connection to learning and then offer multiple learning experiences that meet the learning objective.

SAMPLE QUESTIONS

35) **Which of the following is an example of using short-term memory?**

   A.   memorizing a phone number to write it down

   B.   learning a foreign language

   C.   learning to multiply single-digit numbers

   D.   memorizing the letters of the alphabet

   Answers:

   A.   **Correct.** Typically, phone numbers are put into short-term memory long enough to write them down or dial them but then forgotten.

   B.   Incorrect. Foreign languages are put into long-term memory for later use.

   C.   Incorrect. Multiplying single-digit numbers is a math fluency skill that must be encoded into long-term memory.

   D.   Incorrect. Learning the letters of the alphabet belongs to long-term memory.

36) **Which instructional method helps students move from short-term to long-term memory?**

   A.   taking notes

   B.   reading a textbook

   C.   activating prior knowledge

   D.   listening to a lecture

   Answers:

   A.   Incorrect. Taking notes does not promote long-term memory unless the student rereads them repetitively.

   B.   Incorrect. Reading a textbook will not move information into long-term memory unless the student connects with the material.

   C.   **Correct.** Activating prior knowledge helps students assimilate or accommodate new information into existing schema, which helps the learner store information into long-term memory.

   D.   Incorrect. A lecture will not help students remember information unless the information is repeated or connected to student experiences.

THE ROLE OF TEACHABLE MOMENTS

In a **teachable moment**, an unplanned event occurs, triggering interest in learning more about that or a related topic. Typically, teachable moments will sidetrack traditional lesson plans; therefore, it is imperative to be able to recognize a teachable moment and respond to it without losing sight of learning goals. For example, if Grace's father has just returned from deployment in Afghanistan and has brought back some afghani (Afghan money) for her to show to the class, a responsive teacher may look for Afghanistan on the globe, talk about cultural differences, or compare the afghani to the dollar, depending on the age of the students.

Each day in every classroom there are missed opportunities to enrich students. Keeping an eye open for teachable moments that will enhance learning goals and keep students engaged in learning expands students' knowledge base for future learning opportunities and shows students that their teacher cares about the things that matter to each of them.

SAMPLE QUESTIONS

37) **What is the benefit of recognizing teachable moments?**

    A.   Lesson plans stay on track.

    B.   Learning follows predictable patterns.

    C.   Student engagement increases.

    D.   It focuses on identified learning objectives.

Answers:

    A.   Incorrect. Teachable moments typically throw lesson plans offtrack.

    B.   Incorrect. Teachable moments are unpredictable by nature.

    C.   **Correct.** Teaching students about something that interests them in the moment increases student engagement and broadens students' knowledge base.

    D.   Incorrect. Teachable moments frequently do not follow identified learning objectives; therefore, the time off-task needs to be weighed against the benefit of taking advantage of the moment.

38) **Which of the following is an example of a teachable moment?**

    A.   Students express an interest in current political events during US government class.

    B.   Students have completed all of their work and are given an independent research project for extra credit.

    C.   Students who do not finish work on time take it home for homework.

    D.   Every student works from bell to bell.

Answers:

    A.   **Correct.** Taking advantage of current events in a government class is an example of a teachable moment.

    B.   Incorrect. Independent research is an example of enrichment, not a teachable moment.

    C.   Incorrect. Planned homework assignments are not an example of a teachable moment.

D.   Incorrect. Maximizing instructional minutes is important but is not an example of a teachable moment.

QUESTIONING TECHNIQUES

In this section, various types of questions and methods for selecting questions to meet the learning goals of each student will be reviewed. Teacher candidates will learn how to provide a safe learning environment for open discussions in which students are comfortable articulating their thoughts. Strategies for helping students think critically and creatively will be reviewed.

EFFECTIVE QUESTIONING

Approximately half of instructional time is spent asking students questions; therefore, developing questioning skills is essential for every teacher. Questions are designed to develop critical thinking skills, assess understanding, increase engagement, and activate prior knowledge. Typically, questions in the higher levels of Bloom's taxonomy are more thought-provoking and interesting and should make up more than half of the questions that are asked, but there are times when lower levels of questions are appropriate in moderation, especially in the lower grade levels.

Questions to stimulate prior learning experiences are especially useful when working with older children since they prepare students for learning by helping students connect to learning. A common mistake is not giving students enough time to think about a question before responding. Students need both think time and wait time of at least three seconds to achieve maximum success from the learning experience. **Think time** is the processing time that a learner takes to reflect on new information before responding to it. Students select their own think time as they ponder what they have learned. **Wait time** is the processing time that is intentionally provided by the teacher after asking a question. The quality of responses improves when teachers intentionally give learners think time.

Teachers successfully respond to students' answers when they validate correct answers by repeating them, build on students' responses by asking additional questions related to students' answers, and redirect, rather than admonish, incorrect responses. Feedback should be constructive, specific, and positively phrased.

When teachers randomly select students to answer questions, rather than just those who raise their hands, more students participate in the thinking process. Using pair-share, whiteboards, and signaled responses requires participation from every student to every question.

Teachers can promote a safe, respectful environment by using, and teaching students to use, active listening skills. **Active listening** is a technique that improves listening skills by structuring how a person listens and responding to the person who is talking. Active listening includes making a conscious effort to really hear what another person has to say without a wandering mind or preparation for a response. Good listeners respond to the speaker by reflecting back what the speaker said and asking for clarification. Responses are only given after the original speaker has been heard. Students who are active listeners absorb more background knowledge from one another and demonstrate respect for others.

SAMPLE QUESTIONS

39) **What is the difference between think time and wait time?**

  A.   Think time is initiated by the learner, but wait time is initiated by the teacher.

  B.   Think time is initiated by the teacher, but wait time is initiated by the learner.

  C.   Think time and wait time are the same.

  D.   Think time ends in a written response, but wait time ends in a verbal response.

Answers:

  A.   **Correct.** The learner takes think time before responding. Teachers intentionally provide wait time.

  B.   Incorrect. The opposite is true.

  C.   Incorrect. Think time and wait time differ depending on who initiates it.

  D.   Incorrect. Responses to think time and wait time can be verbal or written.

40) **What do active listeners do when someone is speaking?**

  A.   correct the other person

  B.   formulate a response

  C.   state their opinion

  D.   reflect the speaker's thoughts

Answers:

  A.   Incorrect. Active listeners make a conscious effort to clear their minds.

  B.   Incorrect. Active listeners make sure that they clearly understand what the other person is saying.

  C.   Incorrect. Active listeners listen without judgment.

  D.   **Correct.** Active listeners clarify what the speaker has said by reflecting and asking questions.

USES OF QUESTIONING

Before a learning experience, teachers can use essential questions to focus the learning experience. By putting learning objectives into question form, teachers help students understand what they are supposed to learn and be able to evaluate their own level of mastery by the end of the lesson. Essential questions are typically open-ended questions that begin with stems, such as "When and why would this skill be used?" or "What is the relationship between these two ideas?" Essential questions are introduced at the beginning of a lesson to guide thinking and reviewed at the end of the lesson to motivate students, help them set learning goals, and check for understanding.

Using questions to find out what students already know about the topic will generate interest, give students an opportunity to share their background knowledge, serve as a review of previously learned material, and help the teacher assess whether or not the students are prepared for the new learning experience. During a learning experience, teachers use questions intended to kindle the interest of students and motivate them to learn. Open-ended questions that give the students an opportunity to reflect on their own thoughts, feelings, and knowledge are used to redirect students who are losing interest in the topic. Questions that allow students to brainstorm ideas and share knowledge with a partner, or that ask "What do you think about… ?" are useful for keeping students engaged in learning.

Socratic questions are used to generate discussions and help students think both critically and creatively. Socratic questions are probing questions that prompt students to critically evaluate a topic and provide clear responses that are fully developed, supported by evidence, and explored from multiple points of view. Even elementary-aged students can be taught to participate in Socratic discussions by actively listening to their classmates and asking probing, clarifying questions, such as "Why do you think that?" and "What evidence from the text supports your opinion?"

At the end of a lesson, questions may be used to assess mastery of the learning goal, provide closure through summarization of information, and challenge students to further research a topic on their own. Questions like "What are two things that you learned?" or "How will you apply something you learned to another class?" will help students see value in the learning experience and move information from short-term to long-term memory.

Table 2.3. Questioning Throughout Instruction

Before	During	After
▶ set learning goals through essential questions	▶ engage	▶ assess mastery
▶ activate prior knowledge	▶ motivate	▶ establish closure
▶ review previously learned material	▶ redirect	
	▶ monitor	
	▶ invoke critical thinking	

EXAMPLES

41) Which of the following is the purpose of essential questions?

A.   to assess mastery

B.   to redirect students

C.   to critically evaluate a topic

D.   to focus instruction

Answers:

A.   Incorrect. Students may revisit essential questions to evaluate their own mastery at the end of a lesson, but essential questions are provided before learning takes place.

B.   Incorrect. The questions that are used to redirect students with wandering minds are not necessarily essential questions.

C.   Incorrect. Socratic questions help students critically evaluate a topic.

D.   Correct. Essential questions basically put the learning goal in a question form so that students can focus on what they need to learn during a segment of instruction.

42) Which of the following is an example of a Socratic question?

A.   What is the main idea of this passage?

B.   How did the character resolve the conflict?

C.   Why do you think the author chose this setting?

D.   What is your favorite part of this story?

Answers:

A.   Incorrect. Although it is an open-ended question, the purpose is to apply academic vocabulary rather than to critically evaluate the text.

B.   Incorrect. This is another example of an open-ended question with an exact right answer.

C.   Correct. "Why do you think …?" questions give students the opportunity to critically evaluate the text.

D.   Incorrect. This is a good question for redirecting students who are off-topic by helping them reconnect to the text, but it lacks the depth to be a Socratic question.

HELPING STUDENTS ARTICULATE IDEAS

In preparation for life outside the classroom, students need to be able to clearly articulate not only their thoughts but also new learning and the opinions of others within the context of their own experiences. When asking students questions, teachers may assist students with verbal prompting, nonverbal prompting, or sentence stems. **Verbal prompting** is using words or beginning phonemes to assist students. For example, Mr. Young asks his students to name the New England states and then prompts them by reminding them that they have forgotten one that starts with the letter C. Nonverbal prompting is less invasive to the flow of the lesson and therefore is preferred when possible. **Nonverbal prompting** is using gestures or other physical prompts to assist students. Pointing, head shaking, facial expressions, and body language are examples of nonverbal prompts. Sentence stems guide thinking in order to help students focus their communication. For example, students may explain how they solved a math problem using the sentence stem "I chose _____ strategy to find the solution because _____."

> **TEACHING TIP**
>
> Having tokens that students must surrender to speak limits those who tend to take over the conversation and gives those who are hesitant to participate an incentive to speak up when they have something to say.

Reflective listening helps students broaden their knowledge base by incorporating the thoughts and experiences of others into their schema. **Reflective listening** is hearing a speaker and then repeating back the meaning behind their words to clarify understanding.

A simple way to make articulation a part of the closure of each lesson is to ask a reflective question about the learning segment, such as "What is the difference between capitalism and socialism?" After giving the students adequate wait time to formulate their ideas, students exercise their reflective listening skills during a pair-share. After each speaker has an opportunity to speak, the listener will form a **restatement**, in which the learner or listener repeats what has been learned using his or her own wording.

SAMPLE QUESTIONS

43) **Which of the following is an example of nonverbal prompting?**

   A.   facial expression

   B.   the beginning phoneme

   C.   word association

   D.   sentence stems

   Answers:

   A.   **Correct.** Facial expressions, pointing, and gesturing are examples of nonverbal prompting.

   B.   Incorrect. Providing students with the beginning phoneme of the answer is an example of verbal prompting.

   C.   Incorrect. Word association may be used to verbally prompt students.

   D.   Incorrect. Sentence stems help students articulate their learning by narrowing the focus.

44) How does reflective listening contribute to a student's understanding of new learning?

A.   It narrows the focus of the learning objective.

B.   It incorporates the knowledge of other learners.

C.   It improves self-efficacy.

D.   It broadens the learning objective.

Answers:

A.   Incorrect. Sentence stems may narrow the focus of the learning objective.

B.   Correct. Reflective listening helps students learn from each other.

C.   Incorrect. Self-efficacy comes from a student's achievement of his or her learning goals.

D.   Incorrect. Typically, depth and not breadth of the learning experience is preferred.

ENCOURAGING HIGH LEVELS OF THINKING

Education is so much more than the regurgitation of facts. True learning takes place when students are working at higher levels of thought that can develop the critical thinking skills necessary to transfer knowledge to different content areas and situations. One way teachers can encourage students to think about learning is to provide them with opportunities to reflect. Reflection includes developing metacognitive skills as well as providing wait time for students to absorb the information and integrate it with prior knowledge.

Students develop schema as they compare, contrast, and search for connections between different pieces of information. However, their critical thinking needs to begin with looking at the validity and relevance of the information they have been provided. Students need to be able to ask the question "Why do I believe what I believe?" and challenge themselves to find evidence that supports or changes the way they think. In addition to critical thinking, students need to be able to think creatively to find more than one solution to a problem.

SAMPLE QUESTIONS

45) Which of the following activities encourages creative thinking?

A.   brainstorming new solutions

B.   determining the validity of a source

C.   recalling facts

D.   providing evidence to support an opinion

Go on

Answers:

A.   **Correct.** Brainstorming gives students the opportunity to find more than one solution to a problem using creative thinking.

B.   Incorrect. Critical-thinking skills are used to determine the validity of sources.

C.   Incorrect. Recalling facts is low-level thinking that is neither critical nor creative.

D.   Incorrect. Finding valid evidence to support an opinion is a critical-thinking activity.

46)   **Which of the following activities uses critical thinking to build schema?**

A.   identifying the parts of a cell

B.   comparing and contrasting mitosis and meiosis

C.   listing the phases of a cell cycle

D.   describing the metaphase of mitosis

Answers:

A.   Incorrect. Identifying parts uses low-level thinking skills.

B.   **Correct.** Comparing and contrasting helps students make connections and build schema.

C.   Incorrect. Creating finite lists, such as the phases of a cell cycle, is low-level recall thinking.

D.   Incorrect. Describing is level two on Bloom's hierarchy, but describing exhibits comprehension rather than making connections.

Promoting Discussion

When preparing students for a discussion, the first step is to choose a topic and some resources that inspire them to consider ideas in the text. In a debate, students try to prove their point or state their opinion. A discussion is about learning to listen to others, building existing knowledge, and increasing understanding. Discussions need to be a safe place where a student's thoughts are encouraged and respected by everyone in the class.

Before beginning a discussion, teachers should provide the information that will be discussed and help students prepare for the discussion by modeling how to dive into the text and note key points. Students should formulate a few open-ended questions before the discussion.

Expectations, including using evidence from the text to support statements, asking clarifying questions, listening to each other without interrupting, and creating a judgment-free zone are imperative to making sure that students feel comfortable taking the risks during a discussion. These expectations, as well as the purpose and procedures for listening and speaking, should be explicitly taught before beginning any discussion.

Frequently, teachers will lead a discussion, but students may be taught to develop open-ended questions. In some scenarios, the entire class participates in the discussion. In other scenarios, part of the class discusses the material while other students observe, take notes, and reflect on the discussion.

QUICK REVIEW

What might happen if the teacher forgets to establish norms before a discussion?

Future discussions improve when students are given the opportunity to reflect not only on the learning that took place but also on the discussion process itself. Students need to be given the opportunity, either formally or informally, to evaluate both the process and their own part in the discussion.

SAMPLE QUESTIONS

47) **Which of the following is true about a discussion?**

A.   Students try to prove their point to others.

B.   Discussions are based on the opinions of the participants.

C.   Each student needs to choose a side of an argument.

D.   Students build knowledge by listening to others.

Answers:

A.   Incorrect. Students want to use evidence from the text to back up their statements, but discussions are not about proving a point.

B.   Incorrect. Discussions are based on text evidence, not opinions.

C.   Incorrect. Debates are arguments. Discussions are about finding common ground.

D.   **Correct.** Discussions build student knowledge by listening to the perspectives of others.

48) **What is the teacher's role in building a risk-free environment for students during a discussion?**

A.   The teacher should initiate all questions.

B.   The teacher should not provide the discussion material until the day of the debate to prevent some students from gaining an unfair advantage.

C.   The teacher should end the discussion if a student appears to be unprepared.

D.   The teacher should establish norms for preparedness, listening, questioning, and showing respect.

Answers:

A.   Incorrect. Sometimes the teacher will lead the questions, but students may be taught to write their own questions and should be prepared with a few before the start of the discussion.

B.   Incorrect. The teacher should model breaking down the material before the discussion so that everyone is prepared in advance.

C.   Incorrect. Expectations for preparedness should be set. In some discussions, some students are outside observers who will later reflect on the discussion.

D.   Correct. Teachers should explicitly teach expectations before beginning each discussion.

COMMUNICATION TECHNIQUES

In this section, communication methods, including both verbal and nonverbal, will be discussed. Although diversity is an asset to problem-solving, differences among people can inhibit effective communication, and learning active listening skills will help both students and teachers become better listeners.

VERBAL AND NONVERBAL COMMUNICATION

There are a variety of ways that teachers and students communicate with one another. Some nonverbal forms of communication include body language, eye contact, facial expressions, and gestures. **Gestures** are movements that are intended to nonverbally convey meaning.

During verbal communication, signals are received differently depending on the tone, stress, and inflection of the voice. **Vocal tone** is a way of sounding that expresses meaning. Tone conveys the feeling of the speaker but can often be misinterpreted. **Vocal stress** is emphasizing a word or words in a sentence to express meaning. For example, "*I* never accused Rebecca of lying about you," with the emphasis on the word I, comes across differently than saying "I never accused *Rebecca* of lying about you," with the emphasis on the word *Rebecca*. In the first sentence, it sounds like someone other than the speaker made an accusation of lying, whereas in the second sentence it sounds like the speaker accused someone of lying, but not Rebecca. **Vocal inflection** is a change of pitch or tone to express meaning. For example, a speaker will typically say the last word with a higher pitch to indicate a question compared to a statement. The word *Tabitha* sounds different in the sentence "Your name is Tabitha?" from "Your name is Tabitha" because of inflection. Even aspects such as the amount of personal space one person gives to another can convey meaning. With so many factors that affect the way communication is received, it is important to understand the point of view of each student to effectively understand one another.

SAMPLE QUESTIONS

49) **Which of the following factors affects how communication is received?**

A. tone of voice

B. body language

C. personal space

D. all of the above

Answers:

A. Incorrect. Tone of voice is only one factor that indicates how verbal communication is received.

B. Incorrect. Body language is a form of nonverbal communication, but there is a better answer here.

C. Incorrect. Personal space affects how communication is received, but there is a better choice.

D. Correct. Each of these factors contributes to understanding or misunderstanding of intended communication.

50) **Which of the following is an example of using vocal tone to communicate?**

A. Ms. Short speaks sternly to a student who is off topic.

B. Mr. Blume emphasizes the word *read* when he says, "You must *read* the text to find the answer."

C. Mrs. Black raises the pitch at the end of the sentence "Savannah rides the bus home?"

D. Mr. Williams taps on the desk of a student who is not working.

Answers:

A. Correct. Vocal tone expresses emotion. Ms. Short is expressing disapproval by speaking sternly.

B. Incorrect. Mr. Blume is using vocal stress or emphasizing a word to help students understand that they really have to pay attention to what they are reading to find the answer.

C. Incorrect. Mrs. Black is using vocal inflection so that the listener will understand that she is asking a question.

D. Incorrect. Mr. Williams is using nonverbal communication.

EFFECTS OF CULTURE AND GENDER

Culture and gender affect the way people see the world. To effectively communicate with people from different backgrounds, it is important to understand how diversity affects the way information is transmitted and received. In the event that native language is also a barrier, literal translations may create even further confusion.

High-context cultures, such as those found in most of the Middle East, Asia, Africa, and South America, communicate heavily through relationships, context, and nonverbal cues. However, low-context cultures, which are typically English- and German-speaking countries, rely more on direct messages.

Another way that cultures differ from one another is that some think sequentially, whereas others think synchronically. Sequential cultures, such as those found in the United States, Canada, and northern Europe, typically do one thing at a time and place a large amount of value in being on time and not wasting time. Synchronic cultures, such as Asia, southern Europe, South America, and Mexico, put less value on being on time and are more likely to multitask.

Additionally, some cultures are affective, whereas others are emotionally neutral. Italy, France, the United States, and Singapore are affective and typically condone some expression of emotion. However, neutral countries, such as Japan, Indonesia, the United Kingdom, Norway, and the Netherlands, find expressions of emotion to be irrational and unacceptable in most situations.

In the same way that culture affects communication style, gender also plays a role in how people communicate. It is important to note that not all students communicate according to gender types, but awareness of variations in the way people communicate reduces potential conflicts. Typically, men are more direct, authoritative, and confrontational. They tend to sit at an angle to avoid eye contact. Conversation for men is usually for the purpose of finding solutions rather than to vent. Women are more likely to be vulnerable, take turns talking, ask for help, and talk about their feelings. Some boys may need to be encouraged to show their vulnerabilities by asking for help, just as girls should be encouraged to take on leadership roles that enable them to be more direct.

Table 2.4. Communication Styles by Culture	
Country	**Cultural Communication Styles**
United States	▸ relies heavily on precise language ▸ places value on time and efficiency ▸ is emotionally expressive
Middle East	▸ relies heavily on relationships and nonverbal cues ▸ is less concerned about time, tends to multitask ▸ is emotionally expressive
Japan	▸ relies heavily on relationships and nonverbal cues ▸ is less concerned about time, tends to multitask ▸ considers emotional expressions unacceptable

Country	Cultural Communication Styles
Mexico	▶ relies heavily on relationships and nonverbal cues ▶ is less concerned about time, tends to multitask ▶ is emotionally expressive
United Kingdom	▶ relies heavily on precise language ▶ places value on time and efficiency ▶ considers emotional expressions unacceptable

However, no two people are exactly alike. Although culture and gender can be used to make generalities about expected communication styles, knowing and understanding each individual student is most effective.

SAMPLE QUESTIONS

51) **Which of the following countries has a culture in which expressing emotions is generally acceptable?**

    A.   United States

    B.   Japan

    C.   Indonesia

    D.   United Kingdom

Answers:

    A.   **Correct.** The United States has an affective culture in which expressions of emotions are usually acceptable.

    B.   Incorrect. Japan's culture is generally emotionally neutral.

    C.   Incorrect. The emotionally neutral culture of Indonesia frowns upon public displays of emotions.

    D.   Incorrect. In the United Kingdom, people do not readily display their emotions.

52) **Which of the following is often a typical conversation style for women?**

    A.   blunt

    B.   direct

    C.   taking turns

    D.   confrontational

Answers:

    A.   Incorrect. Men tend to be more blunt than women in their conversation style.

    B.   Incorrect. Women are usually not as direct as men in conversations.

C.   **Correct.** Typically, women take turns speaking.

D.   Incorrect. Generally, men are more confrontational than women.

COMMUNICATION TOOLS

There are tools available to help educators improve communication within the classroom. **Audio aids** are devices that amplify the teacher's speech so that it can be heard clearly by students regardless of the student's position in the classroom. Not only do audio aids help students with hearing deficits, but all students have been shown to be more attentive when these devices are used. Typically, audio aids consist of a microphone that is used by the teacher and projected by speakers on all sides of the room. Using audio aids helps students in the class feel as if they are sitting in the front of the room.

Visual aids are devices that can be shown to students to accompany text or speech to clarify meaning. Visual learners and English-language learners find visual aids particularly beneficial. PowerPoint clips, videos, and props are all examples of visual aids that can enrich the learning experience. Text resources, such as books and reproducible passages, are available both within adopted textbook materials and online for students of every instructional level.

Digital resources include cameras, software, and Internet sites that contain electronic materials, which can be used to enhance the learning experience. Technology is an important part of a student's world that should not stop when the student enters the school building. Some digital resources are able to monitor student progress and adjust to the level of each individual student, whereas others require more guidance and direction from the teacher.

SAMPLE QUESTIONS

53)   **Which of the following is an example of a visual aid in a classroom?**

     A.   a microphone

     B.   a PowerPoint® presentation

     C.   a textbook

     D.   a website

Answers:

     A.   Incorrect. A microphone is an audio aid.

     B.   **Correct.** A PowerPoint® presentation is an example of a visual aid.

     C.   Incorrect. Textbooks are text resources.

     D.   Incorrect. Websites are digital resources.

54) **How do audio aids support communication in the classroom?**

    A.   Students are more attentive.

    B.   They clarify meaning.

    C.   They help students work at their instructional level.

    D.   They monitor student progress.

Answers:

    A.   **Correct.** Audio aids support student attention by making every student feel as if the teacher is speaking directly to him or her.

    B.   Incorrect. Visual aids may be used to clarify meaning.

    C.   Incorrect. Text resources can be found for each student's instructional level.

    D.   Incorrect. Some digital resources provide progress monitoring.

EFFECTIVE LISTENING

Using effective listening skills may reduce communication errors. Teachers can train not only themselves but also their students to be better communicators by using active listening strategies. The first step to being a good listener is to pay attention. Frequently, when another person is talking, the listener will allow his or her mind to wander off topic or to formulate a response. In either scenario, the listener is not really attending to the speaker. The next step is to check for understanding by restating the speaker's key points in the listener's own words. This allows the speaker to clarify any misinterpretations. The listener can further clarify what the speaker has said by asking questions. Once the listener has determined that he or she has fully understood what has been communicated, it is time to begin interpreting the information within the listener's context to form a response that is both supportive and respectful.

SAMPLE QUESTIONS

55) **What is the first step to active listening?**

    A.   to form a response

    B.   to ask questions

    C.   to pay attention

    D.   to form an opinion

Answers:

    A.   Incorrect. When the listener is forming a response, he or she is not focused on what the speaker is saying.

    B.   Incorrect. Clarifying questions should be asked after the speaker has had an opportunity to fully share the message.

C.   **Correct.** The listener's mind should be completely open to what the speaker is trying to say, without judgment.

D.   Incorrect. When listeners begin to form judgments about the speaker's message, they are not truly being attentive.

56)   **A student is asked what motivates a character in the story to make false accusations against a neighbor. The student responds, "This character wants revenge because the community voted against his proposal." Which of the following statements by the listener would demonstrate the first step of active listening?**

A.   The character is upset with the community and wants to get back at them for voting against him.

B.   Why do you think the community voted against his proposal?

C.   This character is using accusations as a means of financial gain so that he can buy his neighbor's land.

D.   What evidence from the text supports this conclusion?

Answers:

A.   **Correct.** The first thing an active listener does after listening to a response is to restate key points.

B.   Incorrect. This question builds context but is only indirectly related to the speaker's message.

C.   Incorrect. By rebutting the speaker's statement, the listener has not shown the speaker that the message has been fully understood.

D.   Incorrect. This is a great clarifying question to ask after restating the key points of the speaker's message.

CONSTRUCTED-RESPONSE QUESTIONS

1)   **Describe the process of writing lesson plans.**

Sample Aswer:

Lesson plans should be written using backward design. The teacher begins by identifying the learning objectives that need to be taught. State standards in conjunction with district materials, such as the scope and sequence and pacing guides, are used to help the teacher identify which objectives need to be taught and to what depth. The next step is to select assessments that are aligned with the learning goal. There should be a combination of summative assessments that outline learner expectations at the end of the unit, and formative assessments that help the teacher monitor and adjust instruction. Once the objectives and assessments are aligned, the teacher will select learning activities and materials that are aligned, research based, and engaging to move students toward mastery.

2)   **How might culture affect communication?**

Sample Answer:

The way culture is imprinted on a person can make a big difference in how that person transmits and receives information. For example, if a student is from a synchronic culture, where people frequently multitask and time is not considered to be as important, and a teacher is from a sequential culture, which completes things one at a time and puts a great emphasis on time, there may be an issue when the student misses deadlines. The student will likely not understand why the teacher is upset, whereas the teacher may feel that the student is distractible and irresponsible. Understanding the perspective of the other party is the first step in resolving conflict that may occur as a result of diversity.

Go on →

TERMS

active listening: This technique improves listening skills by structuring how a person listens and responds to the person who is talking.

affective domain: The affective domain controls the development of emotions, values, and attitudes.

analyze: Analyzing is the process of inspecting something critically.

artifacts: These consist of genuine objects or articles created by a person.

assessment: This is the process of gathering data to determine the extent to which learning goals have been met.

audio aid: This device amplifies the teacher's speech so that it can be heard clearly by students.

behaviorism: The theory of behaviorism describes how rewards and punishments condition student behavior and learning.

bias: A bias is an unfair inclination toward a person or idea that invalidates objectivity.

Bloom's taxonomy: This classifies cognitive processes from simple to abstract.

brainstorming: This is the process of generating ideas related to a specific problem or concept.

categorize: This is the practice of sorting into groups by characteristics.

cloze procedures: This is the practice of omitting words from the text as a reading comprehension activity.

coaching: This training occurs when one person receives support from another toward the achievement of a goal.

cognitive domain: The ways students process new information, store knowledge, and retrieve it to apply to new circumstances fall within this domain.

compare: This is when students note the similarities between two or more things.

computer-mediated instruction: Learning activities are facilitated through computer technology.

concept learning: A form of learning that involves classifying information by topic.

concept mapping: This is the practice of using graphic organizers to present thoughts or information.

constructivism: Students construct their own knowledge through learning experiences.

contrast: This is when students note the differences between two or more things.

creative thinking: This form of thinking describes cognitive processes, such as brainstorming, that are designed to generate new thoughts, ideas, and solutions.

critical thinking: This form of thinking involves looking at evidence from an objective viewpoint to make inferences or draw conclusions.

debates: Debates are formal discussions about opposing arguments.

deductive reasoning: Certain conclusions are drawn by using known information and narrowing it to a specific circumstance.

demonstration: This is the practice of providing evidence of an observable conclusion.

direct teaching: This form of teaching is centered on the teacher and instruction is based on disseminating facts.

discovery learning: Students perform experiments or research information to comprehend new concepts.

distance learning: This type of learning involves provisions for educating students that are not in attendance at a school facility.

enrichment: This is the opportunity to learn objectives at a deeper level than outlined in the curriculum standards.

evaluate: This is when something or someone is assessed.

experiential learning: This type of learning happens through experiences and may include hands-on learning.

explicit teaching: This centers on focused and unambiguous teaching of a specific skill or standard.

extrinsic rewards: These are external rewards, such as trinkets, praise, or recognition, bestowed upon someone for doing a good job.

generalize: This is the practice of applying what is known from a small sample and assuming it to be true about a larger group.

gesture: This movement is intended to nonverbally convey meaning.

guided practice: Students practice a new concept with scaffolded support from the teacher.

independent learning: Learning experiences are completed autonomously by the student.

indirect teaching: This term describes student-centered instruction in which the teacher facilitates opportunities for students to construct their own learning.

inductive reasoning: Likely conclusions are drawn by putting together known concepts and applying them to a new situation.

infer: When students infer, they draw a conclusion using reasoning skills.

inquiry: Inquiry is the process of finding the answers to questions.

integrative framework: This framework entails a plan for achieving goals in all subject areas by combining content across disciplines.

interactive learning: This learning approach relies heavily on social interaction and cooperative grouping.

interdisciplinary unit: This is a unit of study in which content from all subject areas is integrated.

intrinsic rewards: Learners are internally satisfied by doing work because it is interesting, challenging, or relevant, or makes them feel successful.

learning centers: These centers are segments of the classroom in which independent learning activities are provided to students.

learning contracts: These types of contracts are agreements negotiated between a student and a teacher, with possible input from other school personnel or parents, designed for the improvement of an objective.

learning domain: The three domains of learning are cognitive, affective, and psychomotor.

lecture: This is teacher-led instruction; the teacher talks while the students listen and possibly take notes.

lesson objective: This objective establishes the student's learning goals for a lesson.

listening guides: These are statements or questions that provide instructional focus when listening to a lecture or other form of auditory instruction.

long-term memory: Information is stored for a long period of time and may be recalled.

manipulatives: These include items that students are able to move or change during hands-on instruction.

mapping: This is the practice of graphically organizing thoughts by starting with a main idea and organizing thoughts and ideas around the main idea.

memory: This is a cognitive process of storing and retrieving information that has been learned.

modeling: Modeling involves demonstrating for others so that they can learn through mimicry.

models: These include representations or examples.

nonverbal prompting: The teacher uses gestures or other physical prompts to assist students.

occupational therapist: This is a certified professional who assesses and provides treatment for the development of life skills among disabled individuals.

one-on-one: This is a type of instruction in which a teacher works with one individual student on a concept.

pair-share: Students work with a partner to discuss learning as it is taking place.

paraprofessional: This is a trained teacher assistant.

peer practice: This is the practice of using social interaction among students to promote learning goals.

physical therapist: This type of therapist is a certified professional who evaluates and treats mobility issues.

planning: This involves having forethought in implementation and design to achieve a desired outcome.

predict: This is the act of anticipating what will happen.

problem-based learning: Children learn by solving open-ended questions.

problem-solving: This is the process of finding answers to difficult questions.

psychomotor domain: The psychomotor domain controls motor skill development.

punishment: Punishment is used to penalize for the purpose of extinguishing behavior.

questioning: Questioning involves inquiries that are used to help focus instruction and assess understanding.

reading guides: These guides include statements or questions that lead students through the text, providing instructional focus.

recall: This is the act of retrieving facts.

reciprocal determinism: This theory by Albert Bandura states that behavior is determined by a combination of cognitive factors, the environment, and stimuli.

reflective listening: The teacher hears a speaker and then repeats back the meaning behind his or her words in order to clarify understanding.

reinforcement: This is the process of strengthening behavior through rewards or consequences.

remediation: Remediation is the additional support provided to regular education students to bridge gaps in learning.

research projects: These types of projects are studies of specific concepts using scientific principles for gathering information.

restatement: The learner or listener repeats what has been learned using his or her own wording.

role-play: This involves using play-acting to demonstrate a concept.

scaffolds: This term describes the supports that allow a child to work above his or her independent level and are gradually removed as the learner gains mastery.

schema: This term indicates the framework of understanding in a child's brain.

scope: The scope of planning outlines the learning objectives that will be taught to students, including all supporting standards and the level of complexity.

sequence: Sequence refers to the order in which learning objectives are taught to maximize student success.

short-term memory: Information enters the conscious memory but is not stored for recall at a later time.

simulations: These models mimic real-world processes.

small group: Instruction is provided to a group composed of learners with similar instructional needs.

speech therapist: This type of therapist is a certified professional who diagnoses and treats communication disorders.

standards-based education: This form of education involves a set of learning outcomes clearly set by the district and state that all students are expected to achieve.

summarize: When an individual provides a condensed version of a story or an explanation, he or she is summarizing.

synthesize: This is the process of combining information from various sources and applying it to a new area.

teachable moment: In a teachable moment, an unplanned event occurs, triggering interest in learning more about a related topic.

thematic unit: This kind of unit involves integrating curricula across content areas under a general theme.

think time: This is processing time that a learner takes after receiving new information before responding to it.

verbal prompting: The teacher uses words or beginning phonemes to assist students.

vicarious learning: This theory by Albert Bandura involves learning by observing the consequences to others that evokes emotion from the observer.

viewing guides: These guides include statements or questions that provide instructional focus while students are watching films or clips.

visual aid: This is something that can be shown to students to accompany text or speech in order to clarify meaning.

vocal inflection: This is a change of pitch or tone to express meaning.

vocal stress: This involves emphasizing a word or words to convey meaning.

vocal tone: This involves a certain way of sounding that expresses meaning.

wait time: This is processing time that is intentionally provided by the teacher after asking a question to give learners think time.

whole class: Instruction is delivered to all of the students in the class at the same time in the same way.

3

Assessment

Why are there so many different assessments in education? Each type of test uses different criteria for item selection and grading strategies that match the intent. This chapter explores different types of assessments that are used for educational purposes. Some tests are intended for teachers to use in the classroom to make instructional decisions, whereas other tests provide data for accountability or student placement decisions. Teachers need to clearly understand the purpose of each test, the grading strategy, and basic statistical information that is provided on score reports to articulate results to stakeholders and make sound educational decisions with the information provided.

ASSESSMENT AND EVALUATION STRATEGIES

Throughout the learning process, teachers use a variety of assessments for many purposes. Teachers use formal assessments, such as standardized tests, to evaluate a student's progress against a statistical average of other students of the same age. Typically, formal assessments are purchased at a hefty price from a publisher or testing company that will put the assessment through a series of research studies to standardize information.

Teachers use informal assessments to help make daily instructional decisions. An informal assessment can take place before, during, or after instruction and can be used to guide instruction or evaluate student progress.

Diagnostic assessments may be formal or informal. They are used to assess a student's background knowledge prior to a learning experience. Throughout instruction, formative assessments help teachers monitor students' progress so that instruction can be adjusted to meet the needs of the students. Typically, formative assessments will be informal. Summative assessments are used after learning occurs. Summative assessments may be formal or informal. In general, teachers use summative assessments for accountability purposes and grades. However, if more than 20 percent of students fail a summative assessment, it may indicate that the material needs to be retaught in a different way; therefore, it may be used to guide instruction. Another reason for an unexpected number of failures could be alignment issues among the standards, the learning activities, and the assessment.

In addition to the type and purpose of the test, the format of a test should be based on the type of evidence the teacher hopes to glean from the assessment. Essay tests give students the freedom to creatively articulate their learning at a deep level. However, they are time-consuming both to take and to grade, so they are better used when there is not a lot of material to cover. Selected responses cover a great deal of material and are easier to grade, but students may guess some answers, and error analysis is difficult.

> **TEACHING TIP**
>
> If the curriculum is solid, well delivered, and aligned to the standards, approximately 80 percent of students should not need additional intervention to meet standards.

Portfolios, conferences, performances, and observation provide information that can be assessed only in these ways. However, they are time-consuming to grade. Checklists, rubrics, or anecdotal notes should accompany these types of assessments so there is evidence of the grading methods.

Peer assessment and self-assessment are tools for helping students internalize the criteria for quality work. These assessment methods help students use their critical thinking skills to evaluate work products and articulate feedback.

FORMAL AND INFORMAL ASSESSMENT

Assessments used for educational purposes can be formal or informal. **Formal assessments**, using standardized calculations, measure a student's progress against a statistical average of other students the same age. Both achievement and aptitude tests are examples of formal assessments. Formal assessments may be oral, written, or computer based. Annual state tests, ACT/SAT tests, and Wechsler Scales are commonly used formal assessments. In general, formal assessments are purchased from a publisher who has specified both administration and scoring procedures. An advantage of a formal test is that a great deal of effort went into ensuring that it accurately measures what it claims to measure; however, formal assessments are expensive and time-consuming and therefore are not practical for daily application.

Informal assessments are regularly used to assess classroom performance and drive instruction. Teacher-made tests, anecdotal records, portfolio assessments, error analysis, interest inventories, and project-based assessments are all examples of informal assessments that are used in the classroom. Typically, informal assessments are created by teachers or committees of teachers but have not endured the rigorous validation processes of formal assessments. Most districts use informal benchmark tests but provide some degree of standardization in the administration and scoring of the test.

Table 3.1. Formal Versus Informal Assessments

Formal Assessments	Informal Assessments
standardized scoring and administration	varied scoring and administration techniques
purchased from test publishers	created by educators for classroom use
used to compare students to each other or standards for placement and accountability	used to make classroom-level instructional decisions and to assign grades

Formal assessments are frequently used to make educational placement decisions and measure the effectiveness of educational programs, whereas informal tests are used to help districts, schools, and teachers make informed classroom decisions.

SAMPLE QUESTIONS

1) **Which of the following is an example of an informal assessment?**

    A. an annual state test

    B. a college admissions test

    C. an IQ test

    D. a portfolio assessment

    Answers:

    A. Incorrect. An annual state test is a formal test that is used primarily for accountability purposes.

    B. Incorrect. A college admissions test is a standardized, formal assessment.

    C. Incorrect. An IQ test is a formal assessment.

    D. **Correct.** A portfolio assessment is an informal test used by teachers to make instructional decisions.

2) **Mr. Clayborne wants to informally gather information about Charity's progress in reading to help her target her flexible small-group instruction. Which assessment is most appropriate for him to use?**

    A. a state standardized test

    B. an aptitude test

    C. anecdotal records

    D. an intelligence test

Answers:

A. Incorrect. State standardized tests provide accountability information to agencies.

B. Incorrect. Aptitude tests help determine a student's strengths compared with other students of the same age.

C. **Correct.** Anecdotal records are an informal assessment that helps guide instruction.

D. Incorrect. Intelligence tests help diagnose exceptionalities.

DIAGNOSTIC, FORMATIVE, AND SUMMATIVE ASSESSMENTS

Depending on the goal of the assessment instrument, teachers may use diagnostic, formative, or summative assessments. **Diagnostic assessments** are given before a learning experience, and they provide teachers with a baseline of students' skills. Diagnostic assessments may be formal or informal. Formal diagnostic assessments include the Developmental Reading Assessment (DRA), Dynamic Indicator of Basic Early Learning Skills (DIBELS), and the Comprehension Attitude Strategies Interests (CASI). Each of these formal diagnostic assessments provides teachers with information about student reading levels; however, diagnostic assessments may also be used in other content areas.

TEACHING TIP

Anticipation guides and KWL charts can serve as both diagnostic assessments and learning tools to activate prior knowledge.

Informal diagnostic assessments include student self-assessments, anticipation guides, KWL charts, and pretests. Anticipation guides ask students questions about the content they are about to learn to spark student interest and activate prior knowledge. These guides can also be used as a diagnostic assessment to determine what students already know before launching a new unit.

Formative assessments are informal assessments that are used throughout the learning experience to help teachers make instructional decisions and to provide feedback to students. Examples of formative assessments are anecdotal records, questioning techniques, and pop quizzes. In general, formative assessments do not provide quantifiable data, but they are valuable for providing information necessary to help teachers target instruction based on students' needs.

Table 3.2. Examples of Formative Assessments

anecdotal records	These are notes that teachers keep concerning student performance according to learning or behavior goals.
observation	Teachers watch students' learning activity to determine strengths and weaknesses so that students may receive targeted remediation.

pop quizzes	Pop quizzes are short, unexpected assessments used to indicate students' strengths and weaknesses regarding newly learned material. Pop quizzes should be used to give the teacher and the students feedback rather than for grades.
ticket out the door (exit ticket)	This is a short summary of learning or answer to an open-ended question that students write as part of closure for a lesson that provides insight about students' strengths and challenges regarding new learning.
think-pair-share	This method engages students by having all students think about a question related to content and then articulate their answers to a partner. When combined with active listening skills, students can learn from one another. This can be used as a formative assessment if the teacher listens to discussions and then asks partner groups to share their answers.
learning logs	Students keep learning logs throughout a learning experience to journal their thoughts and questions. Monitoring learning logs can help teachers assess students' level of understanding.
discussion	Discussions help inform the teacher about the degree of general understanding of learning topics. Care must be taken during a discussion to prevent some students from dominating the conversation as others avoid participation.
questioning	Asking questions helps teachers gain insight about how much students understand. However, care must be taken to engage students because, in general, students will check out when it is not their turn. Randomizing which students will answer the question and giving think time to everyone before calling on someone to answer increase engagement.
signaled responses	Signaled responses involve asking students questions and then asking them to perform a gesture to indicate their answer. Gestures could include thumbs up/thumbs down, stand up/sit down, or choosing a corner of the room to walk to depending on the answer. Signaled responses require everyone to engage on a physical level; however, some students will copy one another rather than think about their answer.
choral responses	Choral responses are when everyone in the class gives the answer at the same time. For short-answer questions, choral responses can improve student engagement. If this method is used, students need to be explicitly told before each learning experience whether the expectation is to raise their hands or call out answers.

Summative assessments may be formal or informal and evaluate student achievement after learning takes place. Standardized state tests are an example of a formal summative assessment. End-of-unit tests and benchmark tests are examples of informal summative assessments. Summative assessments may be used for accountability and grades as they are a measure of student performance in relation to the objectives.

Diagnostic, formative, and summative assessments are an integral part of planning any unit. Frequent monitoring and quality feedback are some of the most effective ways to improve student achievement. Regardless of the type, an assessment will be an accurate measure only if it is aligned with the instructional objectives and learning activities. Therefore, how the teacher uses assessments is crucial to the planning process.

SAMPLE QUESTIONS

3) Ms. Randle is gathering information about her students at the beginning of the school year to determine their reading levels. She wants to find out what skills they are entering school with. Which assessment tool should she choose?

A. a diagnostic assessment

B. a formative assessment

C. a summative assessment

D. an aptitude test

Answers:

A. **Correct.** Diagnostic assessments test students before a learning experience.

B. Incorrect. Formative assessments take place throughout a learning experience to provide information for instructional decisions.

C. Incorrect. Summative assessments take place after a learning experience to evaluate learning.

D. Incorrect. Aptitude tests measure students' talents.

4) Mr. Ferguson's students are taking an end-of-course examination that they must pass as a graduation requirement. Which type of assessment are they taking?

A. a diagnostic assessment

B. a formative assessment

C. a summative assessment

D. an intelligence test

Answers:

A. Incorrect. Diagnostic assessments determine background knowledge and skills before a learning experience.

B. Incorrect. Formative assessments provide information that guides instruction.

C. **Correct.** Summative assessments evaluate what students have learned.

D. Incorrect. Intelligence tests help diagnose exceptionalities.

ASSESSMENT FORMATS

For each type of assessment, there are a variety of formats that may be used to evaluate students' learning.

Essay tests are written responses that provide students the opportunity to fully articulate their learning. Essay tests are easy to write but time-consuming and subjective to grade. Student responses are more likely to be based on knowledge and creativity rather than best guesses. Essay tests demonstrate depth rather than breadth of knowledge. Essay questions are more practical to use either as a summative assessment with five or fewer questions or in conjunction with other types of questions. These can also be used as formative assessments that can be quickly reviewed.

Selected-response, or multiple-choice, tests allow students to choose the best answer from the available choices. Selected-response assessments are easy to grade and versatile, which makes them a popular choice among educators. However, they can be difficult to write and leave some room for students to guess. It is also difficult to determine why students made errors, so it is challenging to find a solution. Selected-response can be used in any subject to provide information about student content knowledge.

Students collect a variety of artifacts as evidence of learning to be evaluated when using **portfolio** assessments. Written work, photographs of projects, and video evidence may all be used as artifacts in a portfolio. Portfolios have the advantage of providing a holistic view of student learning but are time-consuming and difficult to grade. For example, a portfolio assessment might be used in a technology class in which students are asked to submit their best work from each of the applications.

Conferences are meetings between the teacher and student in which learning is orally assessed and evaluated. Conferences can be beneficial to students because teachers can prompt students toward the correct answer, but they can also be uncomfortable for students who are not accustomed to this method. A student may not know what the teacher wants from him or her. Conferences can be difficult to grade and do not provide a trail of evidence to justify a grade; therefore, some type of checklist or rubric can be used when using a conference as part of a student's grade.

> **QUICK REVIEW**
>
> When would performances be an appropriate assessment?

Observation is when a teacher watches a student engaged in a learning activity to find evidence of learning. Like conferences, observation does not leave a paper trail and is difficult to grade but can provide information to make instructional decisions. Anecdotal records, checklists, or rubrics should be used when employing this method.

Performances give students the opportunity to present their learning while teachers assess mastery of learning goals. Performances provide students the opportunity to present skills in ways that cannot be assessed in another manner. Performances do not work for all subject areas but are a great way to demonstrate abilities in athletics, history, and the arts. Performances can be time-consuming and difficult to grade, but they provide opportunities for students to tap into an area of intelligence that may be neglected using other assessment formats.

Table 3.3. Advantages of Assessment Formats

Assessment Type	Easy to create	Easy to grade	Thorough	Provides documentation of student learning
Essay	✓		✓	✓
Selected-response		✓	✓	✓
Portfolio			✓	✓
Conference			✓	
Observation	✓		✓	
Performance	✓		✓	

Providing students some choice in evaluation methods they may use to demonstrate their knowledge can be motivating. Choice provides opportunities for students to take advantage of their learning style and express creative and critical thinking. However, there may be challenges in providing consistent scoring when a variety of assessment methods are used in a summative assessment. Checklists that outline which information must be included can help create more consistent outcomes.

SAMPLE QUESTIONS

5) Mrs. Franco's students meet with her individually so that she can ask them questions about what they have learned. Which assessment format is Mrs. Franco using?

A. performance

B. observation

C. conference

D. portfolio

Answers:

A. Incorrect. Performances give students the opportunity to present their learning as teachers watch to assess mastery of learning goals.

B.   Incorrect. Observation is when a teacher watches a student engaged in a learning activity to find evidence of learning.

C.   Correct. Conferences are meetings between the teacher and each student in which learning is orally assessed and evaluated.

D.   Incorrect. Students collect a variety of artifacts as evidence of learning to be evaluated when using portfolio assessments.

6)   **Mr. Diego, the history teacher, will be giving a final test the day before grades are due for the semester. He needs an assessment that will cover all of the information that has been learned so far this year in a format that will be quick and easy to grade. Which format would work best for Mr. Diego?**

A.   essay

B.   selected-response

C.   conference

D.   portfolio

Answers:

A.   Incorrect. Essay tests do not cover as much information as other types of tests and therefore could not cover an entire semester of instruction.

B.   Correct. Selected-response tests are easy to grade and cover a breadth of information.

C.   Incorrect. Conferences are time-consuming and difficult to grade.

D.   Incorrect. Portfolios take a great deal of time to grade.

ASSESSMENT TOOLS

In addition to different types of assessments used for different purposes, different assessment tools can be used to help teachers gather the information they need.

Rubrics are a fixed scale that measures performance with detailed descriptions of criteria that define each level of performance. Rubrics define the expectations of an assignment, thereby clarifying the standards of quality work. The use of rubrics improves consistency and reliability compared with more subjective evaluations. Rubrics not only measure student progress but also can be used as a learning tool to outline what it takes for students to move to the next level. When using rubrics, it is helpful for students to see exemplars that demonstrate the work at each level. Rubrics work best with writing, projects, and performance-based learning activities.

Analytical checklists outline criteria of student performance that teachers can mark as students show mastery of each required skill in standards-based education. Checklists should be written in a language that can be easily understood by students and their parents but based on state standards. Analytical checklists answer simply the yes-or-no question regarding whether students have accomplished the learning goals. They do not provide information regarding the degree to which students have met proficiency. Typically, the teacher would date the checklists so that progression can be seen over time. Checklists work best in activities that require the incremental mastery of skills, such as athletics, instrumental music, languages, math fluency, and prereading skills.

Objective	Date of Mastery
Rides a tricycle	
Matches objects by shape	
Matches objects by color	

Figure 3.1. Sample Analytical Checklist: Pre-K

Frequently, anecdotal notes will accompany checklists. **Anecdotal notes** are written records of the teacher's observations of a student. Records should be specific, objective, and focused on outlined criteria. Anecdotal notes provide cumulative information about how each individual performs and may include information about learning and/or behavior. Anecdotal notes are particularly useful for targeting remediation; however, it can be overwhelming for a teacher to attempt to observe every action of every student in this way.

Scoring guides are similar to a rubric because they outline criteria for quality work and define levels of proficiency; however, they differ from rubrics in that each criterion is weighted with a multiplier. For example, a rubric may measure writing scores based on mechanics, word choice, and organization. A scoring guide may indicate that word choice is more important than mechanics, and so the score on the word choice portion of the rubric will be multiplied by two.

As students make progress, they proceed on a continuum. A **continuum** is a progression of learning. Sometimes while moving through the continuum, students will reach a plateau or even regress slightly before continuing to move forward. Computer-based programs are available that adapt to student progress and regression by providing questions slightly more difficult than the question they just answered correctly or one slightly less complex than the question they missed.

Rating scales are used to rate attitudes and opinions on a continuum. Typically, a rating scale will ask participants to rate an idea or an experience on a number scale or a category, such as "strongly agree," "agree," "neutral," "disagree," and "strongly disagree." The most commonly used rating scale is the Likert scale. A Likert scale should be interpreted using the mode rather than the mean and then displayed using a bar graph. The advantage of using rating scales is that students are required to rate the degree to which they feel a certain way. However, students are not always honest. Rating scales can be used for self-assessment or peer assessment, or to gather student input to evaluate learning activities and overall understanding of concepts. For example, the teacher may ask students to rate the participation of their peers during a cooperative learning activity.

To gather information about challenging behaviors, a teacher can develop a **behavior scale**. To create a behavior scale, the teacher should clearly identify the behavior to be observed. Typically, a teacher targets between one and three behaviors. Next, a method for measuring the behavior must be developed. Is information about frequency, duration, and/or intensity going to be part of the data collected? Next, a baseline is established by measuring the behavior before any interventions begin. From there, goals are set. For example, if a student typically has three temper tantrums every hour, the first goal might be to reduce the number of temper tantrums to one per hour.

SAMPLE QUESTIONS

7) **Ms. Frisillo notates the progress of her kindergarten students by indicating the date at which children can master skills such as writing their name, identifying basic shapes, and memorizing their parents' phone number. Which assessment tool is Ms. Frisillo using?**

  A. rubric

  B. checklist

  C. anecdotal notes

  D. portfolio

Answers:

  A. Incorrect. A rubric is a fixed scale that measures performance with detailed descriptions of criteria that define each level of performance.

  B. Correct. Checklists outline criteria of student performance that teachers can mark as students show mastery of each required skill.

  C. Incorrect. Anecdotal notes are written records of the teacher's observations of a student. They are specific, objective, and focused on outlined criteria.

  D. Incorrect. Students collect a variety of artifacts as evidence of learning to be evaluated when using portfolio assessments.

8) **Mr. Amendt, the English teacher, provides students with detailed descriptions of criteria that define each level of writing performance. Students use the descriptions to learn what they can do to be better writers, and then the student's level of performance is graded according to the criteria. Which assessment tool is Mr. Amendt using?**

  A. rubric

  B. selected-response

  C. checklist

  D. anecdotal notes

Answers:

A. **Correct.** A rubric is a fixed scale that measures performance with detailed descriptions of criteria that define each level of performance. Rubrics can be used to guide students and to grade performance.

B. Incorrect. Selected-response are multiple-choice tests.

C. Incorrect. Checklists outline criteria of student performance that teachers can mark as students show mastery of each required skill.

D. Incorrect. Anecdotal notes are written records of the teacher's observations of a student in relation to a learning standard.

SELF–ASSESSMENT AND PEER ASSESSMENT

The teacher is the primary evaluator of students' work, but there are times when training students to be evaluators will improve outcomes. When students evaluate their own work and the work of their peers, they are using metacognitive skills that help internalize the distinguishing characteristics of a quality work product from one of lesser quality. Students become active participants in the evaluation process and develop into autonomous learners.

Self-assessment describes methods by which students monitor their own progress toward learning goals. Students must have a clear understanding of their learning goals to determine whether they are making adequate progress. Goals should follow the SMART goal format. In other words, they should be specific, measurable, attainable, relevant, and time-bound. With the use of learning contracts, students and teachers work together to determine how students will monitor their own progress. Students may use checklists or rubrics as they develop a portfolio to document their growth. Self-assessment is frequently used with writing assignments and projects to help students internalize the criteria outlined for their assignment. Self-assessment gives students the opportunity to reflect on their work and use critical thinking skills to evaluate their work product. Are there any drawbacks to self-assessment? It takes a great deal of effort on the part of the teacher to effectively train students to be reliable evaluators since the tendency of students is to inflate their own grades. Self-assessment helps to motivate students to learn as they see themselves moving toward their goals.

Many of the same benefits of self-assessment occur with peer assessment. **Peer assessment** is when students evaluate one another and offer feedback. Students need a great deal of training to properly use peer assessment since they are unable to help one another if they do not have a clear understanding of what constitutes quality performance. It is recommended that students participate in guided practice using a sample of writing provided by the teacher before their first independent peer assessment. Rubrics, checklists, and rating scales

TEACHING TIP

Peer assessment should be used cautiously to prevent embarrassment or confidentiality issues.

may be used as a guide to help students evaluate one another. Peer assessment requires a safe learning atmosphere in which students trust one another and feel comfortable providing and receiving critical feedback. Frequently, peer assessment is used as part of group work and may improve participation of all group members. Peer assessment improves critical thinking skills because students must not only evaluate one another's work but also articulate and defend the reasons behind the scores they assign. Students involved in peer assessment feel a greater sense of responsibility for the achievement of their classmates. Teachers should be mindful that students may feel peer pressure to mark students higher or lower than the accurate score or may be reluctant to provide any type of feedback to their peers.

The goal of both self-assessment and peer assessment should be to improve student performance and help students critically evaluate what constitutes quality work, rather than assign grades.

Table 3.4. Self–Assessment Versus Peer Assessment

	Self-Assessment	Peer Assessment
Students gain a clear understanding of learning objectives.	✓	✓
Students use critical thinking skills to evaluate work.	✓	✓
Teachers must train students to be effective evaluators.	✓	✓
Students feel responsible for ensuring that all students are successful.		✓
Students may feel uncomfortable sharing feedback.		✓
Students may give inaccurate scores.	✓	✓

SAMPLE QUESTIONS

9) **Ms. DiCristafaro is considering using peer assessment to help students edit their writing assignments. Which of the following steps should she take first?**

A. establish a safe learning environment

B. pair students by ability level

C. teach students active listening skills

D. remind students of the importance of grades

Answers:

A.   **Correct.** Students must feel safe and trust their peers to participate in peer assessment.

B.   Incorrect. Students will not be paired for editing until after all students have had a chance to practice their editing skills with teacher support.

C.   Incorrect. Active listening skills will be helpful when receiving feedback, but that is the last step in the editing process.

D.   Incorrect. Peer assessments should be used to improve learning, not assign grades.

10)   **Mr. Patrick would like his students to self-assess their history projects before turning them in. Before beginning the project, which of the following should take place?**

A.   set learning goals

B.   locate resources

C.   critically evaluate their work

D.   articulate learning

Answers:

A.   **Correct.** Students should write SMART goals to drive their learning experience.

B.   Incorrect. Resources will not be selected until after the goals are set.

C.   Incorrect. Once the project is complete, students will evaluate their work.

D.   Incorrect. By the end of the project, students can articulate their learning.

National, State, and District Standardized Assessments

Standardized tests may be used to measure achievement, aptitude, or ability. Some are norm referenced, and they rank students or provide them with a grade or age-equivalent score that is calculated in comparison with other students who have taken the examination. Other tests are criterion referenced and provide scores that are based on mastery of identified objectives regardless of how others score.

Teachers need a basic understanding of how reliable and valid a test is for its intended purpose. Navigating through raw scores and percentile rankings can be confusing, but is necessary to explain scores to parents and develop next steps based on student and classroom score reports. How an assessment is scored can be as important for an educator to understand as knowing how test items were selected. Holistic scores provide general information about how a student scored, compared with analytical scores that provide specific feedback regarding the student's strengths and weaknesses.

STANDARDIZED TESTS

In January 2008, the No Child Left Behind Act was signed into law by President George W. Bush, ushering in an era of accountability. In December 2015, the Every Student Succeeds Act was signed by President Barack Obama to replace the No Child Left Behind Act. The Every Student Succeeds Act also requires annual state testing for accountability purposes, but some of the changes in legislation give more power to the states to determine student performance targets and interventions. Each state selects and adopts curriculum that will be taught and tested at each grade level. After the standards are set, the state contracts with a testing company to provide a standardized test that matches the curriculum standards for that state.

Standardized tests are administered to all students in a consistent way and then graded in the same way so that score comparisons may be made. Typically, the public considers only wide-scale, formal assessments to be standardized, but district benchmarks may also be considered standardized if testing methods are consistent. Throughout their educational experience, students will take a variety of standardized tests. Standardized tests may be used to measure achievement, aptitude, or ability.

> **QUICK REVIEW**
>
> What are the differences between achievement, aptitude, and ability tests?

The annual accountability test is an example of an achievement test. **Achievement tests** measure acquired knowledge or skills. They are intended to determine what students know at the end of a learning experience. The learning experience may be a unit, a semester, a year, or some other specified time segment during which a specified number of learning objectives should have been mastered. Some examples of well-known achievement tests include the American College Test (ACT), the Iowa Test of Basic Skills, and STAR Early Literacy. Achievement tests are popular because they provide a fairly accurate snapshot of student learning that can be used to compare students against the norm. However, many criticize the emphasis that has been placed on achievements tests, which creates undue stress on students and schools and should be considered only as one of multiple measures that indicate student learning. Cultural biases persist, particularly between socioeconomic groups, although efforts are made to minimize their impact. Informal achievement tests are used by classroom teachers to evaluate students and assign grades. Formal achievement tests are used for accountability and for college admissions.

Another type of test that most students will take at some point during their education is an aptitude test. **Aptitude tests** are used to measure a person's ability to develop a particular skill if properly trained. Aptitude tests may measure academic ability, clerical speed, or mechanical reasoning. Aptitude tests are often used to guide secondary students toward careers in which they are successful. Some examples of aptitude tests include the Differential Aptitude Test and the Armed Services Vocational Aptitude Battery. Increasingly, employers in technical fields use aptitude tests when choosing new hires. Some aptitude tests assess a variety of skills, whereas others are specialized for a specific occupation or program. Aptitude tests provide some objectivity, but aptitude does not always translate into ability because work ethic and training also contribute.

Ability tests measure a person's ability to perform a particular skill. The difference between aptitude and ability is that aptitude indicates natural talent that can be developed over time, whereas ability measures how capable a student is to perform a skill without training. The CogAT, or Cognitive Abilities Test, measures a student's ability to use reason to solve verbal, quantitative, and nonverbal problems and is used to place students in gifted programs. Intelligence tests, such as the Woodcock-Johnson, fall under the umbrella of cognitive abilities tests, which assess reasoning and comprehension skills, as well as the ability to think abstractly. Intelligence tests are used to identify and place students in need of special services. Employers use a variety of ability tests to measure dexterity, speed, and general abilities. Ability tests are expensive and can be invalidated if used incorrectly, but they provide more consistent results than more subjective selections.

Table 3.5. Standardized Tests

Test Type	Definition	Examples
achievement	Achievement tests measure acquired knowledge or skills.	▸ American College Test (ACT) ▸ Iowa Test of Basic Skills ▸ STAR Early Literacy
aptitude	Aptitude tests measure a person's ability to develop a particular skill.	▸ Differential Aptitude Test ▸ Armed Services Vocational Aptitude Battery
ability	Ability tests measure a person's ability to perform a particular skill without any training.	▸ CogAT (Cognitive Abilities Test) ▸ dexterity tests ▸ typing speed tests ▸ Woodcock-Johnson

Another form of assessment that is used to identify students for special education services is the adaptive behavior scale. **Adaptive behavior scales** are used to measure the ability of a person with an identified disability to become self-sufficient. Adaptive behavior scales may include information about reading, money, time, social skills, ability to follow rules, ability to stay safe, and ability to work. There are several adaptive behavior scales that have met standards for validity and reliability. Some examples of adaptive behavior scales are Scales of Independent Behavior—Revised (SIB-R), Vineland Adaptive Behavior Scales, and AAMR Adaptive Behavior Scale 2nd edition. Adaptive behavior scales generally produce results based on age equivalency, because what is considered appropriate for a six-year-old will vary greatly from what is expected from an eighteen-year-old.

SAMPLE QUESTIONS

11) **Mrs. Grand is searching for a test that will compare her students' content knowledge with other students in the state. Which type of assessment should she use?**

A. achievement

B. aptitude

C. ability

D. informal

Answers:

A. **Correct.** Achievement tests measure acquired knowledge or skills.

B. Incorrect. Aptitude tests measure a person's ability to develop a particular skill.

C. Incorrect. Ability tests measure a person's ability to perform a particular skill.

D. Incorrect. Informal tests do not compare students against a norm.

12) **Mr. Cavanaugh, the school counselor, would like information that will help him determine which students should be placed in the preengineering program. He does not expect students to have the skills but is looking for students who have the potential to develop engineering skills. Which of the following types of assessment should he use?**

A. intelligence

B. achievement

C. aptitude

D. ability

Answers:

A. Incorrect. Intelligence tests specifically assess existing reasoning and comprehension skills.

B. Incorrect. Achievement tests measure acquired knowledge or skills.

C. **Correct.** Aptitude tests measure potential to develop a skill.

D. Incorrect. Ability tests measure innate ability.

Norm–Referenced and Criterion–Referenced Scoring

When school or state officials want information about how students or schools are performing against a national average, norm-referenced tests are used. **Norm-referenced tests** measure each student's performance in comparison with other students of the same age or grade. The data provided help schools distinguish between high and low students for program placement. They also can indicate which students are working at grade level and which ones need remediation or enrichment. In norm-referenced tests, test items range in difficulty and may be pulled from outside the state-adopted curriculum. Each student's score is assigned as either a percentile or a grade equivalent based on the student's performance in comparison to the norm. Norm-referenced tests are used to determine school readiness, academic progress, eligibility for special-education services, or college admission.

Criterion-referenced tests are used to measure students according to performance on preset standards. Criterion-referenced tests may be given as a pretest and/or a posttest to indicate students' mastery of the learning objectives. Test items come from state-adopted curriculum with several items of similar difficulty from each objective included for reliability. Each student's score is assigned a percentage based on the mastery of objectives as determined by criteria that disregard how other students score. Criterion-referenced tests are better for determining the level of academic achievement of students since they measure what the students actually know. In addition to annual state tests, most teacher-made tests are criterion referenced.

SAMPLE QUESTIONS

13) **Which of the following is a characteristic of a norm-referenced test?**

    A. Questions are based on adopted curriculum.

    B. Questions do not range in difficulty.

    C. Student scores are based on mastery of objectives.

    D. Student scores are based on comparisons with others.

Answers:

    A. Incorrect. Norm-referenced tests may draw questions from a variety of resources outside of the adopted curriculum.

B.   Incorrect. Norm-referenced tests include items that range in difficulty to determine the student's level of mastery.

C.   Incorrect. Criterion-referenced tests base scores on the mastery of objectives.

D.   **Correct.** Norm-referenced tests score students in comparison with other students of the same age or grade level.

14) **After taking a reading test, Jensen was provided a grade-equivalent score that indicated she is performing above grade level. What type of test did Jensen take?**

A.   norm referenced

B.   criterion referenced

C.   formative

D.   informal

Answers:

A.   **Correct.** Norm-referenced tests compare students with other students of the same grade or age level.

B.   Incorrect. Criterion-referenced tests provide scores based on mastery of identified objectives regardless of how others score.

C.   Incorrect. Formative assessments are informal assessments that are used throughout the learning experience to help teachers make instructional decisions and to provide feedback to students. This is not the best answer choice.

D.   Incorrect. Informal assessments are collected in the classroom to monitor student performance. Again, this is not the best answer choice.

TESTING AND SCORING TERMINOLOGY

What additional criteria should be considered when selecting or creating a test? Test scores must be both reliable and valid to provide quality information to make educational decisions. Frequently, it is not the test itself but the way the test scores are used that determines whether it is valid. **Validity** refers to how well an assessment measures its intended purpose. Degrees of validity may exist, which makes determining the validity of a test much more complicated. As with any science, over time, information may be collected that either supports or contradicts the validity of a test. First of all, test items must be aligned to the test goals. For example, if a test is intended to assess a student's performance in relationship to Common Core Standards in Algebra I, the test items must match the standards. In addition, the weighting of the questions should be aligned to the depth and significance of each standard. Therefore, students should theoretically have a test score that is similar to their class grade if the grade is based on mastery rather than participation. An additional aspect of validity involves the social consequences of how the test is used. For example, are high school students who pass the End of Course Exam in Algebra I ready for Algebra II? If so, does that mean that students who have not taken Algebra I but can pass the test are ready for Algebra II? The goal of testing instruments is to measure a sample from which valid inferences about a student may be drawn.

Reliability refers to the consistency of similar results if the test were repeated. A test can be reliable even if it is not valid, however. For example, students may repeatedly fail a test that is too difficult, which means that it is reliable enough to get consistent failing scores. However, it would not be valid because it is not aligned with what students have learned.

Score reports provide a wealth of information for educators who understand how to interpret them. Frequently, student scores come in the form of raw scores, percentiles, grade equivalents, and/or age equivalents. **Raw scores** refer to the number of questions a student answered correctly. No calculations are made directly to raw scores, and they are not dependent on how other students score.

> **HELPFUL HINT**
>
> A test is not considered valid if it is not reliable.

Percentile scores rank students by indicating the percentage of students who measured higher and the percentage who measured lower. For example, if a student scores better on a test than 83 percent of the other students, that student is in the eighty-third percentile.

Grade-equivalent scores are calculated using the average score of students who fall into that grade level. For example, if students who are in the fourth month of sixth grade have an average raw score of 45 on a fourth-grade test, fourth-grade students who score a 45 will receive a grade-equivalent score of 6.4. It is important to note that this score is assigned by calculating the average of sixth-grade students doing fourth-grade work and in no way indicates how well a fourth grader receiving this score would fare on sixth-grade work.

Age-equivalent scores are calculated similarly to grade-equivalent scores. **Age-equivalent scores** use the average score of students within an age group. For example, if the average score for a student who is twelve years and three months of age is 45, students who receive a 45 raw score will be assigned the age-equivalent score of 12.3.

Table 3.6. Testing and Score Terminology

Score Type	Definition
raw scores	refers to the number of questions a student answered correctly; no mathematical calculations have been applied
percentile scores	indicates how a student ranks in comparison with other students who took the same test

Score Type	Definition
grade-equivalent scores	assigns a grade level to a student based on that student's score matching the norm for students at that grade level
age-equivalent scores	indicates how a student's score compares with the norm of students of a particular age

An indicator of the validity of a test is its variability. The variability of test scores is measured using standard deviation. **Standard deviation** is a mathematical calculation that indicates the variability of scores in comparison with the average. A large degree of variability of scores is an indicator that the test measures a wide range of performance levels. Scores with a low standard deviation may indicate that the test is either too difficult or too simple, but it could also mean that all students mastered the content knowledge.

Standard deviation is calculated in the following way:

1. The mean for a group of scores is calculated. For the scores 65, 80, 85, and 100, the mean is 82.5.

2. For each score, the difference between the score and the mean is calculated. For the above scores, 17.5, 2.5, 2.5, and 17.5 are the differences, respectively.

3. The square root of each of these differences is calculated, which gives 4.18, 1.58, 1.58, and 4.18, respectively.

4. The mean of each of these squares is calculated, which is 2.88.

Measures of central tendency are used to identify norms. Norms are determined by calculating the mean, median, or the mode, which are explained in Table 3.7.

Table 3.7. Calculating Mean, Median, and Mode	
mean	The mean is the average score. It is calculated by adding together all the scores and dividing the sum by the number of scores added. For example, in Mr. Roger's class, students made the following scores: 65, 80, 85, and 100. To find the mean, he adds together all the scores. $65 + 80 + 85 + 100 = 330$ Then he divides the sum by the number of tests. $330 \div 4 = 82.5$ The mean is 82.5.

Go on →

Table 3.7. Calculating Mean, Median, and Mode (continued)

Median	The median is the middle score when scores are put in order from least to greatest. In this example, there are two scores in the middle; therefore, they are averaged to find the median. 65, 80, 85, 100 $80 + 85 = 165$ $165 \div 2 = 82.5$ The median and the mean are not always the same number, but in this case, 82.5 is also the mean.
Mode	The mode is the score that appears most frequently. For this example, a few additional scores have been added. 65, 80, 80, 80, 85, 85, 100 Although two students scored 85, there are three students who scored 80, and therefore the mode is 80.

SAMPLE QUESTIONS

15) **Which of the following statements on a score report may be true?**

   A.   A test may be valid, but not reliable.

   B.   A high standard deviation means that students performed well on the test.

   C.   A test may be reliable, but not valid.

   D.   Percentile refers to how many questions the students answered correctly.

   Answers:

   A.   Incorrect. If consistent scores are not achieved during a retest, the test is not valid.

   B.   Incorrect. High variability means that scores are clustered neither high nor low.

   C.   Correct. Reliability is dependent on the likelihood that a retest would net similar results. A test does not need to be valid to be reliable.

   D.   Incorrect. Raw scores provide information about how many questions the students answered correctly.

16) **Dennis scored in the sixty-fifth percentile. Which of the following best describes what this score means?**

   A.   Dennis missed 65 percent of the questions.

   B.   Dennis ranked higher than 65 percent of the test takers.

   C.   Dennis answered 65 percent of the questions correctly.

   D.   Dennis ranked lower than 65 percent of the test takers.

Answers:

A. Incorrect. Percentages measure the number of questions answered correctly. Percentiles refer to rankings.

B. **Correct.** Percentiles rank students compared with other test takers.

C. Incorrect. Percentiles refer to rankings rather than the number of questions answered correctly.

D. Incorrect. Percentile scores are based on what percentage of students the test taker scored better than.

HOLISTIC AND ANALYTICAL SCORING

When grading multiple-choice, true/false, matching, or short-answer quizzes, it is simple to calculate grades using a percentage. However, for writing assignments, projects, and performances, it becomes much more difficult to be objective. What is the solution? There are different types of scoring tools that can be used depending on the measurement goal.

Holistic scoring uses general categories to rate the overall outcome. A holistic scoring rubric has between three and five levels of performance with general statements that indicate achievement at each level. Holistic rubrics are easier to create and use than analytical rubrics but also provide only limited feedback.

Table 3.8. Holistic Scoring Rubric

Score	Description
below expectations	illegible and difficult to understand; severe grammatical and spelling errors
progressing	clear and logical, but may contain some organization issues and several grammatical errors
proficient	organized, clear, and logical; contains few grammatical errors
exceeds expectations	organized, clear, and logical; contains no grammatical errors; correctly uses two or more literary devices

Analytical scoring breaks down the general scoring categories into more specific parts. The breakdown allows students and teachers to review strengths and weaknesses with more precision so that feedback is targeted. Creating analytical rubrics is challenging because the creator must anticipate all possible errors as well as all ways that students could exceed expectations. They can also become lengthy, which may limit their usability, but they provide detailed feedback that can be used to justify a score and as a tool for guiding students toward making improvements.

→

Go on

Table 3.9. Analytical Scoring Rubric

	Below Expectations	Progressing	Proficient	Exceeds Expectations
grammar and spelling	contains severe grammatical and spelling errors	contains several grammatical errors	contains few grammatical errors	contains no grammatical errors
organization and engagement	lacks organization; makes no attempt to engage the reader or attempts serve as a distraction	organized; does not use or incorrectly uses literary devices	organized; correctly uses one or more literary devices	organized; correctly uses two or more literary devices
clarity	illegible and difficult to understand	clear and logical; has to work on handwriting	clear and logical; neatly written	clear and logical; neatly written; includes illustrations that match text

This analytical rubric could easily be converted into a scoring guide by adding multipliers to the criteria (see Figure 3.2.).

Another type of scoring rubric is a single-point rubric. Single-point rubrics break down the categories similarly to an analytic rubric, but rather than make an attempt to predict every possible answer, single-point rubrics outline only the necessary criteria for meeting proficiency. If students exceed or do not meet proficiency, anecdotal notes are included that describe the reason for the score. Grading a single-point rubric can be time-consuming because it requires a lot of writing, but the open-ended opportunities for feedback have been shown to improve student work over time.

Table 3.10. Single-Point Scoring Rubric

	Below Proficient	Proficient	Above Proficient
grammar and spelling		contains few grammatical errors	
organization and engagement		organized; correctly uses one or more literary devices	
clarity		clear and logical; neatly written	

	1	2	3	4	Total
grammar and spelling (multiply by 1)	contains severe grammatical and spelling errors	contains several grammatical errors	contains few grammatical errors	contains no grammatical errors	× 1
organization and engagement (multiply by 3)	lacks organization; makes no attempt to engage the reader or attempts serve as a distraction	organized; does not use or incorrectly uses literary devices	organized; correctly uses one or more literary devices	organized; correctly uses two or more literary devices	× 3
clarity (multiply by 2)	illegible and difficult to understand	clear and logical; has to work on handwriting	clear and logical; neatly written	clear and logical; neatly written; includes illustrations that match text	× 2
Add the total of all 3 boxes: highest score possible is 24 (4 × 1) + (4 × 2) + (4 × 3) = 24					

Figure 3.2. Scoring Guide

SAMPLE QUESTIONS

17) **Mr. Jarod wants to create a rubric that he can easily grade for the final examination of the year. Which type of scoring should he use?**

   A.   holistic scoring

   B.   analytical scoring

   C.   single-point scoring

   D.   analytical checklist

Answers:

   A.   **Correct.** Holistic scoring is the easiest to grade but provides less feedback than other types of scoring.

   B.   Incorrect. Analytical scoring provides a great deal of feedback but is difficult to make and to grade.

   C.   Incorrect. Single-point scoring provide a good amount of feedback and are easier to create than analytical rubrics, but they are time-consuming to grade.

D.   Incorrect. Analytical checklists are not rubrics. They are used to mark whether students have mastered an objective.

18)   Mrs. Kimberly has created an analytical-scoring rubric. Which of the following would be true about this rubric?

A.   It is limited to indicators of proficiency.

B.   It provides detailed feedback to help students improve.

C.   It will be easy to grade.

D.   It was simple to create.

Answers:

A.   Incorrect. Analytical rubrics include every possible way a student could fail to meet or exceed proficiency.

B.   Correct. Analytical rubrics are detailed enough to provide feedback.

C.   Incorrect. Analytical rubrics are much more complicated to grade than holistic rubrics.

D.   Incorrect. Analytical rubrics are complicated to create since educators must include every possible deviation from proficiency.

INTERPRETING AND COMMUNICATING ASSESSMENT RESULTS

When interpreting test results, the most important aspect is understanding the purpose and limits of the assessment. For example, if the purpose of the assessment is to determine the test taker's ability to pursue a career as a surgeon based on dexterity, the results will not include information regarding how training might support the test taker's aptitude. One measurement on one day should not be used to limit the possibilities of students. Big decisions that affect the education and the future of students should be based on multiple measures in an effort to have a comprehensive view of the child's talents and challenges. Depending on the type of test, scores may be used for program placement, to help teachers make instructional decisions, or for accountability.

Educators should familiarize themselves with all assessments that their students take so they can answer any questions that arise regarding the validity, reliability, and variability of scores. Teachers should provide answers about what content is being tested and how it will be graded. Is it based on the state curriculum or a mixture of national curriculum resources? Does it measure the student's content knowledge or does it measure reasoning skills or other abilities? Teachers should also understand how it is graded and scored. Are scores based on a student's mastery of content or in comparison with other students?

When speaking with students and parents about test scores, the teacher should clearly and simply explain the purpose of the test, describe the meaning of student scores, and propose next steps toward applying those scores to the educational context for which the test was intended. When speaking with school personnel about test scores, the assumption is that colleagues have similar understanding of the purpose and meaning of student scores, but next steps should focus on how the teacher and other professional staff intend to support students both collectively and individually.

With the degree of accountability that is placed on the annual state tests for states, districts, schools, and teachers, it is easy to lose track of their intended purpose. Placing too much weight on standardized tests for guiding instruction is a disservice to students who need targeted support or enrichment.

SAMPLE QUESTIONS

19) **Mrs. Plumley is meeting with Erika's parents to discuss the results of her Cognitive Aptitude Test (CogAT). Erika's parents are concerned that her low scores will affect her ability to be successful in postsecondary education. Which of the following is the best response?**

   A.   Aptitude tests do not measure content knowledge or work ethic.

   B.   Erika will need to work harder to overcome her gaps in content knowledge.

   C.   Erika will be most successful in a career in civil service.

   D.   Erika may want to consider technical school to learn a skill in lieu of college.

   Answers:

   A.   **Correct.** Work ethic and content knowledge are big contributors to student success in school.

   B.   Incorrect. The CogAT does not measure content knowledge; it measures reasoning skills.

   C.   Incorrect. The CogAT tests reasoning skills rather than aptitude toward a particular career.

   D.   Incorrect. The CogAT is used to place students in gifted and talented programs, not for college admissions.

20) **Madeline's achievement scores indicate that she is in the top 25 percent of test takers. What can school officials determine from this score?**

   A.   Madeline is more intelligent than most of the other students who have taken this test.

   B.   Madeline has retained more content knowledge than most of the other students who have taken this test.

   C.   Madeline will be more successful in any chosen profession than most other students.

   D.   Madeline does not have an exceptionality.

Answers:

A.   Incorrect. Achievement tests measure content knowledge, not intelligence.

B.   Correct. Madeline has answered content questions more accurately than 75 percent of the other students.

C.   Incorrect. Achievement tests do not measure aptitude toward a specific profession.

D.   Incorrect. Aptitude, ability, and intelligence tests are generally used as tests for exceptionalities.

CONSTRUCTED-RESPONSE QUESTIONS

1)   **Ms. Canary uses a combination of formative and summative assessments in her classroom. Describe each type of assessment as well as examples of each.**

Sample Answer:

Formative assessments take place throughout the learning segment so that teachers can make sound instructional decisions. Examples of formative assessments are anecdotal notes, observation, and pop quizzes. Summative assessments take place after learning has occurred to evaluate the student's mastery of learning objectives. Examples of summative assessments are unit tests, benchmark tests, and annual state tests.

2)   **Mr. Hughes is creating a unit test. He is trying to decide whether to use an essay format or selected-response. Describe each format and indicate the advantages and disadvantages of each.**

Sample Answer:

Essay tests provide opportunities for students to give written responses to test questions. Students must articulate their thinking and have the opportunity to explore each question at a greater depth. Because each essay question takes longer to answer, essay tests should not be used if a great deal of material needs to be covered. Essay questions also are time-consuming to grade. Selected-response questions ask students to choose the best answer of those provided. Selected-response tests are easy to grade and can be used when lots of questions need to be asked to assess understanding of a wide range of information. However, students may guess answers to test items. Further, it is difficult to determine why students missed certain questions because they do not have the opportunity to explain their thinking.

TERMS

ability test: Ability tests measure a person's ability to perform a particular skill.

achievement test: These tests measure acquired knowledge or skills.

age-equivalent score: Age-equivalent scores are found using the average score of students within an age group.

analytical checklist: Checklists outline criteria of student performance that teachers check off as students show mastery of each required skill.

analytical scoring: Analytical scoring breaks down the general categories to be scored into more specific parts.

anecdotal notes: Anecdotal notes are written records of the teacher's observations of a student. Records should be specific, objective, and focused on outlined criteria.

aptitude test: These tests measure a person's ability to develop a particular skill.

conference: This is a meeting between teacher and student in which learning is orally assessed and evaluated.

continuum: A continuum is a progression of learning.

criterion-referenced test: Criterion-referenced tests measure students according to performance on preset standards.

diagnostic assessment: Diagnostic assessments are given before a learning experience to measure students' baseline knowledge.

essay test: Essay tests are written responses to questions that provide students the opportunity to fully articulate their learning.

formal assessment: Formal assessments are measures of progress that are supported by data to be statistically accurate.

formative assessment: Formative assessments are informal assessments that are used throughout the learning experiences to help teachers make instructional decisions and to provide feedback to students.

grade-equivalent scores: Grade-level equivalents are found using the average score of students who fall into that grade.

holistic scoring: Holistic scoring uses general categories to rate the overall outcome.

informal assessment: Informal assessments are collected in the classroom to monitor student performance.

mean: Mean is the average score.

median: Median is the middle score if all scores were lined up from least to greatest.

mode: Mode is the score that appears most frequently.

norm referenced: Norm-referenced tests measure students in comparison with other students of the same age.

observation: Observation is when a teacher watches a student engaged in a learning activity to find evidence of learning.

peer assessment: This means evaluation and feedback among students.

percentile: Percentile ranks a student in comparison with what percentage of students measured higher and what percentage of students measured lower.

performance: Students present their learning as teachers watch to assess mastery of learning goals.

portfolio: Students collect a variety of artifacts as evidence of learning to be evaluated when using portfolio assessments.

raw score: This indicates the number of questions a student answered correctly.

reliability: Reliability is the consistency of similar results if the test were repeated. A test can be reliable even if it is not valid.

rubric: A rubric is a fixed scale that measures performance with detailed descriptions of criteria that define each level of performance.

scoring guide: This guide measures performance with detailed descriptions of criteria that define each level of performance and that are weighted with multipliers.

selected-response: Selected-response is sometimes called multiple-choice. Students choose the best answer from the available choices.

self-assessment: This is a method by which students monitor their own progress toward learning goals.

standard deviation: Standard deviation is a mathematical calculation that indicates the variability of scores in comparison with the average.

standardized test: This is a test administered to all students in a consistent way and then graded in the same way so that score comparisons may be accurately made.

summative assessment: Summative assessments may be formal or informal. Summative assessments evaluate student achievement after learning takes place.

validity: Validity indicates how well an assessment measures what it is intended to measure. A test is not considered valid if it is not reliable.

Professional Development, Leadership, and Community

4

Chapter four will review professional development practices and resources, school leadership, collaborative relationships, and relevant legislation. The professional development practices in which educators engage include joining professional associations, attending workshops and conferences, furthering their education, collaborating with colleagues, and reflecting on their own practices.

A variety of professional associations are available to fit the needs of every branch of educational practice. Some focus on providing research-based teaching strategies, whereas others place a greater emphasis on being advocates for education professionals. Most professional associations offer magazines, journals, or newsletters, as well as sponsor online courses, webinars, workshops, and conferences to keep their members informed and up-to-date.

Although professional associations offer the opportunity for teachers to network with professionals in other districts and states, teachers should also collaborate with the other teachers in their building. Many schools will provide new teachers with a mentor who can offer guidance, support, and feedback related to finding materials, understanding building protocols, and developing professionally. Many grade-level or content-area teams engage in collaborative planning, either formally through professional learning communities (PLCs) or through informal lesson planning meetings. Some teams find it helpful to create shared drives in which lesson plans, common assessments, and other artifacts may be easily accessed. Other ways that teachers help each other improve are critical friends groups, study groups, and peer observations and assessments.

In addition to collaborative relationships, many teachers improve their practice through reflection. Teachers can use reflective journaling, incident analysis, self-assessment, and action research to examine what happens in their own classroom and create plans for improvement. Teachers may engage in many other types of professional development, including internships, independent research, and advanced studies, in their effort to be role models as lifelong learners.

Teachers also have a responsibility to advocate for their profession, their students, and the community. Professionalism and collegiality help the community feel secure about teachers making professional decisions and also improve teacher retention rates. Often the profession is judged by the actions of a few; therefore, it is imperative that teachers hold themselves and their colleagues to a high standard.

Community leaders and parents have a stake in ensuring the success of local schools. Members of the community need to feel involved through volunteerism, shared decision making, and fund-raising efforts. Positive, two-way, home-to-school connections benefit student achievement, attendance, and the dropout rate.

Finally, this chapter will discuss some important legislation that protects students' rights during school hours. This includes legislation regarding students with disabilities as well as gender and racial equality. Students have the right to keep their confidential information protected. Furthermore, the First Amendment includes the right to intellectual freedom that is not restricted by censorship.

There is also legislation on federal and state levels that regulates the profession. One of the laws that each teacher should review for his or her state regards mandated child abuse reporting. Every state requires it, but whether the reporting is done directly by the teacher to Child Protective Services or whether it is sufficient for the teacher to report it to a supervisor is determined by state law. Each state also has different teacher licensing requirements; however, all states require teachers to meet certain standards before working as a school teacher. Federal legislation requires state tests that are used for federal accountability. Failure to meet minimum professional standards may result in an educational malpractice lawsuit. Beacause anyone working with students could face risks, professional liability insurance coverage is recommended for all educators.

PROFESSIONAL DEVELOPMENT PRACTICES AND RESOURCES

When the undergraduate experience is over and a teacher obtains his or her first job, professional growth is still in its infancy. Throughout a teacher's career, the body of research surrounding educational practices will continue to grow and change. The best educators are willing to evaluate new practices and implement those that are relevant and research based. During the first few years in the classroom, many teachers are surprised by how much they have left to learn about managing students, timing and pacing lessons, and record keeping. Fortunately, many options are available for teachers who are dedicated to being lifelong learners.

DID YOU KNOW?

Some well-respected professional associations for each content area are National Council for Teachers of Mathematics, National Science Teachers Association, National Council of Teachers of English, and National Council for the Social Studies.

Professional associations are nonprofit organizations that support the members of a particular profession by setting standards and advocating for associates. Membership and participation in professional associations provide a variety of benefits. First of all, membership in an association is a great networking opportunity. Members have the chance to connect with others within their profession and learn from one another. Second, professional associations provide support, such as helping members search for jobs. Some provide job boards that connect potential employers with employees. Some provide advice to help job seekers build a résumé and improve their interviewing skills. Finally, these associations provide literature and organize conferences and workshops that help members stay abreast of the latest research and best practices within their profession. Some well-known professional associations for teachers are the Association for Supervision and Curriculum Development (ASCD), the National Education Association (NEA), and the National Council for Teachers of Mathematics (NCTM). Each of these associations has a unique mission and can provide its members with different services.

QUICK REVIEW

Why would it be important for a beginning teacher to be part of a professional organization that specializes in his or her content area?

Typically, professional associations publish literature such as magazines, journals, and newsletters that contributes to the collective growth of its members. In addition, they offer workshops, conferences, and other professional development opportunities. **Workshops** are discussions or meetings in which a small number of participants exchange information about best practices. **Conferences** are formal meetings in which a large number of members of a particular profession learn from one another and discuss important topics within the field.

Table 4.1. Professional Associations for Educators

Association for Supervision and Curriculum Development (ASCD)	▶ provides professional development through workshops and conferences ▶ specializes in research-based programs for teacher leaders ▶ publishes *Educational Leadership* magazine
Association of American Educators (AAE)	▶ advocates for teachers ▶ nonunion ▶ provides professional development opportunities ▶ provides liability insurance and legal protection ▶ offers grant and scholarships to improve practice ▶ publishes *Education Matters* newsletter

⟶
Go on

Table 4.1. Professional Associations for Educators (continued)

Association for Middle Level Education (AMLE)	▶ advocates for middle school teachers ▶ holds professional development workshops ▶ specializes in the unique developmental needs of early adolescents ▶ publishes *The Middle School Journal*
National Education Association (NEA)	▶ provides liability insurance and legal support ▶ holds professional development through workshops ▶ offers grants and scholarships to support instruction ▶ offers online courses ▶ conducts research on trending educational issues ▶ has union services
National Association of Biology Teachers (NABT)	▶ holds professional development workshops and conferences ▶ allows access to *The American Biology Teacher* journal ▶ provides access to lesson plans and experiments ▶ specializes in biology content and pedagogy
National Science Teachers Association (NSTA)	▶ offers a choice of peer-reviewed journals based on grade level of students ▶ provides online courses ▶ provides professional development through conferences ▶ specializes in science content and pedagogy
American Association of Physics Teachers (AAPT)	▶ publishes two professional journals annually ▶ offers insurance ▶ has a career advice center ▶ holds professional workshops, conferences, and discussion boards ▶ specializes in physics content and pedagogy
National Council of Teachers of Mathematics (NCTM)	▶ holds professional development workshops ▶ has online teaching resources ▶ publishes five mathematics journals ▶ specializes in mathematics content and pedagogy
National Council of Teachers of English (NCTE)	▶ publishes research journals ▶ offers the Pathways Professional Development Program ▶ holds professional development workshops and webinars ▶ specializes in English and language arts content and pedagogy

National Council for the Social Studies (NCSS)	▶ publishes professional journals ▶ provides US History Collection lesson plans and activities ▶ provides professional development through conferences and workshops at national, state, and local levels ▶ specializes in social studies content and pedagogy
National Council for History Education (NCHE)	▶ holds professional development workshops and conferences ▶ publishes CDs and documents with lesson plans and activities ▶ specializes in history content and pedagogy
Council for Exceptional Children (CEC)	▶ publishes the *Teaching Exceptional Children* magazine ▶ hosts an annual conference ▶ offers insurance ▶ offers identity theft protection ▶ offers retirement planning ▶ specializes in support needs of disabled children
National Association of Special Education Teachers (NASET)	▶ provides more than fifty professional development courses ▶ publishes *The Practical Teacher* monthly ▶ offers home, auto, and health insurance ▶ specializes in supporting the needs of special education teachers
National Association for Gifted Children (NAGC)	▶ publishes a quarterly journal ▶ offers networks for various specializations, including early childhood education and counseling ▶ holds an annual convention ▶ specializes in the unique needs of gifted and talented students
National Association for the Education of Young Children (NAEYC)	▶ offers discounts on books, posters, and other teaching materials ▶ publishes a monthly newsletter ▶ publishes *Teaching Young Children* ▶ holds professional development workshops and conferences ▶ offers insurance ▶ offers online forums ▶ specializes in developmental needs of children in third grade and below

In an effort to help teachers take control of their own professional learning experiences, PLCs have become a popular option for educators. **Learning communities** are small groups of professionals who share common goals that meet to collaborate about instructional practices. During the first PLC meeting, teachers will identify SMART (specific measurable achievable relevant timely) goals and develop a plan that focuses on the essential questions that will be reviewed at each meeting. What do we expect students to learn? How do we know that they are learning? How will we respond when they don't learn? How will we respond if they already know the subject? To be effective, a PLC must include members who are willing to share leadership, take ownership of the collective improvement of student learning, and be vulnerable when students do not meet expectations.

Study groups are different from PLCs; these learning communities focus their meetings on student achievement, whereas study groups are focused on learning more about a specific subject. Study groups may work together on a book study, or each member may be assigned research that is brought back to the group and discussed.

Another way that teachers can take responsibility for their own development is through independent research. If a teacher has a specific educational topic that he or she is interested in finding out more about, independent research may be a viable option. Some graduate school programs offer credit for independent research that follows their guidelines.

Colleges and universities have a variety of professional development options available that teachers can earn graduate credit for attending, whether the teacher is enrolled in a graduate school program or not. Earning a graduate degree can increase career options for teachers who enroll in programs to become a school counselor, administrator, or library media specialist, and this can also help teachers improve their practice within their profession with degrees available in every content area.

As part of the teacher education program, most prospective teachers participate in one or more unpaid internships to help prepare them for the classroom. **Internships** are positions that offer on-the-job training either in addition to or in lieu of a salary. A quality internship depends on a quality mentor. A **mentor** is a more experienced professional who guides someone new to the profession. The mentor offers support and guidance as the new teacher gradually becomes more independent. Not all internships are through a teacher education program. The US Department of Education, curriculum publishers, educational television programs, museums, and overseas teacher-exchange programs also offer internships that provide unique experiences to teachers.

Typically, in the first one to three years of teaching, school administrators will match the new teacher with a mentor in the building. This person is available to advise on how to navigate the first years of teaching, including where to find resources, how to handle classroom management issues, and how to write effective lessons. New teachers should observe their mentor, ask their mentor to observe them and provide feedback, and regularly meet with the mentor to discuss classroom issues.

If the school does not match the teacher with a mentor, or if a teacher–mentor relationship is expired, it is recommended that each teacher find a colleague to discuss instructional issues and learn from. Frequently, mentor–mentee relationships develop into a mutually beneficial relationship in which both teachers improve.

SAMPLE QUESTIONS

1) **Which of the following professional organizations would be most appropriate for a second-grade teacher?**

   A.   Association for Middle Level Education

   B.   National Council for the Social Studies

   C.   National Council of Teachers of English

   D.   National Association for the Education of Young Children

   Answers:

   A.   Incorrect. The Association for Middle Level Education advocates for middle school teachers and students.

   B.   Incorrect. While social studies is part of second-grade education to some degree, it is more appropriate at this grade level for teachers to understand child development.

   C.   Incorrect. The National Council of Teachers of English supports language arts curriculum development at all grade levels, but most English and language arts instruction at the second-grade level relates to reading and writing.

   D.   Correct. The National Association for the Education of Young Children specializes in instruction to suit the developmental needs of PK–3 students.

2) **Which of the following professional development opportunities includes a group of teachers who are working toward a specific student-learning goal?**

   A.   independent study

   B.   internships

   C.   PLCs

   D.   conferences

Answers:

A. Incorrect. Independent study is for a teacher who has an interest in learning more about a particular topic in education, therefore embarking on independent research of that subject.

B. Incorrect. Internships provide on-the-job training under a mentor.

C. Correct. PLCs share a common goal.

D. Incorrect. Conferences are formal meetings where people from a particular profession come together to learn from each other and discuss educational issues.

Implications of Research, Views, Ideas, and Debates

Homework, common core, voucher programs, and childhood obesity are among the hundreds of topics that are highly debated within schools. There appear to be valid arguments on all sides of controversial topics from educators and noneducators. However, what does the research say?

The education community includes professionals who collect, interpret, and report research to support teachers and other educational professionals who are making instructional decisions. The World Education Research Association (WERA) and the American Educational Research Association (AERA) advocate for the use of research-based practices in education and promote professional standards for collecting and distributing research findings.

Educational researchers work for colleges and universities, are graduate or doctoral students, or work for publishing companies, testing companies, and educational associations that research a variety of topics in education from adult literacy to bilingual education to teacher evaluation systems. All types of educational research include the use of scientific method, but when reviewing research, it is important to consider the intent behind it. Basic academic research is for the purpose of finding out information, which is typically the goal of university researchers and professional associations. Applied research is for the purpose of proving a point, usually to sell a product. Further, qualitative research tends to be more subjective since it uses observations, interviews, and case studies, but quantitative research attempts to analyze findings through statistics.

With so many sources claiming to use research, how does a teacher know whether he or she is genuinely accessing research-based information? Typically, professional journal articles and other peer-reviewed materials provide more accurate information than secondary sources, such as newspapers, magazines, and encyclopedias. However, peer reviews provide only minimal verification that scientific principles were followed. Replication of results by a second party is a better measurement of validity.

The following are some examples of peer-reviewed journals:

▶ *American Educational Research Journal*

▶ *Child Development*

▶ *Developmental Psychology*

▶ *Early Childhood Research and Practice*

▶ *Early Education and Development*

▶ *Educational Researcher*

▶ *International Journal of Early Childhood Special Education*

▶ *Journal of Applied Developmental Psychology*

▶ *Journal of Early Childhood Teacher Education*

▶ *Journal of Early Intervention*

▶ *Journal of Educational Psychology*

▶ *Journal of Research in Childhood Education*

A big consideration when interpreting research is whether the intended purpose of the research is aligned with the intended use. Further, teachers need to understand statistical terminology, such as measures of central tendency (mean, median, and mode), range, variance, and distribution, to thoroughly understand quantitative displays of data. Next, to what degree inferencing is used by the researcher to draw conclusions should be considered. Was inductive or deductive reasoning used to connect data to the conclusion? Inductive reasoning applies what is known about a small population to a larger context, which is often accurate but not always. Deductive reasoning takes what is known generally and applies it to a smaller population, which can be fairly accurate. The higher the degree of inferencing used, the more likely the results are skewed.

> **QUICK REVIEW**
>
> How can a teacher differentiate between research-based practices and opinions?

Even if the research is solid, what good is it if classroom teachers are not sure how to use it? Many teachers engage in classroom instructional practices that are not research based because valid research seems inaccessible. Research is overabundant, expensive, and written in a complicated statistical language that is not frequently used by classroom teachers. Teachers sometimes have a hard time distinguishing the latest educational fad from solid research. However, expectations of teachers have shifted so that developing an engaging lesson that is not grounded in scientific principles is no longer good enough.

Teacher preparation programs introduce educators to available research, but as teaching practices change over time, teachers need to stay current to ensure their practices are grounded in research. Teachers must be able to reflect on their own practice and justify their instructional decisions.

As teachers begin thinking scientifically about their instructional practices, many will engage in action research. **Action research** is researching the teachers' own instructional practices to improve student learning. Action research links new discoveries to existing knowledge as teachers gather evidence to support their conclusions. The first step to action research is developing a guiding question that is clear and will likely yield results that can be used to develop a solution. Next, teachers need to decide how to gather evidence to answer the guiding question. Anecdotal records, observations, work samples, interviews, conferences, surveys, and journals may all be part of data collection. At least three forms of data collection should be used. Data should then be organized and displayed graphically using a chart, table, or graph to demonstrate patterns. Finally, teachers must analyze the data to draw a conclusion. Once a conclusion has been drawn, they can take what they have learned and put it into practice while selecting another guiding question for the next action research project.

QUICK REVIEW

What are the benefits of action research?

Table 4.2. Action Research

1. Develop a guiding question and data collection technique.
2. Gather evidence.
3. Display the data.
4. Analyze the data and draw a conclusion.
5. Use the information to guide one's teaching practices.

SAMPLE QUESTIONS

3) **Which of the following sources of research is the most reliable?**

   A. peer-reviewed journals
   B. mainstream newspapers
   C. professional magazines
   D. online encyclopedias

Answers:

A. Correct. Peer-reviewed journals meet minimal criteria for finding accurate research.

B. Incorrect. Newspapers are secondary sources that may be less accurate than primary sources.

C. Incorrect. Professional magazines include ideas, opinions, and debates about educational issues that may not be research based.

D. Incorrect. Encyclopedias are an example of a secondary source.

4)   **Which of the following best describes action research?**

   A.   A publishing company conducts a research project to prove that their products are effective.

   B.   A teacher researches his or her own practice.

   C.   Doctoral students at a university conduct a study out of academic interest.

   D.   Scientists review a research project and reflect on its accuracy.

Answers:

   A.   Incorrect. This is an example of applied research.

   B.   Correct. Teachers research their own classroom results and draw conclusions about best practices.

   C.   Incorrect. This is an example of basic research.

   D.   Incorrect. This is a peer review.

REFLECTIVE PRACTICES

Reflective practice is intentionally thinking about professional practices as part of one's own professional development. Using reflective practice enables teachers to connect the classroom to recent research. Reflection not only includes a description of a classroom experience but also incorporates the emotions, reactions, and responses of the teacher that either contributed to or detracted from its effectiveness.

> **QUICK REVIEW**
>
> Why should teachers engage in reflective practices?

One way to engage in reflective practice is through the use of reflective journals. **Reflective journals** are written records of a learning experience that are frequently used to provide an opportunity for students to articulate their process as they progress through their learning goals, but the journals also can be used by teachers as a professional development tool. Reflective journals can be written formally or informally and can be used for personal use or shared with colleagues. They may contain reflections about lesson delivery, student achievement, classroom management, content questions, and/or ideas regarding remediation or enrichment of students. Although recording thoughts in a reflective journal can take time, it has been proven to be a useful metacognitive tool for improving practice. Journal entries can take several forms, including observations, questions, speculations, critiques, or inspirations. The format, purpose, and content of a reflective journal may be individualized to meet the needs of each teacher.

Aspects of reflective journaling are as follows:

- ▶ record of what happened
- ▶ reflection on reactions, feelings, and thoughts associated with a lesson or event

- ▸ an analysis of the situation
- ▸ conclusions
- ▸ a resulting action plan

Self-assessment and peer-assessment are learning tools used to help students internalize the characteristics of quality work; they can also be used as professional development tools for teachers. Prewritten self-assessment scales are available from a variety of Internet sites and professional books. A formal self-assessment may also be part of the teacher evaluation process in some districts. However, there is nothing magical that makes those that are published any more informative than a self-assessment that a teacher writes. Self-assessments may address goals regarding classroom environment, classroom management, parent involvement, collabora-tion, lesson plans, student engagement, grading practices, or any other area that a teacher may want to reflect upon. However, just as students tend to inflate their grades when using self-assessments, teachers need to be careful about their own blind spots to more objectively select areas to improve.

Peer assessment can similarly give teachers an opportunity to look at teaching from a more objective viewpoint. However, there must be a degree of mutual trust between teachers because there is a risk in both providing and receiving critical feedback. If teachers are unwilling or unable to respectfully and honestly identify areas for growth in one another, the process is meaningless.

When working with students, colleagues, parents, and supervisors, hopefully most experiences are positive, but some less-than-positive incidents can occur. Someone may get hurt, or angry, or perhaps a student stops progressing; regardless of the type of incident, reflective practices should be used to prevent it from happening again. An **incident analysis** formally reviews a situation to determine why it happened and how to reduce the likelihood of another similar event. The first step in an incident analysis is to write a detailed description of what happened. The next step is to write down reactions, emotions, and thoughts about the event.

QUICK REVIEW

When might a teacher use incident analysis?

The third step is to apply critical thinking skills to evaluate and assess the situation. During the analysis, the teacher must be prepared to challenge not only his or her own thinking patterns but also widely held beliefs about how things are tradition-ally done. A properly executed incident analysis will increase self-awareness on both a personal and a professional level as teachers begin to understand why they follow particular patterns of behavior.

Just as teachers maintain student portfolios to assess student growth and performance, keeping a professional portfolio can assess professional growth and performance. Although portfolios may be time-consuming to create and maintain, they provide a more comprehensive view of professional practice than other forms of evaluation. Portfolios create unique opportunities for teachers to document, reflect, and share their professional experiences. Portfolios may include lesson plans, student work, formal evaluations, anecdotal records, and clips of teaching. Portfolios are intended to reflect professional practice, not be a storage for keepsakes: this is not the place to keep notes, gifts, and photos of memorable students. A teaching portfolio should be documentation of accomplishments and growth opportunities. Portfolios generally contain a combination of artifacts and reflections of the teacher's beliefs about education and his or her goals for growth. Portfolios are an effective tool for teachers who strive for continuous improvement through reflective practices.

Peer observation is a collaborative approach to professional development in which teachers improve their practice by watching each other and offering feedback. Observations are beneficial for the person who is observing, who will inevitably pick up on new techniques, and also benefit the one who is being observed if followed by a meaningful, professional conversation. Like peer assessment, peer observation requires a degree of mutual trust and respect. The advantage that peer observation has over other forms of professional development is that it is practical rather than philosophical. However, if the observation is not immediately followed by a discussion and a plan to apply what has been learned, then it is meaningless.

Professional educators who value the opportunity to reflect on their professional growth with a trusted peer will often find a critical friend. A **critical friend** is someone who supports growth by providing objective and honest feedback. The philosophy aligned with finding a critical friend contradicts the outdated notion that teachers work in isolation. Teachers actually request and provide constructive criticism to one another to help each other learn and grow. Harmony Education Center, as part of National School Reform, has developed a formal professional development program in which four to seven educators voluntarily come together, led by a trained critical friends group (CFG) coach, to observe and consult with one another and build the collective efficacy of the group.

The CFG process is as follows:

- ▶ A CFG coach opens the meeting and reviews the process.
- ▶ A teacher presents an issue and asks a question of the group.
- ▶ Other members ask questions to clarify the issue.
- ▶ While the teacher that presented takes notes, other members of the group discuss the issue and offer suggestions.
- ▶ The presenter responds to the group's suggestions.
- ▶ The CFG coach discusses the process and either closes the meeting or introduces the next presenter.

Go on

SAMPLE QUESTIONS

5) **Which of the following reflective practices requires respect, trust, and collegiality among staff to be effective?**

    A.   observation

    B.   reflective journals

    C.   incident analysis

    D.   portfolios

Answers:

   A.   **Correct.** Observation is effective only if it is followed by a meaningful, professional conversation, which requires both trust and respect.

   B.   Incorrect. Reflective journals allow teachers to reflect in writing on their own practices.

   C.   Incorrect. Incident analysis allows teachers to review a negative experience in a way that will help them grow personally and/or professionally.

   D.   Incorrect. Portfolios are records of teaching practices that are built over time. They may be shared or used for personal reflection.

6) **Mr. Reed develops a scale to help him rate the usability of his substitute lesson plans. Which of the following reflective practices is he using?**

    A.   reflective journaling

    B.   self-assessment

    C.   incident analysis

    D.   a portfolio

Answers:

   A.   Incorrect. Reflective journals are composed of the teacher's written notes, which include descriptions of events, related emotions, and analysis.

   B.   **Correct.** Self-assessment involves the use of scales or rubrics to identify areas for improving practice.

   C.   Incorrect. Incident analysis is a written observation, reflection, and analysis that is used to prevent the event from being replicated.

   D.   Incorrect. A portfolio contains ongoing documentation of teaching artifacts accompanied by reflective notes.

THE TEACHER'S ROLE IN THE COMMUNITY

In addition to maintaining a growth mindset for one's own professional practice, teachers are called upon to be advocates for the profession at large as the field of education continues to be politicized. In the face of so many sweeping changes in education, fewer students are enrolling in teacher preparation programs, leading to an ever-increasing teacher shortage. Teachers must come together to educate both the public and legislators about not only the needs of students but also the impact that professional educators continue to make on the lives of students.

Parents, students, and future educators look to those who are currently in the profession as role models. Teachers set expectations for the profession that include using research-based practices, collaboration, collegiality, and a commitment to continued growth.

QUICK REVIEW

How might teachers positively influence enrollment in teacher education programs?

Positive parent–teacher relationships benefit the student, the parent, and the teacher. Students who have parents involved in their child's education demonstrate higher academic achievement, better behavior, lower dropout rates, and better attendance. Parents benefit not only from learning how to help their child at home but also from a greater sense of trust that their child is well-cared for during school hours. Teachers flourish when parents hold them in high regard. Further, parent communication allows the teacher to learn more about each child and how to guide him or her to success. The key to all positive relationships is communication. Communication can happen through conferences, student work folders, phone calls, email, home visits, newsletters, open houses, and other parent involvement. Ideally, positive communication should outnumber negative communication. It is a good idea for a teacher to find a way to connect with all parents within the first weeks of school, before any problems occur. If there are issues, the best approach entails the teacher making contact as quickly as possible and relayimg facts to parents in a nonemotional, solution-oriented style. To maintain trust, teachers must follow through with the solutions that have been agreed upon. Whether the contact is intended to be a positive report, a negative report, or informational, specific and positive communication about a student goes a long way toward building rapport with a parent.

Whenever possible, two-way communication is preferred. **Two-way communication** is communication in which both parties are given the opportunity to speak and listen to one another. Newsletters, calendars, notes to parents, and Web pages all provide valuable information to parents in an efficient way but do not give parents the opportunity to ask questions or provide information about the student. Phone calls, emails, home visits, conferences, and interactive journals, planners, and take-home folders provide two-way communication.

The following are tips for a successful parent conference:
- Be prepared with observations of students working and interacting in a variety of settings.
- Maintain a portfolio of student work to share.
- Invite other school personnel who work with the child to attend.

▶ Be prepared to share anecdotal stories about things the child does well or enjoys.

▶ Ask parents for help with any challenges in a nonjudgmental way that indicates care and concern for the student.

▶ Be prepared for questions.

▶ Never give out information about other students or parents.

Although written communication can often be tempting as a primary means of communication because of its simplicity, teachers should be extra careful to avoid a perceived tone in written communication that is not intended. Particularly when a teacher has a problem to report, face-to-face communication is best. Phone contact is second best. If email communication is used, it should be used cautiously.

Schools have a responsibility to develop partnerships not only with parents and guardians but also with day-care centers, churches, businesses, and community groups. Each of these members of the community have an interest in providing the best possible education for students. To close the achievement gap, students must have more than just academic support. Community resources are tapped to provide for students' social service needs. Schools may elicit involvement through communication, volunteer opportunities, and shared decision making. Community involvement is such an important component of successful schools that many states make community partnerships part of the requirement for school improvement grants. Further, schools that receive federal Title 1 funds must use a portion of those funds for parent and community involvement. Efforts to collaborate through surveys, communication translated into home languages, and community involvement events will be rewarded with student improvement.

> **QUICK REVIEW**
>
> How do teachers and students benefit from building strong school–family–community connections?

SAMPLE QUESTIONS

7) **Which of the following activities harms the public perception of professional educators?**

   A.   reporting behavior issues to parents

   B.   contacting legislators about education reform issues

   C.   gossiping about colleagues

   D.   asking parents for help in the classroom

Answers:

   A.   Incorrect. Parents should hear about the behavior issues of their child in a calm, accurate manner. However, it helps if some positive interaction has taken place in advance.

B.   Incorrect. Legislators should hear the voice of teachers when they are making decisions that will affect students.

C.   Correct. Complaining about students, colleagues, and administrators is unprofessional and harmful to the educational community as a whole.

D.   Incorrect. It is okay to need help and a great way to get parents involved.

8)   **Ms. Durant calls Shelly's mother because Shelly has not done any work in two weeks. Ms. Durant is shocked that Shelly's mother becomes angry with Ms. Durant. How could Ms. Durant have made this a more positive interaction?**

A.   Ms. Durant should have handled it herself.

B.   Ms. Durant should not have waited two weeks to make a phone call.

C.   Ms. Durant should call parents only with good news.

D.   Ms. Durant should have sent a note instead.

Answers:

A.   Incorrect. Parents need to know what is happening with their children at school.

B.   Correct. Ms. Durant should have contacted the parent as soon as she realized there was a problem. After two weeks, it will be much harder for Shelly to catch up than if she had known within the first few days.

C.   Incorrect. It is nice if the first contact is positive and if the teacher has something nice to say about the student even when the call is not positive, but parents need honest feedback about how their child is performing at school.

D.   Incorrect. A note would not have improved this situation two weeks into a problem.

THE TEACHER AS COLLABORATOR

To support each other and every child to the best of a school's collective ability, teachers must collaborate. One way that grade-level teams help one another is by creating a shared drive on which they are able to store and access lesson plans, curriculum plans, common assessments, pacing calendars, and other work products. However, it is not enough just to have access to common materials; grade-level teams also need to meet at least weekly, if not more often, to discuss lesson plans, remediation plans, and enrichment. Ideally, grade-level teams will have a common planning time to meet, but in the event that is not possible, it is important for teachers to make the time to benefit their students. Teachers further benefit when they make time to observe one another and attend professional development conferences together. Collaboration can be challenging because personalities may clash, but when teachers share the common goal of making collaboration time about the students and the work, rather than opinions, teachers begin to appreciate and respect one another even when they disagree.

Table 4.3. Faculty

teacher	teaches students in a specialized grade or content area using approved curricula; maintains relationships with students, parents, and colleagues
counselor	provides social skills training and academic counseling; frequently creates class schedules and serves as the testing coordinator
special education teacher	teaches students who have been identified with a disability; writes and implements individualized education plans (IEPs) with the help of an IEP team
library/media specialist	oversees operation of the school library; teaches library and research skills; supports teachers in obtaining resources
reading specialist	provides academic remediation for struggling readers

When teachers and administrators develop an atmosphere of mutual trust and shared responsibility for school improvement, students are more successful. In the most successful schools, teachers and administrators work together to select curriculum materials and instructional practices. Frequent data monitoring as part of the collaborative process is essential for improving test scores over time.

Table 4.4. Leadership

board of education	hires and supervises the superintendent; establishes school board policy; votes on issues that affect the overall function of the school system
superintendent	oversees the day-to-day operation of the school system; maintains communication and makes recommendations to the school board
assistant superintendent	oversees operation of specific areas according to the job description, such as curricula, maintenance, and human resources
principal	oversees daily operation of a specific school building, including supervision of teachers, staff, and students, as well as maintaining community relationships
assistant principal	oversees operation of specific areas as determined by the school principal, such as discipline or a specific grade level
athletic director	oversees the operation of all athletic programs, including hiring and scheduling sporting events

There are a number of other school personnel who teachers interact with regularly to provide quality services to students. The key to successfully working with all personnel is to communicate, stay student focused, understand each person's role, and remain professional and respectful of one another's thoughts, opinions, and viewpoints.

Table 4.5. Support Staff

administrative assistant (school secretary)	greets school visitors; answers phones; maintains organization of the office
encumbrance clerk (financial officer)	maintains financial responsibilities of the school
school nutritionist	creates menus and oversees school nutrition program
cafeteria staff	provides nutritious meals and a sanitary environment for students
paraprofessional	a trained teacher assistant who provides student support as determined by the special education faculty
nurse	provides general first aid; maintains health records of students; administers medication; provides health-related education
custodian	keeps the school building clean; may assist in other areas, such as moving furniture
maintenance	repairs electrical, heating, air, mechanical, and other issues that may affect the physical operation of a school building
computer technician	provides service and maintenance of computer-related equipment
bus driver	provides safe transportation to and from school and to school-related activities, such as field trips and athletic events

In addition to school personnel, teachers will collaborate with parents and community leaders. When people feel involved in a meaningful way, they feel more committed to the success of school programs. Community members can also provide a number of services for students and teachers that might not be available otherwise.

Regardless of the type of planning or who is involved, effective collaborative planning requires hard work, trust, respect, and buy-in from all members of the team. Which **stakeholders** are invited to the meeting depends on the purpose of the meeting. It needs to involve people who have decision-making authority, access to necessary resources, and commitment to success. The team may include students, teachers, parents, staff,

QUICK REVIEW

How might student participation positively impact collaborative decision making?

administrators, and/or community members. At the first meeting, the members need to set the norms for teamwork. Norms may be related to using active listening skills, giving all participants the chance to speak, showing up on time, and completing assigned tasks. The next step is to write an action plan. An **action plan** is a process by which goals and the steps toward achieving those goals are determined. It includes objectives and a shared vision. As the objectives are considered, the team should brainstorm every possible challenge to meeting the goal so that each of these challenges can be turned into an action step. For each action step, the team should decide what success would look like if the step were accomplished. Further, considerations should be made for sustaining positive results. Collaboration is considered successful if each member feels valued, the vision is valued by all team members, the team is making progress, and the action plan is eventually completed in a sustainable way.

SAMPLE QUESTIONS

9) **Which of the following is an example of a stakeholder?**

    A.   a student

    B.   a businessman

    C.   a parent or guardian

    D.   all of the above

Answers:

    A.   Incorrect. Students have a stake in their school.

    B.   Incorrect. Businessmen and community leaders want quality schools to draw new business and quality employees.

    C.   Incorrect. Parents and guardians have a strong desire for quality school programs.

    D.   Correct. Stakeholders may be students, teachers, parents, staff, administrators, and/or community members.

10) **Which of the following is a benefit of collaborating with grade-level team members?**

    A.   Collaborating saves time.

    B.   Students benefit from the collective strengths of the team.

    C.   Teachers are able to agree on the best instructional approach.

    D.   Administrators feel more comfortable when teachers give each other critical feedback.

Answers:

    A.   Incorrect. Teachers need to make time to collaborate because it benefits students.

- B. **Correct.** Teachers are stronger when they work together for the benefit of students.

- C. Incorrect. Teachers do not always agree, but they need to have professional respect for one another.

- D. Incorrect. Collaboration is not for the benefit of administrators; it is for the benefit of students.

IMPLICATIONS OF LEGISLATION AND COURT DECISIONS

Although most legislation related to schools is determined at the state level, teachers need to be aware of some federal legislation that governs schools. In December 2015, No Child Left Behind was replaced by the Every Student Succeeds Act (ESSA). Although annual statewide assessments are still required, more power has been given to the states to determine student performance targets based on multiple measures. Further, states choose support and interventions for schools in the bottom 5 percent with dedicated federal funds for turnaround initiatives. In addition to standardized test scores, other factors, such as school climate, graduation rates, and advanced coursework, must be considered. Although chronically low-performing schools still need to be remediated, state governments rather than federal governments are responsible for teacher evaluation standards. Previous legislation was expanded to include preschool education by ensuring that resources are available to promote quality early childhood programs and provide professional development for teachers and school leaders to help professionals understand the developmental needs of young children while aligning early childhood experiences to the skills that will enhance elementary school experiences. In addition, states have the authority to develop their own opt-out laws as long as at least 95 percent of students take the test; therefore, it is likely that severely disabled children will no longer be forced to endure annual testing.

The Family Educational Rights and Privacy Act (FERPA) protects the confidentiality of a student's education records. **Confidentiality** is the ability to be trusted with private information. Parents have rights until the student reaches the age of eighteen, and then rights are transferred to the child. According to FERPA, parents and students have the right to review the students' educational records. Schools may charge a fee to make copies. Parents and students have the right to request inaccurate or misleading records be changed. If a school concludes that records should remain as is, a student or parent has the right to attach a statement to the record. Schools must have written permission from the parent or student to release records, except to school officials with legitimate interest; schools to which the student transfers; official auditors; financial aid services; organizations conducting studies for the school; accrediting organizations; judicial order, state, and local authorities; and emergency health and safety officials. Schools may publish directory information without consent but must notify parents of the right to have their child's directory information withheld. FERPA guarantees that parents and students have a reasonable right to privacy. **Privacy** is freedom from having personal business shared with others.

The Individuals with Disabilities Education Act (IDEA) ensures that students with disabilities have equal access to a free and appropriate public education. **Equal access** entails providing procedural safeguards to ensure that all students receive the same benefits of public education regardless of disabilities. Part B of IDEA addresses the requirements for schools to service qualified students from three until twenty-two years of age. IDEA outlines parents' rights and the school's responsibility to identify and serve disabled students.

Title II of the Americans with Disabilities Act (ADA) prohibits discrimination based on disabilities for all public entities, including access to educational facilities.

DID YOU KNOW?

Teachers are required to document compliance with accommodations for students on 504 plans.

Section 504 of the Rehabilitation Act prohibits discrimination based on disability in any program or activity that is subsidized by federal funds, including athletics. Under Section 504, all students with a physical or mental impairment that affects one or more major life activities qualify for services.

Title IX of the Education Amendments of 1972 prohibits gender discrimination, including sexual harassment, inequality in athletic opportunity, inequality in STEM (science, technology, engineering, and math) courses, and discrimination based on pregnancy.

Title VI of the Civil Rights Act of 1964 prohibits discrimination based on race, color, or national origin in programs or activities receiving federal financial assistance. This includes racial harassment, segregation, and denial of language services to English learners.

DID YOU KNOW?

Since Title IX's inception, the number of athletic programs, athletic scholarships, and advanced degrees for women has increased. However, critics feel that the reallocation of funds from boys' athletics to support newly created girls' athletics, particularly those with low participation rates, is unfair.

The **First Amendment** guarantees freedom of religion, freedom of expression, freedom of the press, and freedom to peaceably assemble. According to *Tinker v. Des Moines,* teachers and students do not lose their First Amendment rights when they come to school, but the right to free speech is limited if it interferes with the educational mission of the school. In this particular case, students in the Des Moines school district wore black arm bands to protest the Vietnam War. The district restricted the students from wearing the arm bands as part of the school dress code. The court agreed that the students had the right to wear the arm bands because it was not proven that they interfered with the operations of the school.

To balance the student's rights to intellectual freedom with the beliefs of a community, educators are often faced with a dilemma. **Intellectual freedom** is the right to receive information from various perspectives without censorship. Typically, the courts side with the professional judgment of an educator if the educator's decisions are based on sound educational principles rather than on the desire to conform to popular political or religious viewpoints. Whereas the decision that materials should not be purchased for classrooms or libraries because they are not age appropriate is not considered censorship, removing materials already available in the library based on objections to the materials is. The concern is that most relevant literary pieces of literature could be considered offensive to some group based on character explorations of profanity, sex, violence, religion, racism, or political views. If all materials that were objected to by someone were removed from the curricula, there would be little of value left to help students understand the human experience from another viewpoint. Most school districts adopt formal policies for making complaints about materials that clarify the criteria used for removing materials. These procedures help educational professionals better understand the values of the community while protecting the intellectual freedom of teachers and students. Materials should not be removed unless the proper procedure is followed.

> **DID YOU KNOW?**
>
> When a teacher chooses controversial materials for a classroom activity, parents should be given the option of opting out of the assignment and given an alternative assignment that will accomplish the same objectives. Each state or district may have individual policies outlining teacher expectations in this area.

However, in *New Jersey v. TLO*, the court supported the school's decision to search a student's purse after the student was caught smoking in the hall. The assistant principal discovered drug paraphernalia in the student's purse. The court did not consider this a violation of the student's Fourth Amendment right against illegal search and seizure because it was determined that the school had reasonable suspicion.

Each of the US states has legislation in place that mandates reporting of child abuse and neglect to an appropriate agency, such as Child Protective Services or the police. For most states, this includes social workers, teachers and other educational personnel, the medical community, mental health professionals, child care providers, law enforcement officers, and coroners. Some institutions have internal policies for handling child abuse reporting, but for many states, making a report to a supervisor is not sufficient. It is important to understand the laws for the state in which the abuse occurs to determine the appropriate response. The reporter is only responsible for reporting facts that led to the suspicions; he or she is not required to provide proof. Some states allow anonymous reporting, but all states have statutes in place to protect the confidentiality of child abuse records.

Due process means that everyone must be treated fairly and the rights of all must be respected. Due process laws are in place to ensure that each person's rights to life, liberty, and property are not violated without providing that person the opportunity to have his or her side of the story heard. *Goss v. Lopez* determined that students must be given the opportunity to have an informal hearing with school administrators before a suspension from school. If a suspension is for ten or more days, the student has a right to a formal hearing before an impartial body. However, if the school determines that a student poses a danger to other students, he or she may be suspended immediately with a hearing scheduled as soon as possible. Students have the right to have an attorney present when they are questioned.

QUICK REVIEW

Under what circumstances should books be removed from the school library?

Due process is also protected under IDEA as a means of resolving conflicts between parents and the school district. Typically, IEP disputes are resolved using third-party mediation, but if that is not successful, parents may request a due process hearing, which may be appealed through the court system. Students are entitled to remain in their current placement until the dispute has been resolved.

Educators may be held liable for injuries to students or educational malpractice. **Liability** is a legal responsibility. In the event that a teacher is sued based on incidents that occured during employment, teachers may face personal financial responsibility. Professional liability insurance is recommended, either through a professional organization or union or from a private provider, to cover the educator in the event that a claim is made against him or her.

Each state has its own teacher licensure rules that outline minimum criteria for working as an educator within the state. **Licensing** means to be given permission to do something, such as teach. Typically, licenses cover only certain content or grade levels. If an educator wishes to expand his or her options by adding additional content areas to the license, additional criteria, such as passing competency tests or furthering one's education, are required. Typically, licenses last from one to five years before they must be renewed. Ongoing professional development and proof of current experience are frequently required for renewal.

Generally, teachers are hired on a temporary or probationary contract but are able to become tenured in approximately three years. The technical definition of **tenure** means that a person has been given a permanent position, but in reality, tenured teachers have earned only the right to due process. Even after a teacher earns tenure, proof of educational malpractice could result in dismissal.

For teachers it is very important to understand the appropriate use of copyright materials. **Copyright** is the exclusive right to intellectual or creative works, such as literary or musical pieces. Nearly every piece of artistic work is protected by copyright laws whether it has been registered or not. People have exclusive rights to their own creative works. The only creative works that are not protected by copyright laws are those that have not been recorded in any way: works contrived from public documents; familiar names, slogans, and symbols; and ideas. Works in the public domain are also not protected by copyright laws. The fair use doctrine provides teachers some leeway to use copyrighted materials for educational purposes as long as it is not used in a way that will create financial loss for the creator. Typically, educators may copy excerpts from a book, article, short story, or essay that comprise less than 10 percent of the work; copy up to 250 words of a poem; or copy a graphic from a book, magazine, or newspaper. However, teachers may not duplicate a work in lieu of purchasing a class set, copy the same work for more than one class, use the same work more than nine times in a semester, use the work for commercial purposes, or fail to attribute the author. If materials are copied to avoid purchasing class sets, it is a violation. Teachers may use bought or rented videos for instruction, but not for student entertainment. Whenever there is a question about whether certain works may be used, it is better to ask permission.

Copyright materials may be used by teachers under the following conditions:

▶ The material is part of the public domain.

▶ Less than 10 percent of a literary work is used.

▶ The material is not used for more than one class, course, or semester.

▶ The material is not used more than nine times within a semester.

▶ Videos are used for instruction, not entertainment.

▶ A graph or picture is used only with an attribution line.

▶ The material consists of solely public information.

▶ The teacher has secured permission from the author or publisher.

SAMPLE QUESTIONS

11) **Which of the following pieces of legislation protect against gender discrimination in athletic programs at public schools?**

    A.   the First Amendment

    B.   Section 504 of the Rehabilitation Act

    C.   Title IX of the Education Amendments of 1972

    D.   the Family Educational Rights and Privacy Act

Answers:

    A.   Incorrect. The First Amendment guarantees freedom of religion, freedom of expression, freedom of the press, and freedom to peaceably assemble.

    B.   Incorrect. Section 504 of the Rehabilitation Act prohibits discrimination based on disability in any program or activity that is subsidized by federal funds, including athletics.

C. **Correct.** Title IX of the Education Amendments of 1972 prohibits gender discrimination, including sexual harassment, inequality in athletic opportunity, inequality in STEM courses, and discrimination based on pregnancy.

D. Incorrect. The Family Educational Rights and Privacy Act (FERPA) protects the confidentiality of students' education records.

12) **Which of the following is an example of fair use of copyrighted materials?**

A. A teacher shows students a rented video as a reward at the end of the week.

B. A teacher copies one chapter of a novel that contains several literary elements to annotate with students.

C. For a performance, a teacher copies a piece of sheet music she finds on the Internet instead of purchasing it.

D. A teacher creates a PowerPoint presentation with a 500-word poem in its entirety that she uses every semester.

Answers:

A. Incorrect. Rented videos may be used for educational, not entertainment, purposes.

B. **Correct.** Up to 10 percent of a work may be copied for educational purposes.

C. Incorrect. In an emergency for a performance, a single piece of sheet music may be copied as long as it has been purchased. Teachers may not copy music from the Internet to avoid purchasing it.

D. Incorrect. A teacher may not use the same work for more than one class.

CONSTRUCTED-RESPONSE QUESTIONS

1) **Briefly describe two forms of professional development and discuss the benefits of each.**

Sample Answer:

Professional learning communities (PLCs) help teachers take control of their own professional learning experiences by meeting in small groups with common goals that are focused on student achievement. Collectively, teachers take responsibility for the educational progress of all students as they review data from common assessments to determine which instructional practices best meet the needs of students. PLCs are focused on the following questions: What do we want students to learn? How will we know if they have learned it? What will we do if they are not learning? What will we do if they already know the material?

Another type of professional development is attending conferences. Most professional organizations have conferences designed to meet the needs of their members. Professional conferences give teachers the opportunity to meet with other teachers of similar grades or content areas to discuss best practices. Conferences are a great way to network with colleagues and learn more about emerging research surrounding a particular area of teaching.

2) **Ms. Villanueva is a first-year teacher who is about to have her first parent meeting. Discuss some things she should do to prepare.**

Sample Answer:

Ms. Villanueva should have observed the student in a variety of settings so that she can discuss the student's social skill development as well as academic development. She should have a portfolio of work products to share with the parents and anecdotal stories about how the child has excelled or what the child particularly enjoys. Ms. Villanueva should be prepared to ask parents for help with any academic or behavioral challenges in a nonjudgmental way. She should also be prepared for the parents to have a number of questions for her. If there are other school personnel who work with the child, they should be invited to the meeting. Also, she needs to be aware that, even if the parents ask, she should not give out any information about other students.

Go on →

Terms

action plan: An action plan is a process by which goals and the steps toward achieving those goals are determined.

conferences: These are formal meetings that are typically sponsored by a professional association in which members of a particular profession come together to learn from one another and discuss important topics within the field.

confidentiality: Confidentiality is the ability to be trusted with private information.

copyright: Copyright is the exclusive right to intellectual works, such as literary or musical pieces.

critical friend: This is someone who supports growth by providing objective and honest feedback.

due process: Due process means that everyone must be treated fairly, and the rights of all must be respected.

equal access: Equal access provides procedural safeguards to ensure that all students receive the same benefits of public education regardless of disabilities.

First Amendment: This amendment guarantees freedom of religion, freedom of expression, freedom of the press, and freedom to peaceably assemble.

incident analysis: After an incident occurs, an incident analysis is done to formally review the situation and determine why it happened as well as how to reduce the likelihood of another similar event.

intellectual freedom: Intellectual freedom is the right to receive information from various perspectives without censorship.

internships: Internships are positions that offer on-the-job training either in addition to or in lieu of a salary.

learning communities: These communities are small groups of professionals who share common goals and meet to collaborate about instructional practices.

liability: Liability is a legal responsibility.

licensing: Licensing is permission given to someone to do something or to use something that belongs to someone else.

mentors: A mentor is a more experienced professional who guides someone who is newer to the profession.

privacy: Privacy is freedom from having personal business shared with others.

professional associations: These associations are nonprofit organizations formed to support the members of a particular profession by setting standards and advocating for their members.

reflective journal: A reflective journal is a record of a learning experience.

stakeholder: A stakeholder is anyone who has a stake in the school. This includes students, teachers, parents, staff, administrators, and community members.

tenure: The technical definition of tenure means that a person has been given a permanent position, but in reality, tenured teachers have earned only the right to due process.

workshops: Workshops are discussions or meetings in which participants come together to interact and exchange information about best practices.

5

Code of Ethics and Principles of Professional Conduct

Teacher conduct and behavior in the state of Florida is governed at the state, district, and school levels. While both districts and schools are empowered to establish professional norms for teachers and staff that align with their specific educational goals and missions, the majority of professional standards in Florida are set by the state. Derived from two sources—the State Board of Education and the Florida Statutes—these professional standards are codified in the Code of Ethics and Principles of Professional Conduct, which is composed of four sections: values, responsibilities to students, responsibilities to the public, and responsibilities to the profession of education. On the FTCE, applicants must demonstrate professionalism by correctly applying the code to specific professional situations. Therefore, it is less important to memorize the language of the code than to develop a thorough understanding of its intent.

PROFESSIONAL VALUES

The code of ethics lists seven specific values for educators. Teachers will value:

1. the worth and dignity of each person.
2. the pursuit of the truth.
3. devotion to excellence.
4. acquisition of knowledge.
5. the nurturing of democratic citizenship.
6. the freedom to learn and teach.
7. the guarantee of equal opportunity for all.

Together, these principles represent an approach to education that prioritizes the student's safety and well-being, and the development of his or her potential. Teachers must not only adhere to a specific code in their interactions with students but also actively pursue professional development so as to continue to best serve students and support their potential. Teachers must also maintain the respect and confidence of others in the learning community, including colleagues, parents, and community members. Serving the students' interests then encompasses all aspects of the education profession. Drawing on this, the remaining three sections of the Code of Ethics and Principles of Professional Conduct list the specific responsibilities a teacher has to each segment of the learning community.

Responsibilities to Students

Because students and student learning are at the heart of the Code of Ethics and Principles of Professional Conduct, the list in the code of the expected behaviors of teachers toward students is the most important articulation of professional responsibilities. There are nine expectations.

Teachers are expected to:

- use reasonable effort to protect students from harmful conditions.
- protect the confidentiality of personally identifiable information unless it serves a professional purpose or it is required by law.

Teachers must NOT:

- unreasonably restrain student efforts in the pursuit of learning.
- unreasonably deny a student access to diverse points of view.
- intentionally withhold or distort relevant subject matter.
- unnecessarily embarrass or disparage students (or allow others to do so).
- violate students' legal rights.
- discriminate based on race, color, religion, sex, age, ethnic origin, political beliefs, marital status, handicapping condition, sexual orientation, or social and family background.
- exploit students for personal gain or advantage.

It is not particularly important to memorize all nine of these responsibilities. Instead, note that there are two guiding principles behind each of these: ensuring student safety and prioritizing student learning. Teachers in Florida are expected to be open and inclusive and to put the best interests of the student first.

Ethical difficulties teachers encounter generally involve their interactions with students. The following table lists the most likely ethical violations and practices that can help avoid them.

Table 5.1. Ethical Violations and Practices Involving Students

Ethical Violation	Ethical Educator Practice
being the students' "friend"	Do not discuss personal issues with students, including issues with a spouse, friends, or dates.
	Do not socialize with students outside of school events or activities.
	Refer students to an appropriate resource person for personal problems.
inappropriate or questionable interactions with students	Do not exchange personal communications with students via phone, email, social media, etc.
	Always keep the classroom door open when meeting with students one-on-one.
unclear or unfair grading procedures	Know school and/or district grading policies.
	Establish clear grading policy at the beginning of the school year or unit.
	Communicate grading policy clearly to both students and parents
unfair or harsh discipline procedures	Know school and/or district policies on corporal punishment.
	Establish clear behavior policy at the beginning of the school year or unit.
	Communicate behavior policy clearly to both students and parents.
harassment, humiliation, or embarrassment of students	Be careful with the use of humor and sarcasm.
	Avoid using humor at the expense of a student.
	Establish clear classroom guidelines about language and showing respect.
student injuries	Avoid leaving students unsupervised and develop a plan for such situations.
	Use school or public transportation to transport students whenever possible.
	Always develop travel plans in advance and obtain parent and administrative approval.

RESPONSIBILITIES TO THE PUBLIC

Teaching is a very public profession: teachers interact not only with their students but with colleagues, parents, and members of the community. If teachers act unprofessionally in any of these relationships, they not only model inappropriate behavior for their students, but they also diminish their ability to provide a high-quality education to those students. Teachers are expected to:

▸ distinguish between personal and institutional or organizational views.

▸ avoid intentionally distorting or misrepresenting facts related to educational issues in direct or indirect public expression.

▸ refrain from using intentional privileges for personal gain.

▸ abstain from accepting or offering gratuities, gifts, or favors that could influence professional judgment or incur special advantages.

In sum, these four responsibilities emphasize the teacher's need to separate his or her interests from those of the school and a student, and to place the latter first. Each of these expectations is rooted in the belief that if teachers uses their position to advance their own interests, they will inevitably harm the interests of their students.

Because of the public nature of the teaching profession, teachers can encounter ethical problems both in the school building and in their lives outside of school. Since teachers are held to a higher moral standard than other professionals, they must consider their professional responsibilities even when not working.

Below are the most likely ethical violations and practices that can help avoid ethical issues:

Table 5.2. Ethical Violations and Practices Involving the Public

Ethical Violation	Ethical Educator Practices
inappropriate (e.g., drunken) behavior in front of students, parents, or other community members	Be discreet in the timing and location of alcohol consumption and peer socialization.
inappropriate dress	Know and comply with school and/or district dress policies when at work. Do not dress in suggestive or controversial ways when in the community.
imposing an opinion on students	Avoid personal politics in the classroom.
accepting large gifts from families	Limit gifts from students and parents. Do not make public displays of gifts from individual students or parents.

RESPONSIBILITIES TO THE PROFESSION OF EDUCATION

Florida recognizes that the profession of education requires collaboration. In order for a teacher to be effective, she or he must be able to work with other teachers and other adults. Therefore, the code of ethics contains specific responsibilities related to appropriate interactions with colleagues.

Teachers are expected to:

▶ maintain honesty in all professional dealings.

▶ provide a written explanation upon request for recommendations resulting in changes in terms of employment, denial of increments, or termination.

▶ self-report within forty-eight hours any arrests or convictions related to child abuse or the sale and/or possession of controlled substances.

▶ report any known violations of the code of ethics.

▶ comply with all orders of the education practices commission.

Teachers must NOT

▶ discriminate against colleagues.

▶ obstruct the exercise of colleagues' civil or political rights.

▶ contribute to the creation of a hostile, oppressive, offensive, or abusive work environment.

▶ inhibit colleagues' professional responsibilities.

▶ commit slander.

▶ use coercion to influence others' professional judgement.

▶ withhold or distort information about a position.

▶ give employment aid to someone who violates the code of ethics.

▶ retaliate against someone else who reports a code of ethics violation.

Each of these responsibilities establishes an expectation of honesty and integrity in teachers' dealings with each other in order to maintain a professional community of respect and trust. Much like a teacher's responsibilities to the public, these responsibilities reflect behavior teachers should model for their students.

The following are the most likely ethical violations involving collegial interactions and practices that can help avoid them.

Table 5.3. Common Ethical Issues and Practices Involving the Profession

Ethical Violation	Ethical Educator Practices
disrespect for colleagues or administration	Use professional language in all work-related communication. Share resources and give appropriate credit when referencing another teacher or source.
policy interpretation inconsistent with school/district policies	Know and comply with school and/or district policies. Post relevant school policies in the classroom and communicate them to students and parents. Document all parent communication.
mismanagement of student funds	Know and follow school and/or district rules for collecting and storing money. Work with a partner when collecting large sums of money.

SAMPLE QUESTIONS

1) **Which of the following gifts would be LEAST ethical for a teacher to accept?**

    A.   tickets to a sold-out concert

    B.   a gift card for a coffee shop

    C.   a bowl handmade by the student

    D.   a new LCD projector for the classroom

    Answers:

    A.   **Correct.** This is a high-priced gift which could easily be seen as influencing how the teacher views and treats the student.

    B.   Incorrect. While monetary gifts are not the most ethical gifts, a coffee shop gift card is worth little, and so it would be acceptable.

    C.   Incorrect. Handmade gifts carry little monetary value and so pose no ethical issue.

    D.   Incorrect. While an LCD projector is a high-value gift, its designation as a classroom tool means the teacher is not personally profiting from the gift.

REPORTING RIGHTS AND RESPONSIBILITIES OF STUDENT ABUSE

Because teachers have regular direct contact with children—and often develop trusting relationships with them—teachers are among those professionals who are **mandatory reporters**. This means that when a teacher suspects a child has been abused—physically, emotionally, or sexually—neglected, or abandoned by an adult, the teacher is required by law to report this suspicion. Failure to do so is not only a breach of the code of ethics that could result in the revocation of the teacher's certificate, but it is also a crime. Ethically, then, a teacher can never promise students to keep information about their potential abuse, neglect, or abandonment a secret. The Florida Statutes have also been amended; now it is mandatory to report sexual battery among students.

IMPORTANT DEFINITIONS

It is important that teachers understand the types of behaviors that constitute abuse, neglect, or abandonment:

> **Abuse** is any intentional or threatened act that results in injury or harm to a child. The injury or harm may be physical, sexual, or mental, and it must be likely to cause impairment of the child's physical, mental, or emotional health.

For example, a teacher frequently notices bruises on a student; the student's explanations are implausible, or the student is withdrawn. The teacher could reasonably suspect abuse might be taking place.

Alternatively, a teacher overhears a student—who seems otherwise healthy—tell another student about receiving a spanking as punishment for disobedience. This would not need to be reported; standard corporal punishment by parents is not considered abuse.

Neglect is the denial or withholding of physical necessities from a child by a parent. Necessities include food, clothing, shelter, and medical treatment. Refusal of the necessity must be likely to lead to impairment of the child's physical, mental, or emotional health.

There are two important exceptions to this definition of neglect. First, if a parent or guardian is unable to provide a child necessities due to financial instability, this is not neglect. In this case rather than reporting neglect, the teacher should contact a school counselor or other social service liaison to find social services for the family. If the family rejects the offered support, however, the case is then considered neglect.

The second exception is if withholding the necessity is based on the religious beliefs of a legally recognized religious organization. This exception is most often relevant when a parent withholds medical services. While the parent would not be charged with neglect, the government may still intervene to provide medical services, particularly in cases in which the child's life is at risk. If a teacher becomes aware of such a situation, he or she should still report it to seek a government review of the situation.

Abandonment occurs when a parent, legal custodian, or caregiver fails to establish a positive relationship with a child that includes a significant contribution to the child's care and maintenance. Abandonment is primarily identified when the adult fails to maintain regular contact—either through visitation or communication—with the child and/or fails to exercise his or her parental rights and responsibilities.

If, for example, a teacher discovers that a child's parent is absent for weeks at a time, leaving the child to find her own food, transportation, etc., the teacher should report a suspected case of abandonment.

It is important to note that incarcerated parents can be guilty of abandonment if they do not maintain regular contact with their children and provide for their care, even by simply finding a temporary caregiver.

REPORTING PROCEDURES

Upon witnessing suspicious behavior or signs from a student, a teacher should begin documenting the observations and any communication he or she has with the student and parent or guardian. If suspicious of abuse, neglect, or abandonment of a child, the teacher must immediately contact the Florida Abuse Hotline of the Department of Children and Families. Contact can be made by phone, letter, fax, webchat, or an online report; all forms are equally acceptable. Teachers must give their full name when filing a report, and it will be entered into the official report. However, the teacher's name will remain confidential; it will not be released to the student, family, or press.

If it is discovered that a teacher had information about the abuse, neglect, or abandonment of a child and willfully failed to report it, the teacher is subject to criminal prosecution. Under Florida law, this constitutes a third-degree felony with a maximum of five years in jail and a $5,000 fine. In addition, the school which employs the teacher is fined $1 million per offence.

DISCIPLINARY PROCEDURES AGAINST TEACHERS

If a teacher does violate the code of ethics, there are two possible repercussions (which can occur simultaneously): the teacher's employment may be affected or the teacher's certificate may be affected. Because teachers are employed at the district level, the school board of a district determines if a teacher's employment should be affected by an ethical violation. Teaching certificates are issued by the state, so the State Board of Education is responsible for any punishment related to the certificate.

Under Florida state law all employees of district schools, charter schools, and private schools that accept students funded by state scholarships are required to report any misconduct they observe by other teachers, staff, or administrators. All reports are first filed at the district level. The processes that follow depend on whether the school board or the Board of Education—or both—will investigate the claim.

DISTRICT INVESTIGATIONS

Once a complaint is filed with the district, the school board investigates to determine if the claim has merit. If there is sufficient evidence to support the claim, the following steps must occur:

1. **Formal charges**: A formal charge is filed against the teacher, and the teacher is immediately suspended without pay. The teacher also receives notice of the charges.

2. **Hearing request**: If the teacher would like to challenge the charge, he or she must submit a written request for a hearing within fifteen days of receiving the notice.

3. **Schedule of hearing**: The hearing must then take place within the following sixty days. The school board may hold the hearing itself or turn it over to an administrative law judge assigned by the Division of Administrative Hearings of the Department of Management Services.

4. **Hearing**: If the school board conducts the hearing itself, the group will examine the evidence and then make a determination—by majority vote—whether the charges can be sustained. If an administrative law judge is used, the judge makes a determination about the charges and presents it as a recommendation to the school board. The school board then makes the final decision by a majority vote.

5. **Consequences**: There are three possible outcomes to the school board vote:

   ▷ The teacher is dismissed. In this case, the teacher's contract is immediately terminated regardless of the timing during the school year.

   ▷ The teacher is suspended. In this case, the school board sets terms for the teacher's future reinstatement. These can include a set amount of time, remediation, or additional training. Any lost pay from the time of the investigation, the hearing, and the suspension period is not reinstated.

   ▷ The teacher is reinstated. If the charges are not sustained, the teacher is immediately returned to his or her position. The teacher also receives back pay for the time lost from the issuance of charges to the teacher's reinstatement.

6. **Appeal**: If the teacher feels that an error was made in the hearing process, she or he has the right to appeal within thirty days of the decision.

STATE INVESTIGATIONS

Once a school board investigates a complaint and determines there is sufficient evidence to proceed, in addition to conducting its own investigation, the school board has thirty days from the date the complaint was originally lodged with the district to file the complaint with the State Board of Education.

Complaints can also be lodged directly with the State Board of Education for the following:

- ▸ use of a fraudulent teaching certificate
- ▸ failure to report abuse or misconduct
- ▸ inability to teach or perform duties
- ▸ revocation of or sanctions on a teaching certificate from another state
- ▸ being subject to a court order or notice by the Department of Revenue for failure to pay child support

- ▶ violation of the professional code of conduct
- ▶ violation of an order of the Education Practices Commission
- ▶ being found guilty of a crime
- ▶ being guilty of "personal conduct that seriously reduces that person's effectiveness as an employee of the district school board" (Florida Statute 1012.795)
- ▶ being guilty of gross immorality or an act involving moral turpitude, including (but not limited to):
  - ▷ acts that would constitute a crime
  - ▷ intentionally falsifying documents
  - ▷ intentionally violating test or exam security protocols
  - ▷ any act with a level of depravity as defined under Florida law

Teachers with lapsed certificates who allegedly committed one of these violations when the certificate was still active are subject to charges as well.

The State Board of Education then follows a series of steps.

> First it conducts a **preliminary investigation** to determine if **probable cause** exists. At this time, the teacher and the teacher's school are notified of the investigation and its nature (unless that would negatively affect the course of the investigation). Once a complaint has been filed with the Board of Education, it must be pursued until its end even if the original complainant withdraws. The Board of Education prioritizes cases that affect the health, welfare, or safety of a student.

> If probable cause is determined to exist, the commissioner of the Board of Education files a **formal complaint**. An administrative law judge is assigned to complete the investigation and make a determination.

> The teacher is immediately suspended (if he or she has not been already) although with pay in a process that differs from complaints handled at the district level. The teacher is also **reassigned** to a position within the district without direct contact with students.

> Upon reviewing all of the evidence, the administrative law judge makes a recommendation to an **Education Practices Commission** panel. The panel conducts a formal review of the investigation and issues a **Final Order**.

POSSIBLE STATE PENALTIES

If the administrative judge finds the charges to be substantiated, the Education Practices Commission may issue one of the punishments described in the following paragraphs.

Arguably the lightest punishment, the Education Practices Commission can place an **official written reprimand** in an educator's file. While this does not explicitly alter her or his certification, it could limit the educator's ability to find employment.

Monetary fines are also a consequence; in some cases, educators may be required to pay an administrative **fine** of no more than $2,000.

If the teacher is placed on **probation**, the teacher may return to the classroom with certain requirements. Usually teachers on probation are assigned to work with another certified educator or to take additional courses. Teachers on probation must:

> ▸ undergo annual performance reports by a supervisor.

> ▸ fully comply with all school, district, and state policies, rules, and laws.

> ▸ perform their duties professionally and competently.

> ▸ pay all costs of compliance with their probation, including monitoring costs, which must be paid within the first six months of each year.

> ▸ notify the Department of Education immediately if their employment is terminated.

In serious cases, the Education Practices Commission can either suspend or revoke the charged individual's certificate. In cases of **suspension**, a teacher's certificate may be suspended for up to five years, during which time he or she cannot perform any job that requires direct contact with students. In cases of **revocation**, the certificate is revoked, meaning it is not automatically reinstated after a period of time. The certificate can be revoked for up to ten years—at which point the individual is allowed to apply for a new certificate—or it can be revoked permanently. If a teacher has multiple certificates in Florida, a Final Order of revocation of one automatically revokes all others.

Charges may result in a **denial of certificate**. If the charged individual is an applicant for a certificate, or administrative or supervisory endorsement, that application will be denied. The commission may also ban reapplication. Similarly, if the charged individual has an expired certificate, he or she will receive an **administrative sanction**. This prohibits the teacher from applying for renewal of his or her certificate or for a new certificate. A sanction can either be temporary—ten years or less—or permanent.

In other cases, the Education Practices Commission may order **Restriction of Scope of Practice**: rather than being put on probation or having their certificate terminated, educators may be limited by the commission in the duties they are allowed to perform.

Educators who have been found to be impaired by alcohol addiction, drug addiction, or other mental health issues can be ordered to join the Recovery Network Program, which helps individuals access evaluation and treatment. All educators are welcome to voluntarily join the program without a Final Order from the Education Practices Commission.

USE OF TECHNOLOGY

Technology is generally defined as any computer resources in a school or district, including software, hardware, lines, and services that connect the school or district computers to other computers—either internal or external. This includes Internet connections and any digital storage provided by the school or district. Consequently, administrators and others with permission can review any files or communications that take place within the system to ensure its appropriate use.

As technology becomes increasingly important in both classroom practice and professional communication and procedures, its appropriate and ethical use has become relevant to professionalism in education. Each district has its own technology use policy, which applies to anyone with permission to use the network. While there might be slight differences between different district policies, they all include the information described in the following sections.

RESTRICTIONS ON COMMUNICATION

There is no expectation of privacy in communications that occur over the district system. If district equipment (as previously outlined) is used, the system administrator may access the communication at any time—regardless of whether it was sent from a work or personal email account. Therefore, any communication using the district system should be professional. Users may not use the network to discriminate against others, nor may they use profanity, vulgarity, or inappropriate language in their communication.

They are also prohibited from using personally identifiable information about students when communicating, and they cannot disclose information from student records without written parental permission.

Essentially, educators may not use the district network to communicate in ways that would be unacceptable in person. Just as it would be inappropriate for a teacher to use profanity in the halls at school—even if talking to a friend unaffiliated with the school—it is inappropriate for a teacher to do so over the district Internet connections.

RESTRICTIONS ON INFORMATION TRANSFERS

Technology today is used in great part to transfer information: uploading, downloading, sending, and receiving it. Guidelines for appropriate transfer of technology ensure that all information transferred is in line with the district's educational mission and objectives, and to protect equitable access to the system.

When using a district computer or the district network, users must not transmit any material that is in violation of local, state, or federal laws. Among others, this specifically includes materials that are copyrighted or licensed (without the copyright owner's permission) and materials that cause or threaten harm to others. Furthermore, they may not electronically publish materials that have no educational value.

Users may not access or process pornography or other explicit files or text; above all, they cannot access files that may pose a threat to the network (by introducing viruses, etc.). They may not stream media or download games, videos, or audio files with no educational value or without administrative permission. Finally, they may not download, transfer, or install software, images, text, videos, or audio files without administrative permission.

RESTRICTIONS ON SOCIAL MEDIA

Since social media is an increasingly important part of people's lives and daily interactions, most districts have developed specific acceptable-use policies.

Many schools or districts maintain their own social media, and individual educators may even have their own accounts. These accounts may not be used for personal purposes, and any information or communication posted must have educational value, remaining consistent with the district's and school's educational mission and objectives.

Many districts also have specific restrictions on using school or district social media for union purposes.

In general, use of personal social media, including instant messaging, chat rooms, Facebook, or Instagram is prohibited on district networks. Teachers are allowed to maintain personal social media accounts and blogs, but these are considered extensions of the community space. Therefore, the higher moral standard teachers are held to in the community applies in these virtual spaces as well. Teachers are discouraged from "friending" students via their personal social media accounts, and they can be punished for activity on social media, even if that activity occurs off school grounds and outside school time.

BLOGS

If a teacher maintains a blog, the district requires that she or he only blog off school grounds and outside work hours. Even in these circumstances, the individual is considered a representative of the district and is expected to behave in a manner that does not embarrass or disparage the district or the education profession at large.

Teachers are also prohibited from using school or district logos, mascots, etc., on their personal blogs. Finally, they must explicitly state on the blog that the opinions expressed are theirs and do not reflect the opinions of the district.

APPROPRIATE USE OF THE SYSTEM

Regardless of the size of the district, there are numerous users on the district's system. All users are expected to act in a manner that respects the larger community of users and maintains the security of the system. In addition, educators are expected to act in accordance with the code of ethics. Users, then, are NOT allowed to:

▶ compromise account access by using someone else's account without written permission, logging someone else in using their account, helping others access a computer logged into by someone else, or compromising the security of their own password as well as those of others.

▶ use district resources for personal commercial purposes.

▶ bypass the district's content filter without administrative permission.

▶ limit the use of others on the network by monopolizing bandwidth, etc.

▶ use district equipment or connect to non-district wireless networks without administrative permission.

All users are also required to notify the system administrator of any security problem they detect and are prohibited from sharing that security problem with others.

Any users who violate the appropriate use policies of the district can have their access to the system and network restricted or even denied. In addition, users are personally financially responsible for any intentional damage they inflict to the system.

STUDENT RECORDS

The management of student records is one of a teacher's most serious responsibilities. Teachers must ensure not only that student privacy is protected but that parents and students have sufficient access to information pertaining to the student. A federal law called the Family Educational Rights and Privacy Act (FERPA) regulates student record management. FERPA applies at all levels of education and in all educational institutions—district, charter, and private. Most of the requirements of FERPA are fulfilled by the school or district. However, teachers must understand how FERPA affects their own classroom recordkeeping.

STUDENT PRIVACY

Teachers may not disclose information about a student's grades or behavior to anyone other than the student's parents (if the student is a minor); if the student is over eighteen years old, the teacher needs his or her permission to disclose information to the parents. If disclosure is requested by a third party, the teacher must obtain signed consent from the parents (when a minor student is involved) or the adult student. The permission must specifically list the records that can be disclosed and what they can be used for. As previously discussed, teachers must protect the student's identity in electronic communications by removing any identifiable information (unless they have been given permission by the parents in the case of a minor student).

Directory information is the only information that can be disclosed. **Directory information** is information that is not considered harmful: a student's name, phone number, or home address. Parents must be given an access waiver that gives them the chance to opt out of the release of this information annually. This is usually done at the school or district level.

Finally, student work may not be posted or shared with identifying information unless parents have given their permission. This may seem extremely restrictive; however, most schools include a letter with the **access waiver** that requests parent permission for the use of student work or images on school property or in school materials.

There are a few exceptions to these restrictions: other school officials, other educational institutions, the juvenile justice system, and accrediting organizations all have right of disclosure without parental consent. Information can also be disclosed by subpoena, in a lawsuit, or in a health or safety emergency.

STUDENT AND PARENT ACCESS

FERPA also guarantees parents and students full access to student records. To obtain access, the parent or student may file a request. Under the law, this request must be filled within forty-five days. Once they have the records, parents and students are allowed to review them and challenge inaccuracies. This does not mean they have the right to demand grade changes or the removal of disciplinary notes from a student's file. However, if the record does not reflect the student's actual history (e.g., it lists a D in a class in which the student actually received a B) the parents and student have a right to request an investigation and, ultimately, a revision of the record.

To ensure access, FERPA requires all schools to annually notify parents and adult students of their rights. The notice must be written and include information about challenges to records and access to waivers (as previously discussed). Schools are also responsible for making sure that all parents—regardless of native language or disability—can access the notification.

Practice Test

Read the question carefully and choose the most correct answer.

1

In lieu of presenting facts to students, the teacher asks a question to which the students are expected to explore and report back their findings with justifications for their answers. Which teaching method is the teacher using?

A. cross-curricular instruction

B. inquiry-based learning

C. spiral curriculum

D. response to intervention

2

Which of the following is an essential step to help students self-regulate?

A. general feedback

B. setting expectations

C. setting learning goals

D. extrinsic reinforcers

3

Which of the following actions best supports parent involvement in school?

A. inviting parents to be involved in shared decision making

B. posting a calendar of events on the web page

C. inviting parents to after-school community events

D. providing parents with a list of extracurricular opportunities

4

During a science unit on meteorology, the teacher has students do art projects, collect and display data, and read stories about the weather. What teaching strategy is the teacher using?

A.   interdisciplinary learning

B.   inquiry-based learning

C.   constructivist teaching

D.   multimedia instruction

5

Students in Miss Freeman's class ask, "Where does rain come from?" In order to best promote higher-order thinking skills, which response should Miss Freeman give?

A.   Rain comes from clouds.

B.   Let's read a book about it.

C.   Let's see if we can make rain and find out.

D.   You will get extra credit points if you can find out and tell us tomorrow.

6

Miss Gimlin wants to prepare her class to begin using self-assessment for their writing assignments. Which of the following steps would she do first?

A.   Use peer assessment as an introduction to evaluating work.

B.   Have students write their best quality work.

C.   Train students as a class with a sample writing piece.

D.   Start with a holistic rubric with the first piece, gradually working up to an analytical rubric.

7

The teacher would like to begin having formal discussions to help students learn to articulate their learning and become better listeners. Which of the following strategies will help students get the most from the discussion?

A.   Provide information about the topic to students in advance.

B.   Choose a topic that is controversial.

C.   Select a topic that the students know very little about so that they can learn as they are discussing.

D.   Choose a broad topic that has the capacity to go in many different directions.

2

8

Ms. Edwards is a seventh-grade math teacher. She feels comfortable with her content knowledge and pedagogy but would like new ideas to motivate her students and manage her time. Which of the following professional associations would best meet her needs?

A. Association of American Educators (AAE)

B. National Council of Teachers of Mathematics (NCTM)

C. Association for Middle Level Education (AMLE)

D. Council for Exceptional Children (CEC)

9

Which of the following instructional techniques is most effective with visual learners?

A. silent reading

B. pair-share

C. audiobooks

D. mind maps

10

Typically, Ms. Vaught uses essay tests, but she is considering using a selected-response test at the end of the next unit. What is the advantage of a selected-response test?

A. Selected-response test will indicate how deeply students understand the content.

B. Grading is more subjective.

C. Selected-response test can cover a wider range of content.

D. Selected-response test provides a holistic view of student knowledge.

11

When a student who comes to school in the same clothes all week is questioned by the teacher, he says his parents are out of town. The student rarely changes clothes, is often dirty, and is often very hungry. The teacher suspects the student has been abandoned. The teacher is obligated by law to contact:

A. the school social worker.

B. the police.

C. the student's parents.

D. homeless services.

12

What is the primary purpose of the middle column in a KWL chart?

    A.   activate prior knowledge

    B.   set learning goals

    C.   assess understanding

    D.   develop autonomous learners

13

Which of the following theories explains why teenage girls tend to have conflict with their mothers?

    A.   Kohlberg's stages of moral development

    B.   Piaget's stages of cognitive development

    C.   Erikson's stages of psychological development

    D.   Maslow's hierarchy of needs

14

A publishing company is marketing a new teacher evaluation system, so it hires a team of researchers to correlate the use of the evaluation process to increased student achievement. What type of research is this?

    A.   applied research

    B.   action research

    C.   basic research

    D.   qualitative research

15

Which of the following elements of planning is the most important?

    A.   alignment

    B.   engagement

    C.   assessment

    D.   collaboration

16

Mr. Leyman teaches his students how to use a writing rubric so that they can monitor their own proficiency. Which assessment strategy is he using?

    A.   Socratic questioning

    B.   signaled response

    C.   self-assessment

    D.   peer assessment

17

Which of the following scenarios best describes a teacher using analytical scoring?

A. Student work is ranked and then percentile scores are assigned compared with other students.

B. A teacher uses a rubric that gives one or two general indicators of high, medium, and low performance.

C. A teacher counts how many words there are in a student's essay and assigns a score accordingly.

⌄ D. A teacher matches student work to criteria on a scoring rubric. For each of the criteria, the student is assigned a score. The scores are added to assign the overall grade.

18

A teacher is interested in developing an after-school program that focuses on STEM projects. Which of the following should she do first?

⌐ A. meet with building-level administrators about the vision for the project

B. start a fund-raiser to collect materials

C. send a survey to parents to determine whether they are interested in having their child participate

D. schedule a meeting with stakeholders, including parents, students, community leaders, and colleagues

19

A teacher breaks up learning into smaller parts and then provides support to move the student from guided instructional level to independent level. What strategy is the teacher using?

A. constructivism

⌐ B. scaffolding

C. inquiry-based learning

D. spiral curriculum

20

Which behavior theorist would advocate allowing students to sleep when they are tired and providing a safe learning environment?

A. Erikson

B. Watson

⌐ C. Maslow

D. Thorndike

21

Shannon is a first-grade student. She received a grade-equivalency score of 2.6 on a math assessment. Which of the following statements should be communicated to her parent?

A.   Shannon's performance on this assessment compares to students who are in their sixth month of second grade.

B.   Shannon needs to skip to the next grade level.

C.   Shannon scored better than 26 percent of the students who took this assessment.

D.   Shannon's performance compares to students who are six years and two months old.

22

Which of the following is the best example of enrichment?

A.   extra homework

B.   independent study

C.   peer tutoring

D.   higher-order thinking questions

23

Students understand how to fill out a KWL chart in math even though they have never used it in that class. This is an example of which of the following?

A.   accommodation

B.   self-efficacy

C.   transfer

D.   self-regulation

24

Miss Flannigan is frustrated because she does not feel that her mentor, Mr. Ortega, is helping her. Although he is friendly, he views their meetings as a time to socialize rather than as a time to answer her questions and provide feedback. Which of the following is the most productive way to solve the problem?

A.   Miss Flannigan should talk to the principal about getting another mentor.

B.   Miss Flannigan should approach Mr. Ortega and explain her needs.

C.   Miss Flannigan should find another colleague to help her.

D.   Miss Flannigan should make an appointment with the appropriate official in the administration building to express her need for assistance.

25

Which of the following theorists developed social learning theory?

A.   Howard Gardner

B.   Benjamin Bloom

C.   Albert Bandura

D.   Jean Piaget

26

A student listens to a story and recreates it in his own words in the puppet theater. Which of the following domains does this activity represent?

A.   cognitive domain

B.   affective domain

C.   psychomotor domain

D.   moral domain

27

Young students ask questions throughout the day about when various events will occur, including lunch, specials, recess, and the end of the school day. Which of these responses would reflect student-centered responsiveness?

A.   redirecting students back to the learning activity

B.   using the teachable moment to talk about telling time

C.   writing a daily schedule on the board

D.   setting a timer on the smartboard to count down until the next event

28

Students play basketball. In which domain is this learning activity?

A.   cognitive

B.   affective

C.   psychomotor

D.   moral

29

What is the term for a test that accurately measures what it intends to measure?

A.   reliable

B.   valid

C.   variable

D.   consistent

30

During which universal stage of first language acquisition do children begin to produce sounds based upon friction?

A.   pre-speech stage

B.   babbling stage

C.   one-word stage

D.   early multi-word stage

31

Which of the following examples demonstrates the use of a diagnostic assessment?

A.   Mrs. Bittle uses an anticipation guide to introduce a unit on motion.

B.   Mrs. Inbody gives a pop quiz at the end of the first lesson to find out how much her students have learned.

C.   Mr. Wilson conferences with each student at the end of a unit to find out what he or she has learned.

D.   Mr. Sherry gives students a test that measures their cognitive reasoning ability.

32

If a teacher maintains a blog, she may

A.   write funny stories about her students on the blog.

B.   post pictures from her classroom on the blog.

C.   use the school mascot in her page design.

D.   write about lesson plans she uses in her classroom.

33

Ms. Miller wants to use scaffolding to support student learning in US history. Which of the following activities demonstrates scaffolding?

A.   Students use a graphic organizer and a think-pair-share activity to build vocabulary before beginning a writing assignment.

B.   Students take notes while Ms. Miller teaches from a PowerPoint® presentation.

C.   Ms. Miller introduces historical documents using primary sources. A week later, she refers to the lesson on primary sources when students learn about the Declaration of Independence.

D.   Students work in pairs to brainstorm everything they know about the American Revolution before beginning a unit of study.

34

Which of the following is an example of an open-ended question?

A.   Who was the first president of the United States?

B.   How many US presidents have there been?

C.   What are the president's job responsibilities?

D.   What do you think would happen if term limits for the president were abolished?

35

What is the teacher's role in a constructivist classroom?

A.   primary source of facts

B.   determine what pages of the textbook need to be read

C.   lecturer

D.   facilitator of learning

36

One of the students in Mr. Cruz's first-grade class always writes twice as much in his writing journal as any of the other students, but he tends to get off topic. What is this an example of?

A.   divergent thinking

B.   assimilation

C.   accomodation

D.   ADHD

37

Mrs. Paul is not sure whether she should teach exponents before or during the unit on order of operations. Which document should she reference?

A.   scope

B.   sequence

C.   state standards

D.   textbook

38

Which of the following is an example of data collected for qualitative research?

A.   standardized test scores

B.   surveys

C.   teacher retention rates

D.   attendance rates

39

On the unit assessment, there is a high standard deviation. How would the teacher use this information to guide instruction during the next unit?

A. Students need to be remediated.

B. Students need enrichment.

C. Instruction needs to be differentiated to meet the needs of all students.

D. Instruction needs to be better aligned with assessments.

40

Which of the following best exemplifies analytical scoring?

A. A teacher provides a rubric score for criteria in several categories.

B. A teacher uses a simple rubric to evaluate an entire assignment as proficient, not proficient, or exceeds proficient.

C. A teacher writes anecdotal notes to explain whether a paper is above or below proficiency.

D. Students trade papers and grade them according to a rubric.

41

Which of the following is an example of differentiating instruction?

A. offering students choices of learning activity based on their learning styles

B. reteaching the same material at progressively deeper levels throughout the year

C. providing guided instruction at the students' instructional level

D. using assessments as a learning tool

42

Which of the following activities is using zone of proximal development (ZPD)?

A. small-group reading instruction based on students' reading level

B. cooperative learning groups research a topic

C. annotating text before a discussion

D. playing a trivia game to review information before the assessment

43

Which of the following is part of adolescent development?

A. The adolescent is unable to view things from other perspectives.

B. The adolescent is unable to think logically or abstractly.

C. The adolescent is unable to behave responsibly.

D. The adolescent enjoys dramatic, intense experiences.

44

Which of the following is an example of allowable use of copyrighted materials?

A. A teacher makes a class set of a play she finds on the Internet.

B. A teacher rents a movie to play for students during a family night.

C. A teacher copies a poem to display in class that she uses repeatedly over a three-year period.

D. A teacher makes a copy of one chapter of a book to send home with a student who is unable to attend school because of illness.

45

While writing a paragraph describing her house, a student mistakenly uses the following terms: *in the porch, on the basement,* **and** *around the ceiling.* **She needs extra practice with which point of grammar?**

A. prepositions

B. conjunctions

C. pronouns

D. verbs

46

What is the primary purpose of using concept maps during instruction?

A. to visually connect information to schema

B. to help students articulate new learning

C. to increase engagement

D. to help students activate prior knowledge

47

According to cognitive learning theory, how can learning be assessed?

A. through progress monitoring

B. through summarization

C. through application to a different situation

D. through standardized testing

48

Which of the following learning activities will yield the best results?

A. a highly engaging activity that is not grounded in scientific principles

B. a research-based activity that is not aligned with learning standards

C. a highly engaging activity that is aligned with learning standards

D. a research-based activity that is aligned with standards, but less engaging

49

Mrs. Henderson notices that students are distracted and losing interest in the lecture. She changes the volume, tone, and pitch of her voice to draw their attention to a key point. Which of the following strategies is Mrs. Henderson using?

A.   verbal cues

B.   nonverbal cues

C.   conditioned response

D.   remediation

50

Which of the following will be the last skill mastered by a second-language learner?

A.   academic language

B.   sentence structure in writing

C.   receptive social language

D.   expressive social language

51

Which of the following professional development experiences is most focused on learner outcomes?

A.   professional learning communities (PLCs)

B.   critical friends groups (CFGs)

C.   professional association membership

D.   reflective practices

52

What is the term for a test that accurately measures what it intends to measure?

A.   reliable

B.   valid

C.   variable

D.   consistent

53

Which of the following is a necessary part of developing self-motivation?

A.   providing extrinsic rewards

B.   differentiating instruction

C.   inquiry-based learning strategies

D.   goal setting

54

Which of the following teachers is giving students the opportunity to express their First Amendment rights in school?

A. Miss Goodson's students use their cell phones to text their friends during class.

B. Mr. Waters has students who bully other students and call them names.

C. Miss Wood holds formal debates in which students have the opportunity to express their opinions and back them up with facts.

D. Mrs. Griffin's students circulate a petition during class protesting the school lunch menu.

55

Which of the following is an example of an audio aid that may be used to promote better communication in the classroom?

A. PowerPoint® presentations

B. textbooks

C. microphones

D. Internet sites

56

What is the best way to motivate students to do well on their science fair project?

A. emphasize that it will be graded

B. explain that scholarships may be available for national winners

C. provide opportunities for choice and self-assessment

D. provide consequences for students who do not do their best

57

A parent is upset that his minor son received a D in a teacher's class. He requests the teacher's full grade book. According to FERPA, which of the following should happen next?

A. The teacher should provide the parent with a copy of only the son's grades from the year.

B. The teacher should provide the parent with a copy of the entire gradebook.

C. The teacher should inform the father he is not permitted to see any of the individual grades.

D. The teacher should refer the request to the principal, who will make a determination.

58

Which of the following questions about dinosaurs best promotes higher-order thinking?

A. How long are the *Tyrannosaurus rex*'s teeth?

B. In which parts of the United States did the *Stegosaurus* live?

C. Why do you think dinosaurs are extinct?

D. Which dinosaurs are carnivores?

59

In which of the following scenarios would a student's writing journal be used as an informal assessment?

A. when individualized spelling lists are created from misspelled words

B. when it is used to rank students

C. when it is used to qualify students for special services

D. when it is part of a state assessment

60

Which of the following is an example of cognitive learning theory in the classroom?

A. Students brainstorm and categorize things that might be found in a rainforest.

B. Students brainstorm alternatives to logging in the rainforests.

C. The teacher presents information about the food chain in the rainforest ecosystem.

D. Students use an interactive computer program to learn about the rainforest.

61

Mr. Schoen is a fourth-grade math teacher who has emerged as a teacher leader in his school. He is interested in creating a program for new teachers to offer professional development in some of the more challenging areas. He has been allocated funds to join a professional association and attend its national conference. Which association will best meet Mr. Schoen's needs?

A. Council for Exceptional Children (CEC)

B. National Association for the Education of Young Children (NAEYC)

C. National Council of Teachers of Mathematics (NCTM)

D. Association for Supervision and Curriculum (ASCD)

62

Which determines when an English learner no longer requires English language programs and services?

   A.   The student's home survey reports that the primary language is English.

   B.   The student has been enrolled in an English learner program for two years.

   C.   The student's scores on state-selected tests meet designated cutoff points.

   D.   The student has completed an instructional program aligned to ELP standards.

63

Which of the following resources would Ms. Warren use to teach math concepts at a concrete level?

   A.   flashcards

   B.   fluency software

   C.   manipulatives

   D.   individual whiteboards

64

Which of the following learning activities is aligned to cognitivism?

   A.   graphic organizers

   B.   demonstrations

   C.   inquiry-based learning

   D.   scaffolding

65

In which of the following learning theories would a teacher work with a student within the student's zone of proximal development (ZPD)?

   A.   cognitivism

   B.   social learning theory

   C.   constructivism

   D.   behaviorism

66

Which of the following is an example of a formal assessment?

   A.   benchmark tests

   B.   portfolio assessments

   C.   STAR reading test

   D.   performance-based assessments

67

Students role-play the bystander's role in bullying. In which domain is this learning activity?

A.   cognitive

B.   affective

C.   psychomotor

D.   moral

68

Which of the following is most effective for determining learning objectives?

A.   finding fun, engaging activities, and then writing learning objectives to match them

B.   using the teacher's edition of the textbooks

C.   following the guidance of veteran teachers

D.   using state standards with district pacing guides

69

Miss Shannon realizes during the first week of school that her classroom management needs improvement. Which of the following actions should she try first?

A.   Ask her mentor to observe her class and make suggestions.

B.   Send students to the principal's office if they misbehave.

C.   Withhold recess for the entire class until the behavior improves.

D.   Attend a professional development workshop on classroom management.

70

Which of the following activities best serves gifted students?

A.   additional class work

B.   independent study

C.   inquiry-based learning

D.   tutoring struggling students

71

Which of the following contains the most accurate research?

A.   peer-reviewed journals

B.   encyclopedias

C.   second-party replication of results

D.   newspapers

72

Ms. Haley is selecting a summative assessment for a unit about the circulatory system. Which of the following would suit her purpose?

A.   An essay test that covers the key components of the unit.

B.   Learning logs that document a student's learning experiences and questions.

C.   Anecdotal notes that she keeps throughout the unit as she observes students engaged in various learning experiences.

D.   A pop quiz containing five selected-response questions.

73

Which of the following is an example of transfer?

A.   Students use what they know about distance, rate, and time to plan a field trip.

B.   Students use what they have learned about the judicial system to have a mock trial.

C.   Karen begins to psychologically distance herself from her parents as peers become more important.

D.   Matthew is angry with himself because he did poorly on a test, so he behaves disrespectfully to his teacher and peers.

74

Which of the following methods is most effective for redirecting a student who is losing interest during instructional time?

A.   Tell the student to pay attention.

B.   Move closer to the student.

C.   Give other students stickers or tokens.

D.   Send the student to the hall.

75

Mrs. Brandt is a beginning teacher. She has been assigned to work with a more experienced teacher who helps her find materials, understand school procedures, and offers advice. Which of the following best describes this learning experience?

A.   mentoring

B.   internship

C.   peer assessment

D.   professional learning community

Go on →

76

Misty scores in the 45th percentile on a reading readiness test. Which of the following does this score indicate?

A.   Misty failed the test.

B.   Misty correctly answered 45 percent of the test questions.

C.   Misty scored higher than 45 percent of the students who took the test.

D.   45 percent of the students who took the test scored higher than Misty.

77

Students create a word web of life science vocabulary. In which domain is this learning activity?

A.   cognitive

B.   affective

C.   psychomotor

D.   moral

78

Which of the following strategies will work best to motivate struggling readers to read at home?

A.   At a monthly assembly, honor students who complete 400 minutes of outside reading time.

B.   Give a soda to students each time they complete 1000 minutes of outside reading time.

C.   Provide high-interest reading materials and help students set individual goals.

D.   Model reading for pleasure during a daily silent reading time.

79

Miss Wagner wants to learn more about instructional strategies that are specific to the developmental needs of her kindergarten students. Which of the following will most likely meet her needs?

A.   attending a district professional development workshop

B.   joining a social network in which teachers share their ideas

C.   joining the National Association for the Education of Young Children (NAEYC)

D.   reading a peer-reviewed journal article about student engagement

80

In the four phases of acculturation, the humor phase is often marked by what?

   A.   a lot of laughter at the cultural norms of the adopted country

   B.   delight at the newness of the culture of the adopted country

   C.   comfort and feeling like a part of the new culture

   D.   difficulty as the person grapples with feelings of rejecting the old culture for the new

81

Mr. Stick listens as students think-pair-share and then call on pairs to share what they have learned. Which type of assessment is Mr. Stick using?

   A.   summative

   B.   formative

   C.   diagnostic

   D.   formal

82

Which of the following is an appropriate positive reinforcement for a middle school student?

   A.   permission to skip class

   B.   candy

   C.   permission to work with a peer

   D.   movie day

83

Which of the following tools would best help a teacher target instruction for remediation?

   A.   standardized tests

   B.   benchmark tests

   C.   anecdotal records

   D.   error analysis

84

Which type of learning activity would be preferred by an introverted student?

   A.   cooperative learning groups

   B.   active learning

   C.   graphic organizers

   D.   discussion and debate

85

Which of the following is an advantage of using a scoring guide for assessing student projects?

A.   Scoring guides offer a great deal of feedback.

B.   Scoring guides are easy to use.

C.   Scoring guides save time.

D.   Scoring guides are highly subjective.

86

Mr. Estes's students have a take-home folder that goes home with them every day and includes homework, notes, and important information. What is the primary purpose of the take-home folder?

A.   teaching students to be responsible

B.   improving student achievement on homework projects

C.   improving communication between school and home

D.   encouraging parents to volunteer

87

Which of the following learning activities would be most appropriate for a student with verbal-linguistic intelligence?

A.   think-pair-share

B.   word maps

C.   concept sorts

D.   building models

88

In which of the following circumstances is Kanitta's behavior changed because of an intrinsic reward?

A.   The teacher will call Kanitta's mother if she does not turn in her homework.

B.   The teacher will make a positive phone call to Kanitta's mother if she does turn in her homework.

C.   Kanitta is motivated to do her homework because it is engaging and relevant.

D.   Kanitta will get to go to lunch early if she completes her homework.

89

Students play Ping-Pong in physical education class. In which domain is this learning activity?

A. cognitive

B. affective

— C. psychomotor

D. moral

90

Which of the following best explains the primary reason for using an analytical scoring rubric?

A. provides an overall assessment of a work product

⌣ B. provides specific feedback to students

C. provides observable evidence of skill mastery

D. provides a comprehensive view of a student's ability over time

91

Which of the following is true about collecting data and drawing conclusions about research?

⌄ A. Deductive reasoning is more likely to be accurate than inductive reasoning.

B. Inductive reasoning is more accurate than deductive reasoning.

C. Qualitative data are more accurate than quantitative data.

† D. Research may be accurately used to infer conclusions about information that is not aligned with the purpose of the research.

92

Which of the following questions is from the highest level of Bloom's taxonomy?

⌐ A. Which piece of the literature is Charlotte Brontë's best work? Explain your answer.

B. Who wrote *Wuthering Heights*?

C. Summarize chapter three of *Wuthering Heights*.

D. Compare and contrast Charlotte Brontë's *Jane Eyre* to Emily Brontë's *Wuthering Heights*.

93

Which of the following is the *primary* reason a teacher may not install software on a district computer?

A. All software must first be evaluated for educational value.

B. New software could violate district contracts with other vendors.

C. New software could put the system at risk if it contains a virus.

D. All software must be screened for appropriateness.

94

Which of the following learning activities would be most appropriate for a student with bodily-kinesthetic intelligence?

A. think-pair-share

B. word maps

C. concept sorts

D. building models

95

Mr. Nunn gives students a test on the first day of school to find out what they already know. Which type of assessment is he using?

A. summative

B. formative

C. norm-referenced

D. diagnostic

96

Which of the following assessment tools is Mr. Segura using in the example below?

Below Expectations	Progressing	Proficient	Exceeds Expectations
Messy, illegible, difficult to understand	Legible, but may not be neat; some clarity issues may be present	Neat, clear, and organized	Neat, clear, and organized, and contains graphs, illustrations, or other special features that improve understanding

A. analytical checklist

B. analytical rubric

C. holistic rubric

D. single-point rubric

97

Which of the following activities is most appropriate for a mentor teacher?

A. writing a growth plan for the new teacher

B. determining consequences for misbehaving students

C. observing the new teacher and then leading a reflective conversation about instruction

D. providing tutoring services to ensure that every student in the new teacher's class is successful

98

Which of the following is an example of cooperative planning between a content area teacher and an ESOL teacher?

A. A content area teacher follows plans that are written by ESOL teachers and contain both content and language acquisition objectives.

B. A content area teacher writes the lesson plans and the ESOL teacher serves as a classroom aide while working with English learners.

C. An ESOL teacher pulls small groups of students into a separate room to deliver the same content area lesson as the native English speakers are receiving.

D. An ESOL teacher and a content area teacher create lesson plans together to incorporate content area objectives for all students and language objectives for English learners.

99

Which of the following formative assessments provides the most information about individual students to the teacher?

A. formal discussion

B. exit ticket

C. signaled response

D. scaffolded questions

100

Ms. Pruitt presented students with an open-ended question and then helped them use experimentation and research to develop a solution. Which of the following describes Ms. Pruitt's approach?

A. vicarious learning

B. modeling

C. scaffolding

D. problem-based learning

101

Mr. Schula challenges Miss Tom's class to a contest to see which class is able to read more books outside of school. The winning class will receive five new, high-interest books for its classroom library. Which of the following theories is Mr. Schula using?

A. constructivism

B. social learning theory

C. behaviorism

D. cognitivism

102

Which of the following best describes holistic scoring?

A. Score indicates overall level of proficiency.

B. Levels of proficiency for multiple criteria are assessed.

C. It provides specific feedback to guide student improvement.

D. Students are given a percentile rank.

103

Which of the following is true about students from poverty?

A. Poverty does not affect the dropout rate.

B. Teacher turnover rates are not affected by poverty.

C. Poverty does not affect achievement.

D. Homes of poverty use less language than middle-class homes.

104

Gabriel was recently released from ESL services. He is having a hard time with the unit on the circulatory system because he is unable to keep up with the vocabulary. What can his teacher do to help him?

A. borrow an elementary school textbook for him to use during this unit

B. move Gabriel to the front of the class

C. use graphic organizers for vocabulary terms

D. ask the ESL teacher to pull him during science during this unit

105

Which of the following activities would work best with whole-class instruction?

A. writer's workshop

B. reading remediation

C. providing feedback

D. reviewing classroom expectations

106

Which of the following would be the reason for taking a criterion-referenced test?

A. to find out whether students are working on grade level

B. to place students in special education

C. to measure mastery on learning goals

D. to place students in gifted education programs

107

Which of the following is most effective in promoting self-motivation?

A. providing fun competitions for students to demonstrate learning

B. allowing the child to choose the entire curriculum

C. providing incentives for completing extra assignments

D. helping the student set SMART (specific, measurable, attainable, relevant, and time-bound) goals

108

Mr. Bryant, the geometry teacher, writes the following on the whiteboard and asks students to duplicate it, but to add at least four more branches. What teaching strategy is Mr. Bryant using?

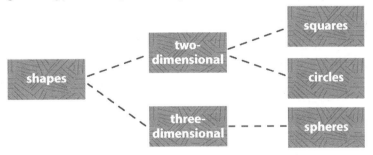

A. lecture

B. listening guides

C. concept mapping

D. learning centers

109

Which of the following is true about the Migrant Education Program (MEP)?

A. It currently has programs in every state.

B. It only serves students in California.

C. It only serves students in California and Florida.

D. It only serves students in California, Florida, and New York.

110

During a discussion about concentration camps during the Holocaust, a student mentions hearing about work camps in North Korea. Which response follows best practice?

A.   redirecting students back to the subject

B.   politely acknowledging the student's contribution before continuing on to the lesson

C.   speaking to the student after class about the interruption

D.   taking advantage of the teachable moment to compare/contrast concentration camps and work camps

Answer Key

A. Incorrect. Cross-curricular instruction is teaching across content areas.

B. Correct. Inquiry-based learning involves asking probing questions that entice students to explore and fact find.

C. Incorrect. A spiral curriculum reintroduces the same material at a deeper level as the year progresses.

D. Incorrect. Response to intervention is a tiered system of intervention.

2

A. Incorrect. Feedback must be specific to be helpful.

B. Incorrect. Expectations are an important part of creating a learning environment, but do not necessarily help students self-regulate.

C. Correct. Setting learning goals and helping students monitor those goals helps students self-regulate.

D. Incorrect. Extrinsic reinforcers can sometimes be used as external motivators, but will not help students self-regulate.

3

A. Correct. Shared decision making, whether through surveys or committees, makes parents feel valued by the school.

B. Incorrect. Posting on the website is an example of one-way communication.

C. Incorrect. Attending after-school events may encourage some parents to come to school and get to know the faculty and staff, but will not bring about a sense of ownership that comes with shared responsibility.

D. Incorrect. Providing a list is an example of one-way communication.

A. Correct. Interdisciplinary learning, also called cross-curricular instruction, is embedding instruction across content areas.

B. Incorrect. Inquiry-based learning involves asking probing questions that entice students to explore and fact find.

C. Incorrect. Constructivist teaching is based on the teacher's role as a facilitator of learning as students work to construct their own meaning from learning activities.

D. Incorrect. Multimedia instruction uses a variety of types of content, such as text, still pictures, and moving pictures.

5)

A. Incorrect. Providing students with facts will not help them become critical thinkers.

B. Incorrect. Books provide invaluable information, but listening to facts in a book is a low-level skill.

C. Correct. Providing students with an experience that gives them enough insight to be able to make inferences and draw conclusions is high-level thinking.

D. Incorrect. Sending students home to find out the answer places some responsibility for the learning experience on the student, but finding the answer through a parent is as low level as if the teacher explained it. Being able to articulate it to the others is a higher skill, but not as high as drawing conclusions from an experience.

6)

A. Incorrect. Peer assessment is somewhat more complicated than self-assessment. It should not be the first step.

B. Incorrect. Students will write a better piece if they have internalized the language of the rubric or checklist that is used for scoring.

C. Correct. Evaluation requires a high level of critical thought. Students need to be trained what to look for.

D. Incorrect. The evaluation tool needs to be used consistently.

7)

A. Correct. Students should know as much information about the topic as possible in advance so that their discussions are relevant and informed.

B. Incorrect. A discussion is different from a debate. A discussion looks for commonalities, whereas a debate stresses differences.

C. Incorrect. Students will find it difficult to discuss a topic with which they are unfamiliar.

D. Incorrect. The topic should be narrow enough that the discussion is focused.

8)

A. Incorrect. AAE offers nonunion professional advocacy for teachers.

B. Incorrect. Ms. Edwards is already comfortable with content and pedagogy related to math; therefore, NCTM would not meet her immediate needs.

C. Correct. AMLE offers professional development that is geared to the developmental needs of middle school students.

D. Incorrect. CEC offers professional development for special education teachers.

9)

A. Incorrect. Some students have a read/write learning style that flourishes using silent reading activities.

B. Incorrect. Pair-shares are good for both interpersonal learners and auditory learners.

C. Incorrect. Audiobooks teach content and fluency to auditory learners.

D. Correct. Mind maps visually represent learning for visual learners.

10)

A. Incorrect. Essay tests allow students to articulate a deeper understanding of content.

B. Incorrect. Selected-response grading is more objective and easier.

C. **Correct.** More questions may be asked during a selected-response test because each question takes less time to answer.

D. Incorrect. Portfolio assessments provide a holistic view of student knowledge as they may contain artifacts from a variety of learning styles.

11)

A. Incorrect. While it is useful to inform the school social worker of a child in need of services, the law does not require it.

B. **Correct.** As a mandated reporter, the teacher must immediately contact law enforcement authorities, the Department of Family and Protective Services, or the abuse hotline.

C. Incorrect. The teacher may choose to determine the status of the student's parents, but this is not a legal obligation.

D. Incorrect. The Department of Family and Protective Services is the responsible organization in this situation.

12)

A. Incorrect. The first column of the KWL chart activates prior knowledge by finding out what students already know about the topic.

B. **Correct.** The second column of the KWL chart helps students set learning goals by finding out what students want to learn about the topic.

C. Incorrect. The third column of the KWL chart assesses understanding by listing what the students learned during the unit of study.

D. Incorrect. Independent learning activities build autonomous learners.

13)

A. Incorrect. Kohlberg's stages of moral development explain the stages children go through as they are developing their value system. In the beginning children behave to keep from getting into trouble, but in later stages they learn to do the right thing because it is the right thing to do.

B. Incorrect. Piaget's stages of cognitive development describe brain development that prevents students from grasping information before they are ready.

C. **Correct.** Erikson's psychosocial development stages explain the issues between self and society that individuals must work through.

D. Incorrect. Maslow's hierarchy of needs demonstrates that motivation comes through fulfillment of needs. Primary needs must be met before students can attend to other needs.

14)

A. **Correct.** Applied research is for the purpose of proving a point, usually to sell a product.

B. Incorrect. Action research is when teachers collect data to analyze their own instructional practices.

C. Incorrect. Basic academic research is for the purpose of finding out information, which is typically the goal of university researchers and professional associations.

D. Incorrect. Qualitative research uses subjective forms of data collection, rather than number-based data, such as test scores.

15)

A. **Correct.** While other elements are also important, alignment between objectives, activities, and assessments is crucial.

B.   Incorrect. Engagement is not to be minimized, but if students are highly engaged in activities that do not match the learning goals, it will be ineffective.

C.   Incorrect. Assessments must be aligned with the learning objectives and activities to be useful.

D.   Incorrect. Collaboration is useful for building connections across the curriculum, but alignment is crucial.

16)

A.   Incorrect. Socratic questioning uses open-ended questions to form a discussion.

B.   Incorrect. Signaled responses use physical gestures to indicate an answer.

C.   **Correct.** Self-assessment helps learners internalize the material by making them responsible for evaluating their own work according to a rubric or checklist.

D.   Incorrect. Peer assessment is similar to self-assessment, except that students evaluate each other's work and provide feedback.

17)

A.   Incorrect. Norm-referenced tests provide percentile rankings compared with other students.

B.   Incorrect. Holistic grading uses a more general rubric to rate student work as a whole.

C.   Incorrect. Word count may be one criterion for an analytical scoring rubric, but several criteria are used.

D.   **Correct.** Analytical scoring uses a rubric that provides detailed information regarding the score a student should be given for meeting criteria.

18)

A.   **Correct.** Decision makers need to be onboard with a project before other steps are taken.

B.   Incorrect. Most school fundraisers require school board approval.

C.   Incorrect. Administrators need to agree to the project before it is presented to parents.

D.   Incorrect. After administrators agree, they should be included in meetings.

19)

A.   Incorrect. Constructivist teaching allows learners to construct their own knowledge.

B.   **Correct.** Scaffolding breaks up the curriculum into manageable parts.

C.   Incorrect. Inquiry-based learning involves asking probing questions that entice students to explore and fact find.

D.   Incorrect. A spiral curriculum reintroduces the same material at a deeper level as the year progresses.

20)

A.   Incorrect. Erikson developed the theory of psychosocial development.

B.   Incorrect. Watson continued Thorndike's work on operant conditioning.

C.   **Correct.** Maslow's hierarchy of needs states that until primary needs are met, individuals cannot attend to other needs.

D.   Incorrect. Thorndike's studies led to operant conditioning.

21)

A.   **Correct.** Shannon's score is equal to the average student in the sixth month of second grade.

B.   Incorrect. One math assessment would not mean that Shannon is ready socially or in other content areas to skip to the next grade level.

C.   Incorrect. Grade equivalents cannot be translated into percentile ranks.

D.   Incorrect. Grade equivalents are based on the student's years in school, not age.

22)

A.   Incorrect. Extra homework is a punishment for having achieved mastery.

B.   Incorrect. Students needing enrichment deserve teacher support at their level.

C.   Incorrect. Higher-level students need challenging learning experiences.

D.   Correct. Asking higher-level questions can make the curriculum more challenging for higher-level students.

23)

A.   Incorrect. Accommodation would be changing through patterns based on new information.

B.   Incorrect. Self-efficacy involves believing in one's ability to achieve learning goals.

C.   Correct. Transfer is applying a skill used in one environment to another setting.

D.   Incorrect. Self-regulation involves maintain control of one's emotions.

24)

A.   Incorrect. Miss Flannigan should attempt to speak with Mr. Ortega directly before going over his head.

B.   Correct. If Miss Flannigan is able to ask for what she needs in a nonemotional, professional manner, Mr. Ortega is more likely to either provide for her needs or find her someone who can.

C.   Incorrect. There is nothing wrong with asking for assistance from another colleague. However, Miss Flannigan should make attempt to get what she needs from Mr. Ortega as well.

D.   Incorrect. It is never appropriate to skip the chain of command in a professional setting.

25)

A.   Incorrect. Howard Gardner's work is in multiple intelligences.

B.   Incorrect. Dr. Bloom outlined the domains of learning.

C.   Correct. Albert Bandura developed social learning theory.

D.   Incorrect. Jean Piaget's work is in child development and constructivism.

26)

A.   Correct. The cognitive domain deals with intellectual development.

B.   Incorrect. The affective domain deals with emotions, motivations, and attitudes.

C.   Incorrect. The psychomotor domain deals with motor skill development.

D.   Incorrect. The moral domain deals with the acquisition of values.

27)

A.   Incorrect. Ultimately, the learning objectives need to be taught, but best practice would take advantage of the students' interest in time.

B.   Correct. Students will more readily absorb a lesson on telling time when they generate a teachable moment.

C.   Incorrect. The daily schedule may reduce distractibility, but it creates a lost opportunity.

D.   Incorrect. Setting a timer may appease students, but it does not take advantage of the moment when students are interested in telling time.

28)

A.   Incorrect. The cognitive domain deals with acquiring knowledge.

B.   Incorrect. The affective domain deals with social skill development.

C.   Correct. The psychomotor domain deals with motor skill development.

D.   Incorrect. The moral domain deals with acquiring values.

29)

A.   Incorrect. Reliable means that it provides consistent results.

B.   Correct. Valid assessments measure what they are supposed to measure.

C.   Incorrect. Variability relates to how scores are scattered.

D.   Incorrect. Consistent is not a testing term.

30)

A.   Incorrect. This stage is characterized by crying and cooing sounds.

B.   Correct. This stage is characterized by the creation of sequences of consonant-vowel sounds that babies often repeat in lengthier spans as they learn to use their mouths to create phonemes.

C.   Incorrect. This stage is characterized by a child's use of a single word to convey a complete idea.

D.   Incorrect. This stage is characterized by the early use of grammatical elements and the repetition of longer sentences.

31)

A.   Correct. An anticipation guide is an example of an informal diagnostic assessment because it measures prior knowledge.

B.   Incorrect. Mrs. Inbody is giving students a formative assessment to help her monitor and adjust.

C.   Incorrect. Mr. Wilson's conferences serve as a summative assessment.

D.   Incorrect. Diagnostic assessments measure content, not ability.

32)

A.   Incorrect. The teacher risks violating her students' right to privacy by writing about them online.

B.   Incorrect. Teachers may not use pictures of students without parental permission either inside or outside of the classroom.

C.   Incorrect. Using the school's logo, mascot, or insignia would be a violation of copyright law.

D.   Correct. Because her specific lesson plans do not refer to the students or the workings of the school, she is free to write about them.

33)

A.   Correct. Scaffolding is breaking up the assignments and providing support to master the pieces.

B.   Incorrect. This is an example of direct teach.

C.   Incorrect. This is an example of a spiral curriculum.

D.   Incorrect. This is an example of activating prior knowledge.

34)

A.   Incorrect. This is a closed question with a short answer.

B.   Incorrect. This is not an open-ended question because there is only one correct answer.

C.   Incorrect. This question is better than the previous choices because there are several possible correct answers, but it is still a closed question because there are a finite number of correct answers.

D.   Correct. This is an open-ended question because students must apply their own knowledge and experience to develop a unique answer.

35)

A.   Incorrect. Constructivism is a student-centered approach. In a constructivist classroom, the teacher facilitates as the students construct their own knowledge.

B.   Incorrect. Students would use authentic learning activities in a constructivist classroom.

C.   Incorrect. This is a teacher-centered approach in which students passively receive information.

D.   Correct. In a constructivist classroom, the teacher facilitates as the students construct their own knowledge.

36)

A.   Correct. Divergent thinkers think differently and more deeply about things. This student should be monitored for giftedness.

B.   Incorrect. Assimilation is applying new knowledge to current schema.

C.   Incorrect. Accommodation is changing schema to accommodate new, conflicting knowledge.

D.   Incorrect. A student with ADHD may exhibit problems completing assignments.

37)

A.   Incorrect. The scope will tell Mrs. Paul how deeply the students need to learn the concepts.

B.   Correct. The sequence will tell Mrs. Paul in which order to teach the material.

C.   Incorrect. State standards indicate what needs to be taught by the end of the school year.

D.   Incorrect. Textbooks should be used as a resource rather than as a guide.

38)

A.   Incorrect. Data that collect numbers, such as standardized test scores, are quantitative.

B.   Correct. Surveys are somewhat subjective; therefore, they are qualitative.

C.   Incorrect. Teacher retention rates may be measured using numbers.

D.   Incorrect. Attendance rates are quantitative data.

39)

A.   Incorrect. A high standard deviation means that students are clustered neither high nor low.

B.   Incorrect. A high standard deviation is an indication that there is a large amount of variability among the scores.

C.   Correct. The high variability that is evident in this assessment indicates that students need differentiation.

D.   Incorrect. Instruction appears to be aligned.

40)

A.   Correct. This is an example of analytical scoring.

B.   Incorrect. This is an example of holistic scoring.

C.   Incorrect. This is an example of a single-point rubric.

D.   Incorrect. This is an example of peer assessment.

Go on →

41)

A. **Correct.** Differentiation provides instruction to meet the needs of all learners.

B. Incorrect. This is spiraling the curriculum.

C. Incorrect. This is using the zone of proximal development.

D. Incorrect. This is mastery learning.

42)

A. **Correct.** During small-group reading, the teacher is using texts at the students' ZPD, or instructional level.

B. Incorrect. Cooperative learning groups provide students with social learning opportunities that help them benefit from one another's background experiences. However, these activities are not necessarily geared to individual student needs.

C. Incorrect. Annotating text can help students prepare for a discussion by providing knowledge from which the students will draw during the discussion. However, there is nothing that indicates that annotations are geared to specific students' needs.

D. Incorrect. Whole-group activities that are presented to everyone in the same way do not work within each student's ZPD.

43)

A. Incorrect. The child should have accomplished this milestone in a previous stage.

B. Incorrect. The child is beginning to think logically and abstractly.

C. Incorrect. The child should be able to take on more responsibilities.

D. **Correct.** Adolescence is filled with emotionally intense experiences.

44)

A. Incorrect. Creative works belong to the author whether they have been registered or not.

B. Incorrect. Fair use allows teachers to teach from videos, but not to use for entertainment.

C. Incorrect. Teachers may not use the same literary work under fair use for more than one class.

D. **Correct.** Teachers may copy less than 10 percent of a work for use in the classroom.

45)

A. **Correct.** Her mistakes are in the use of prepositions.

B. Incorrect. There are no conjunctions in the terms.

C. Incorrect. There are no pronouns in the terms.

D. Incorrect. There are no verbs in the terms.

46)

A. **Correct.** Concept maps help students view information visually in a way that connects with schema.

B. Incorrect. To articulate learning is to put new information into unique words.

C. Incorrect. For students who are visual learners, concept mapping may be more engaging, but that is not the primary purpose.

D. Incorrect. Concept maps help connect prior knowledge to new knowledge visually, but are not intended to activate new knowledge.

47)

A. Incorrect. Progress monitoring is part of social learning theory.

B. Incorrect. A KWL (know, want to know, learned) chart may be used as part of social learning theory to summarize what learning has taken place.

C. **Correct.** Cognitive learning theory advocates that learning has taken place when the student is able to apply new knowledge to a different setting.

D. Incorrect. Standardized testing does not occur in an authentic setting.

48)

A. Incorrect. Engaging students in research-based activities that are aligned with learning standards is ideal.

B. Incorrect. Even if students are involved in a great activity, if it is not aligned with learning standards, it will not help them achieve mastery of learning goals.

C. Incorrect. Teachers want students to be engaged, but alignment is a critical component for mastering standards.

D. **Correct.** Ideally, students will be engaged in learning activities, but it is not enough for an activity to be fun. Teachers must be able to justify their practices according to scientific principles.

49)

A. **Correct.** Volume, tone, and pitch are parts of verbal communication.

B. Incorrect. Nonverbal cues include proximity, gestures, and body language.

C. Incorrect. Conditioned responses are trained responses to stimuli.

D. Incorrect. Remediation is targeted instruction to fill gaps in learning.

50)

A. **Correct.** Academic language takes five to seven years to master.

B. Incorrect. Sentence structure in writing is one of the most complex

skills to master, but is typically evident before academic language.

C. Incorrect. Receptive social language is the first skill that ELLs will demonstrate.

D. Incorrect. Expressive social language comes after receptive social language, but before sentence structure in writing.

51)

A. **Correct.** PLCs choose a SMART goal based on learner outcomes.

B. Incorrect. CFGs improve teacher practices through critical feedback.

C. Incorrect. Professional associations offer information about research-based instructional practices.

D. Incorrect. Reflective practices are when teachers examine their own practices.

52)

A. Incorrect. Reliable means that it provides consistent results.

B. **Correct.** Valid assessments measure what they are supposed to measure.

C. Incorrect. Variability relates to how scores are scattered.

D. Incorrect. Consistent is not a testing term.

53)

A. Incorrect. Extrinsic reward provide external motivation.

B. Incorrect. Differentiating instruction may be intrinsically motivating for some students.

C. Incorrect. Inquiry-based learning may be intrinsically motivating for some students.

D. **Correct.** Goal setting and the achievement of subgoals is the key to self-motivation.

54)

A. Incorrect. Schools must have rules about the appropriate time and place to socialize to preserve the mission of the institution.

B. Incorrect. Students may not use freedom of speech as an excuse to violate another person's rights to an appropriate education.

C. Correct. Formal debates in which students express their opinions in a respectful manner are appropriate.

D. Incorrect. Using instructional time to protest against a department of the educational institution is disruptive to the mission of the school.

55)

A. Incorrect. PowerPoint presentations are visual aids.

B. Incorrect. Textbooks are text resources.

C. Correct. Microphones may be used to help students hear the teacher more clearly.

D. Incorrect. Internet sites are digital resources.

56)

A. Incorrect. Grades are not motivating for many students.

B. Incorrect. Extrinsic rewards are less motivating that intrinsic rewards.

C. Correct. Student choice and self-monitoring are motivating.

D. Incorrect. Consequences are negatively extrinsic.

57)

A. Correct. If the child is under eighteen years of age, the parent has the right to see his son's full educational record—including grades.

B. Incorrect. While the father has the right to see his minor son's grades, disclosing the grades of the rest

of the students would be a FERPA violation.

C. Incorrect. FERPA guarantees parents full access to their child's educational record, so the teacher must comply.

D. Incorrect. The principal does not have the authority to approve or deny a FERPA request. All requests from parents for educational records must be recognized.

58)

A. Incorrect. This is a low-level, recall question.

B. Incorrect. This question does not require students to think, but only asks them to remember facts.

C. Correct. This question requires students to use critical thinking skills by evaluating possible theories and making a judgment regarding which they believe is most likely.

D. Incorrect. Generating a list takes a little more brain power than short-answer questions, but it is still recall.

59)

A. Correct. Informal assessments are given by teachers to guide instruction.

B. Incorrect. Formal assessments are used to rank students.

C. Incorrect. Formal, standardized assessments are primarily used for making student-placement decisions.

D. Incorrect. State assessments are formal assessments.

60)

A. Correct. Students are assimilating information into an existing framework.

B. Incorrect. Inquiry-based learning is a pragmatic approach.

C. Incorrect. This is an example of direct teach.

D.   Incorrect. In this scenario of social learning, the MKO is the technology program.

61)

A.   Incorrect. CEC offers professional development that is specific to special education teachers.

B.   Incorrect. NAEYC offers professional development for teachers of PK to third-grade students.

C.   Incorrect. NCTM offers professional development for content and pedagogy of math teachers. Although Mr. Schoen is a math teacher, he is not looking for a program that is specific to math teachers.

D.   Correct. ASCD offers professional development for industry leaders. Mr. Schoen is seeking information as a leader of teachers.

62)

A.   Incorrect. A home survey is an initial screening method for determining if a student should be assessed for English learner placement. A student whose home language is English would not be place in an English learner program.

B.   Incorrect. Scores on state-selected tests provide the criteria for removing an English learner designation from a student, not time spent in an English learner instructional program.

C.   Correct. Specific scores on state-selected language and achievement tests are designated as cutoff points that determine when English learners no longer require English language programs and services.

D.   Incorrect. English learners remain in instructional programs aligned to ELP standards until their scores on state-selected language and achievement tests meet designated cutoff points.

63)

A.   Incorrect. Flashcards bring fluency to abstract concepts.

B.   Incorrect. Fluency work is typically abstract.

C.   Correct. When students can actually move objects around to help them grasp concepts, learning at a concrete level has taken place.

D.   Incorrect. Whiteboards are used to guide students through representational or abstract problems.

64)

A.   Correct. Graphic organizers help students connect new learning to existing schema.

B.   Incorrect. Demonstrations are aligned to social learning theory.

C.   Incorrect. Constructivism advocates for inquiry-based learning.

D.   Incorrect. Scaffolding falls under the constructivist theory.

65)

A.   Incorrect. Cognitivism promotes connecting learning to schema.

B.   Incorrect. Social learning theory advocates learning by imitating the example of a more knowledgeable other.

C.   Correct. Constructivism uses scaffolding within a student's ZPD.

D.   Incorrect. Behaviorism advocates changing behavior through reinforcement.

66)

A.   Incorrect. Benchmark tests are generally district created and do not have standardized measures.

B.   Incorrect. Portfolio assessments are not standardized.

C.   Correct. The STAR reading test does have standardized measures to compare students statistically to other students within the same grade level.

D. Incorrect. Performance-based assessments allow students to demonstrate a skill and are not standardized.

67)

A. Incorrect. Cognitive deals with acquisition of intellect.

B. Correct. Affective deals with emotions and attitudes.

C. Incorrect. Psychomotor deals with motor skill development.

D. Incorrect. Moral deals with the acquisition of values.

68)

A. Incorrect. The learning activities are chosen based on the standards and assessments as the final part of planning.

B. Incorrect. Teacher's editions are helpful resources, but they are not always aligned to state and district guidelines.

C. Incorrect. Veteran teachers are an invaluable resource for developing teachers. However, all teachers need to follow state and district guidelines for determining objectives.

D. Correct. State standards in combination with district guidance provide teachers with required learning objectives.

69)

A. Correct. Miss Shannon needs direct assistance as soon as possible to improve her practices.

B. Incorrect. Sending students to the office for minor infractions sends the message to students that the teacher is unable to handle them.

C. Incorrect. Punishing the entire class will interfere with teacher–student

relationships and may make the situation worse.

D. Incorrect. Professional development workshops will help, but Miss Shannon cannot wait as classroom management issues can easily become safety concerns.

70)

A. Incorrect. The student needs the opportunity to think deeply, not work harder. Extra work may be viewed as punishment.

B. Incorrect. Independent study has been proven ineffective.

C. Correct. Opportunities to construct knowledge at a deeper level provide the degree of challenge needed for gifted students.

D. Incorrect. The gifted student deserves the same opportunities to grow as other students. In addition, the gifted student may not make the best tutor because he or she may be a divergent thinker.

71)

A. Incorrect. Peer-reviewed journals offer minimum criteria for professional use by having researchers review the research process to verify accuracy.

B. Incorrect. Encyclopedias are secondary sources.

C. Correct. Even more valid than peer-reviewed research, second-party replication of results proves accuracy.

D. Incorrect. Newspapers are a secondary source.

72)

A. Correct. Essay tests may be used as a summative assessment at the end of a unit.

B. Incorrect. Learning logs are used as a formative assessment to help teachers monitor student progress during a learning experience.

C.   Incorrect. Anecdotal notes are formative assessments that are used to guide teachers as they support students.

D.   Incorrect. Pop quizzes are formative assessments that occur during a learning segment.

C.   Incorrect. Peer assessments are ratings done by teachers with similar experience levels to help one another improve.

D.   Incorrect. Learning communities are small groups of professionals with common goals who meet to collaborate about instructional practices.

73)

A.   Correct. Transfer is applying knowledge to a different setting.

B.   Incorrect. This would not be an example of application to a new setting. It is a model of the original setting.

C.   Incorrect. Tranfer is related to cognition.

D.   Incorrect. Tranfer is related to cognition.

76)

A.   Incorrect. Percentiles do not measure students compared to mastery of objectives.

B.   Incorrect. Percentages, not percentiles, indicate how many questions were answered correctly.

C.   Correct. Percentiles rank students by how many other students they outscored on an assessment.

D.   Incorrect. 55 percent of students scored higher than Misty.

74)

A.   Incorrect. Verbal redirection may help, but will interrupt the flow of the lesson.

B.   Correct. Proximity redirects students nonverbally without interrupting the learning process.

C.   Incorrect. External rewards may work, but may potentially interrupt the lesson.

D.   Incorrect. Removing the student from class will interrupt the lesson and prevent the student from learning with his or her peers.

77)

A.   Correct. Cognitive deals with acquisition of intellect.

B.   Incorrect. Affective deals with emotions and attitudes.

C.   Incorrect. Psychomotor deals with motor skill development.

D.   Incorrect. Moral deals with the acquisition of values.

78)

A.   Incorrect. External motivators are less effective than internal motivators.

B.   Incorrect. In addition to being an external motivator, sugary snacks, like soda, may violate federal, state, and/or local nutrition policies.

C.   Correct. Engaging materials in combination with achievable learning goals is self-motivating.

D.   Incorrect. Modeling is a great teaching technique, but less motivating than intrinsic rewards.

75)

A.   Correct. A mentor is a more experienced professional who guides someone who is newer to the profession.

B.   Incorrect. Internships are positions that offer on-the-job training either in addition to or in lieu of a salary.

79)

A. Incorrect. District professional activities will usually target generic learning goals rather than a specific grade level.

B. Incorrect. Teachers have great ideas, but those that appear on social networks and blogs may not be research based.

C. **Correct.** NAEYC has professional development activities that are geared to early childhood development.

D. Incorrect. An article about student engagement will not increase her knowledge about student development.

80)

A. Incorrect. This is not a phase of acculturation.

B. Incorrect. This is the honeymoon phase.

C. Incorrect. This is the home phase.

D. **Correct.** As people begin to accept their new culture, they also experience this difficulty.

81)

A. Incorrect. Summative assessments evaluate mastery of objectives at the end of a learning segment.

B. **Correct.** Formative assessments take place throughout a learning segment to help teachers monitor students and adjust instruction.

C. Incorrect. Diagnostic assessments evaluate prior knowledge.

D. Incorrect. Formal assessments have standardized measures.

82)

A. Incorrect. Students are required by state compulsory education acts to attend class during required times.

B. Incorrect. Candy as a reward violates nutrition guidelines regarding giving students foods of minimal nutrition value.

C. **Correct.** Most middle school students enjoy having the opportunity to socialize as part of the learning experience.

D. Incorrect. Spending an entire class period watching a movie that is not related to a learning experience wastes instructional time.

83)

A. Incorrect. Standardized tests provide limited information for making instructional decisions.

B. Incorrect. Benchmark tests, like standardized tests, provide information after learning has taken place, which limits its use for guiding instruction.

C. Incorrect. Anecdotal records may provide some insight into which students need additional support.

D. **Correct.** Error analysis is a tool for targeting instruction based on the challenges each student faces.

84)

A. Incorrect. Extroverted students are likely to prefer learning activities that include discussion and cooperative grouping

B. Incorrect. Extroverted students may prefer more active learning to quiet reflection.

C. **Correct.** More introverted students, who are likely to be less comfortable speaking in groups, might prefer visuals, such as graphic organizers, over more active or linguistic activities.

D. Incorrect. Introverted students may not be comfortable engaging in lively conversations in the class, and benefit more from graphic organizers.

85)

A. **Correct.** Scoring guides detail what students should do to move to the next level of proficiency.

B. Incorrect. Scoring guides can be intimidating.

C. Incorrect. Scoring with a scoring guide can be time-consuming.

D. Incorrect. Scoring guides are objective.

86)

A. Incorrect. The habit of taking the folder back and forth to school may have the benefit of teaching students responsibility, but the primary purpose is to communicate with parents.

B. Incorrect. The main purpose of homework in the early grades is to keep parents informed about what students are working on at school.

C. **Correct.** Students benefit when there is a system of two-way communication established between school and home.

D. Incorrect. There may be some communication in the folder about volunteering, but that is not why schools communicate with parents.

87)

A. **Correct.** Think-pair-share gives verbal-linguistic students the opportunity to talk about their learning.

B. Incorrect. Word maps help spatial-visual students see new concepts as pictures.

C. Incorrect. Sorting activities help logical-mathematical thinkers organize information into patterns.

D. Incorrect. Building models helps those with bodily-kinesthetic intelligence make connections to learning.

88)

A. Incorrect. The teacher is using punishment in this scenario.

B. Incorrect. This teacher is using praise for positive reinforcement.

C. **Correct.** Kanitta is intrinsically motivated because the work is interesting.

D. Incorrect. This is an example of an extrinsic reward.

89)

A. Incorrect. Cognitive deals with acquisition of intellect.

B. Incorrect. Affective deals with emotions and attitudes.

C. **Correct.** Psychomotor deals with motor skill development.

D. Incorrect. Moral deals with the acquisition of values.

90)

A. Incorrect. Holistic scoring rubrics provide an overall assessment.

B. **Correct.** Analytical scoring rubrics provide detailed feedback to students.

C. Incorrect. Analytical scoring rubrics do not provide observable evidence; rather, they provide written feedback for students.

D. Incorrect. Analytical scoring rubrics are a measurement tool rather than an assessment.

91)

A. **Correct.** Deductive reasoning applies what is known about the whole to a smaller sample to draw an accurate conclusion.

B. Incorrect. Inductive reasoning assumes that what is true about a sample is true in general. It is often, but not always, accurate.

C. Incorrect. Quantitative data are more objective than qualitative data.

D.   Incorrect. There are times that research is skewed to make it fit a purpose not originally intended.

92)

A.   **Correct.** Evaluating and justifying are in the highest level of Bloom's taxonomy.

B.   Incorrect. This is a level one recall question.

C.   Incorrect. Summaries are level two questions.

D.   Incorrect. Comparing/contrasting is a level four analysis question.

93)

A.   Incorrect. While software used should have educational value, a formal evaluation is not required.

B.   Incorrect. Vendor agreements do not prohibit use of other software.

C.   **Correct.** The administrator must approve all software to ensure it does not endanger the system.

D.   Incorrect. Teachers may not use resources that are inappropriate for students, but no official screening is required.

94)

A.   Incorrect. Think-pair-share gives verbal-linguistic students the opportunity to talk about their learning.

B.   Incorrect. Word maps help spatial-visual students see new concepts as pictures.

C.   Incorrect. Sorting activities help logical-mathematical thinkers organize information into patterns.

D.   **Correct.** Building models helps those with bodily-kinesthetic intelligence make connections to learning.

95)

A.   Incorrect. Summative assessments are given after a unit has been taught.

B.   Incorrect. Formative assessments are given throughout instruction to monitor student progress.

C.   Incorrect. Norm-referenced tests provide scores that are based on how a student scored in relation to other students.

D.   **Correct.** Diagnostic assessments are pretests.

96)

A.   Incorrect. Analytical checklists simply mark correct or incorrect use of each criterion rather than breaking down levels of proficiency.

B.   Incorrect. Analytical rubrics measure the level of proficiency as well as multiple criteria.

C.   **Correct.** Holistic rubrics measure the level of proficiency on overall, general criteria.

D.   Incorrect. A single-point rubric identifies only proficiency.

97)

A.   Incorrect. Mentor teachers are there to help, not evaluate new teachers.

B.   Incorrect. The new teacher needs to learn to handle discipline for his or her students.

C.   **Correct.** Mentors offer support by observing the new teacher and offering feedback.

D.   Incorrect. The mentor is not responsible for providing remediation to students, but for helping the new teacher discover ways to remediate students as needed.

98)

A.   Incorrect. Though the plans were developed by one teacher and implemented by another, the plans were not written together and therefore have not been developed cooperatively.

B.   Incorrect. The plans have been developed by the content area teacher, so the ESOL teacher cannot fully exercise his or her expertise in shaping the language objectives.

C.   Incorrect. Though the plans were developed by one teacher and implemented by another, the plans were not written together and therefore have not been developed cooperatively.

D.   **Correct.** When content and ESOL teachers work together on plans, they are working cooperatively.

99)

A.   Incorrect. Formal discussions can provide information about how much students have internalized information; however, not every student will participate with every question.

B.   **Correct.** Exit tickets or tickets out the door offer individualized information about what students have gained from a learning experience.

C.   Incorrect. Signaled responses have each student physically engaged, but some will not attend and will mimic the answers of their peers.

D.   Incorrect. Questions inform teachers of the level of mastery of objectives for the students who answer, but do not provide information about how each student is performing across the content.

100)

A.   Incorrect. Vicarious learning is learning by watching the consequences of others as they learn.

B.   Incorrect. Modeling is when a teacher shows students how to solve a problem.

C.   Incorrect. Scaffolding is providing support within the student's instructional level to move them toward mastery.

D.   **Correct.** Ms. Pruitt is using problem-based learning to help students construct their own learning.

101)

A.   Incorrect. Constructivism relates to student-centered learning experiences.

B.   Incorrect. Social learning is learning by watching the teacher modeling.

C.   **Correct.** Behaviorism is using reinforcements to change behavior. He is using competition as a reinforcement to persuade students to read outside of class.

D.   Incorrect. Cognitivism relates to how knowledge is received and stored.

102)

A.   **Correct.** Holistic scoring scores the piece as a whole rather than breaking it up by criteria.

B.   Incorrect. Analytic scoring breaks up the piece by criteria for scoring.

C.   Incorrect. Analytic scoring provides a great deal of feedback.

D.   Incorrect. Norm-referenced tests compare students and provide a percentile rank as the score.

103)

A.   Incorrect. The dropout rate is higher among students of poverty.

B.   Incorrect. Teacher turnover rates are higher in poverty-stricken areas.

C.   Incorrect. Students of poverty begin school with fewer experiences and continue to suffer from the achievement gap through the high school years.

D. **Correct.** Homes of poverty provide fewer literacy experiences.

104)

A. Incorrect. There is no reason Gabriel should not learn the curriculum at the same depth as his peers if he is provided accommodations.

B. Incorrect. Proximity will probably not help this student.

C. **Correct.** Organizing information within existing schema is a great tool for improving vocabulary.

D. Incorrect. ESL classes are not intended to teach the academic vocabulary for every content area.

105)

A. Incorrect. Writer's workshop is typically done with one-on-one conferences with students, but could be accomplished within a small group.

B. Incorrect. Small homogeneous groups with similar learning needs are formed for reading remediation.

C. Incorrect. Feedback is private and should be one-on-one.

D. **Correct.** Developing and reviewing expectations for the classroom is generally a whole-group activity. If a student does not meet expectations, that is a one-on-one conversation.

106)

A. Incorrect. Norm-referenced tests provide grade-level equivalencies.

B. Incorrect. Cognitive abilities tests are used for identification of learning disabilities.

C. **Correct.** Criterion-referenced tests measure content knowledge.

D. Incorrect. Cognitive abilities tests are used to make placement decisions in gifted programs.

107)

A. Incorrect. Winning competitions can be extrinsically rewarding, but not self-motivating.

B. Incorrect. Opportunities for choice within the framework of the curriculum can be intrinsically motivating.

C. Incorrect. Incentives are extrinsic rewards.

D. **Correct.** Achievement toward goals is the biggest promotor of self-efficacy.

108)

A. Incorrect. Lectures are teacher-led dissemination of information.

B. Incorrect. Listening guides sometimes accompany lectures to help students focus on the key points.

C. **Correct.** Concept mapping is using graphic organizers such as this one to make connections to learning.

D. Incorrect. Learning centers are areas of the room that are set aside for independent learning activities.

109)

A. **Correct.** The MEP currently serves migrant students in every state.

B. Incorrect. While it is true that there are many migrant workers in California, this answer is not complete.

C. Incorrect. Florida and California are both large agricultural states with high numbers of migrant workers, but they are not the only states that the MEP serves.

D. Incorrect. These are all states with high numbers of immigrants as well as migrants, but the MEP does not exclusively serve students in these states.

110)

A.   Incorrect. Redirecting students away from an area of interest equates to a missed opportunity.

B.   Incorrect. In this scenario, the student is somewhat validated, but the teacher still misses out on a valuable chance to enrich and engage students.

C.   Incorrect. Students should not be reprimanded for their contributions.

D.   **Correct.** The best response is to use this opportunity to expand their learning and relate it to present-day human rights violations.

Follow the link below to take your FTCE Professional Education practice test and to access other online study resources:

www.cirrustestprep.com/ftce-professional-education-online-resources

Made in the USA
San Bernardino, CA
04 June 2018